SUPPORTING POST-COVID-19 ECONOMIC RECOVERY IN SOUTHEAST ASIA

MAY 2022

ADB

ASIAN DEVELOPMENT BANK

Notes:
In this publication, "$" refers to United States dollars.
ADB recognizes "China" as the People's Republic of China and "Vietnam" as Viet Nam.

On the cover: Crucial to the recovery phase is the introduction of reforms and strategies to strengthen resilience of tourism, agro-processing, and garments as well as develop evolving sectors with a high potential for growth such as electronics and digital trade. Scenic background inspired by the Borobudur Temple in Indonesia.

Cover design by Cleone Baradas.

Contents

Tables, Figures, and Boxes

Boxes

Foreword

This publication is the first of four reports from a regional study completed in 2021 and funded by the technical assistance of the Asian Development Bank (ADB) on Policy Advice for COVID-19 Economic Recovery in Southeast Asia. The project supports the recovery efforts of Southeast Asian countries to return to their economic performance before the coronavirus disease (COVID-19) pandemic. It also assists countries in preparing for national, regional, or global transformations that may take place post-COVID-19. The focus countries are Cambodia, Indonesia, Myanmar, the Philippines, and Thailand, which tapped ADB's COVID-19 Pandemic Recovery Option facility.* The study produced four reports on the following thematic areas:

1. **Supporting post-COVID-19 economic recovery in Southeast Asia.** After analyzing different sectors, their potential for growth, and the strengths of economies in Southeast Asia, ADB identified five key sectors: tourism, agro-processing, and garments are well-established sectors needing transformation or improvement; while electronics and digital trade are evolving sectors with a high potential for growth. This allows the development of more targeted policies given the constraints to governments' financial and administrative resources.
2. **Strengthening domestic resource mobilization in Southeast Asia.** COVID-19 exacerbated the struggles of some governments to generate tax revenue to meet public expenditure needs. ADB proposes policy actions to expand the tax base, increase tax compliance, and strengthen tax administration to create a healthy fiscal space.
3. **Implementing a green recovery in Southeast Asia.** Green recovery from the pandemic is crucial to ensure an economically and environmentally resilient future for Southeast Asia. Well-designed policy measures can simultaneously achieve socioeconomic and environmental goals.
4. **Harnessing the potential of big data in post-pandemic Southeast Asia.** Digitalization gained more prominence amid COVID-19 and highlighted the value of big data for the effective and efficient delivery of key public services such as health care, social welfare and protection, and education. A range of policy enablers for big data adoption in policy making—from strategic governance to building a data driven culture—were examined.

This publication provides policy makers with a baseline to understand the scope of policy options available in their pursuit of economic recovery. There is still much uncertainty on timing, particularly as the trajectory of the pandemic (i.e., new COVID-19 mutations) remains unclear and countries await the development and distribution of more vaccines. While COVID-19's impact on Southeast Asia has been significant, the report provides hope. The medium-term growth opportunities are strong. Taking advantage of those opportunities, however, will require a significant rethink of current approaches. This series of publications will hopefully inspire governments to think beyond the containment stage and lay the groundwork for opportunities that will ensure a sustainable recovery underpinned by more resilient economies and societies.

The research benefited from the insights and perspectives of government officials, the private sector, the academe, and other key stakeholders and experts working in the region who convened in thematic workshops, roundtable consultations, and focus group discussions. We are grateful for their support and collaboration.

---

*   ADB's stance on Myanmar since 1 February 2021 is outlined in its public statements of 2 February 2021 and 10 March 2021.

The ADB resident mission offices of the focus countries have effectively coordinated all country consultations to inform the study. We look forward to ADB's continued engagement with these countries, in line with its current approaches, to carry out the policy recommendations to support the region's recovery efforts. These recommendations align with the operational directions on fostering regional cooperation and integration under ADB's Strategy 2030. Strengthening regional cooperation is crucial for dealing with future crises more effectively.

Ramesh Subramaniam
Director General
Southeast Asia Department
Asian Development Bank

Acknowledgments

The research was supported by regional technical assistance on Policy Advice for COVID-19 Economic Recovery in Southeast Asia (TA 9964). The team from the Regional Cooperation and Operations Coordination Division (SERC), Southeast Asia Department (SERD) of the Asian Development Bank (ADB) led by Thiam Hee Ng, former principal economist, SERC, with support from Dulce Zara and Georginia Nepomuceno, managed the study and coordinated the preparation of this publication under the supervision of Alfredo Perdiguero, director, SERC. Jason Rush provided technical support. Maria Theresa Bugayong and Hannah Estipona extended administrative assistance.

The study is a collaboration between ADB and AlphaBeta (SG) PTE LTD led by Fraser Thompson. Bingxun Seng, Cheng Wei Swee, and Mohak Mangal from AlphaBeta prepared the report. Several ADB staff members provided invaluable comments, including: David Freedman, Yurendra Basnett, Joel Mangahas, Kyaw Thu, Cristina Lozano, Teresa Mendoza, Jay Roop, Chitchanok Annonjarn, Jiangfeng Zhang, Srinivasan Ancha, Omer Zafar, Takeshi Ueda, Hyunyoung Song, Steven Schipani, Arndt Husar, and Abdul Abiad.

The team gratefully acknowledges the views and suggestions of government officials, the private sector, the academe, researchers, development partners, and other stakeholders in the region. They generously extended their support and cooperation during the thematic workshops, roundtable consultations, focus group discussions, and related events at the Southeast Asia Development Symposium 2021 conducted as part of the stakeholder engagement undertaken for this project. Special thanks to the ADB resident mission offices in Cambodia, Indonesia, Myanmar, the Philippines, and Thailand for coordinating the participation of in-country stakeholders in the workshops and consultation meetings. Very thoughtful insights were also provided by Larry Wong, Anbumozhi Venkatachalam, Phouang Parisak Pravongviengkham, Ken Loo, Do Thi Thuy Huong, Sang Uk Nam, Montira Horayangura Unakul, Mario Hardy, Jens Thraenhart, Deborah Elms, Andrew Staples, and Sriganesh Lokanathan.

Effective 1 February 2021, ADB placed a temporary hold on sovereign project disbursements and new contracts in Myanmar. The bank continues to monitor the situation in the country. All of the background assessments in this study were undertaken before 1 February 2021.

The Knowledge Support Division of ADB's Department of Communications facilitated the publishing of this study.

Abbreviations

3D	three-dimensional
4IR	Fourth Industrial Revolution
ADB	Asian Development Bank
AI	artificial intelligence
APEC	Asia-Pacific Economic Cooperation
ASEAN	Association of Southeast Asian Nations
CMP	cut-make-pack
COBP	Country Operations Business Plan
COVID-19	coronavirus disease
CPS	Country Partnership Strategy
EU	European Union
FDI	foreign direct investment
FOB	free-on-board
FTA	free trade agreement
GAP	good agricultural practices
GDP	gross domestic product
GMS	Greater Mekong Subregion
HDD	hard-disk drive
IBPAP	IT & Business Process Association of the Philippines
ICT	information and communications technology
ILO	International Labour Organization
IoT	Internet of Things
IP	intellectual protection
ISIC	International Standard Industrial Classification
IT-BPO	information technology and business process outsourcing
MSMEs	micro, small, and medium-sized enterprises
PPP	public–private partnership
PRC	People's Republic of China
R&D	research and development
SEZ	special economic zone
UNCTAD	United Nations Conference on Trade and Development

Executive Summary

Governments introduced accommodative monetary policies to expansionary fiscal policies to manage the short-term impacts of the pandemic. However, the impacts and assistance differ by sectors and demographic groups. As the policy discussions move toward recovery, it is important for a sector approach to develop targeted recommendations for this medium-term growth phase. After analyzing different sectors, their potential for future growth, and the strengths of Southeast Asian countries, the Asian Development Bank (ADB) identified five key sectors. Three are well-established sectors that need to be transformed or improved: tourism, agro-processing, and garments; and two are evolving sectors with a high potential for future growth: electronics and digital trade. While our policy analysis focused on supporting the recovery and expansion of these sectors individually, crosscutting policies, such as support for an enabling business environment and improved infrastructure, will be needed. Strengthening regional cooperation in Southeast Asia is important to help countries deal with future crises more effectively.

Tourism

Even prior to the pandemic, the industry was beset with four structural challenges: (i) overreliance on foreign tourists from a limited number of countries focused on a few destinations led to reduced resilience and overcrowding; (ii) the lack of infrastructure outside major destinations limited the potential for diversification; (iii) a significant share of low-wage and informal employment made achieving and maintaining high-quality standards more difficult; and (iv) the amount of spending per tourist was below regional targets resulted to lower tourism revenues.

The coronavirus disease (COVID-19) created new challenges for the industry. For example, tourists are now more aware of the importance of health precautions, making these considerations crucial in selecting travel destinations. There are indications that COVID-19 could lead to a fundamental decline in long haul international tourism, an issue exacerbated by the adoption of digital tools for virtual meetings, incentives, conferences, and events tourism. Finally, environmentally sustainable tourism is not new; there is evidence that the pandemic has strengthened demand for it.

This report proposes four policy response areas for tourism. The first focuses on restoring demand and includes strengthening domestic tourism by developing marketing campaigns to convince travelers it is safe to travel. This requires coordinating and implementing proper procedures to reduce information gaps and minimizing risks. Second is building new channels of demand to diversify tourist destinations and develop lesser-known points of interest, while tapping into high growth segments like ecotourism, health and premium wellness experiences, and halal tourism. The third involves building capacities to support future digital demand, touching on the need for authorities to invest in training workers in both digital and nondigital skills to tackle the issues of low pay and informality. The fourth calls for increasing industry resilience, where the tourism industry in each country must work closely with central and local governments to improve communication channels. Creating a permanent crisis management task force may also ensure that a country's tourism sector is better able to cope with future shocks.

Agro-Processing

This report identifies five major existing challenges for agro-processing: (i) inconsistent supply of raw materials due to factors such as adverse weather conditions, diseases, fluctuations in global market prices and exchange rates, and post-harvest food waste; (ii) low adoption of automation and technology, which hinders productivity; (iii) underdeveloped utility, transport, and logistics infrastructure hampering industry development, especially in rural areas; (iv) lack of access to key enablers including financing, new technologies, and skilled labor; and (v) environmental unsustainability. As countries imposed travel restrictions, closed borders, and curtailed business activities and transportation networks, fluctuations in production factors like labor and raw materials followed. Labor shortages at factories, warehouses, and logistics hubs caused disruptions in supply chains, and some countries imposed restrictions on food product exports and imports to prioritize domestic needs. Some of these measures were only short term and were removed after a few months. While agriculture was less affected by COVID-19, the region's governments must now support efforts to move toward higher value-added activities like agro-processing.

There are four areas of potential policy responses for agro-processing. First, enhancing the efficiency and transparency of supply chains. Harmonizing food product standards, for example, may reduce delays and compliance costs. Second, expanding sales channels and addressing new consumer trends and markets could add significant value to the industry. The third is improving productivity, quality, and safety by focusing on research and enabling policies to ensure a more consistent supply of high-quality raw materials and safety, promoting the adoption of processing equipment, and facilitating digital transformation in the agro-processing industry. The fourth involves building industry resilience by streamlining regulatory functions, strengthening the local agro-processing ecosystem, promoting partnerships, and pursuing food-related circularity policies to tackle post-harvest and supply chain waste.

Garments

Many Southeast Asian countries are competitive in the labor-intensive textile, apparel, and footwear manufacturing industries with their relatively low labor costs, strategic locations, preferential market access, and supportive government policies. Some countries continue to focus on high volumes of low value-added products, relying on cheap labor as their primary competitive advantage. Southeast Asian garment manufacturers are vulnerable to supply chain disruptions due to a reliance on a few key raw materials suppliers; insufficient reliability, timing, and scale of local input production that deepen their dependence on foreign supplies; and irregular electricity supplies. Rising labor costs amid low labor productivity are adding economic pressure on some countries. The garment industry in Southeast Asia has been severely affected by COVID-19. The cancellation of orders and production restrictions forced many Southeast Asian companies to cease operations and lay off employees. Workplace closures in other countries prevented imported inputs from reaching garment production in time and disrupted garment manufacturing, exacerbating existing supply chain problems. The COVID-19 crisis also highlighted the lack of support services for vulnerable workers in the industry, worsening inequalities.

This report proposes four areas of support to the industry. The first is enhancing competitiveness to maintain the industry's growth. This could include (i) reviewing policies that restrict growth like high raw material tariffs and cumbersome export permit procedures contributing to high production costs; (ii) upgrading vocational curricula and increasing access to training, particularly in rural regions; and (iii) promoting the adoption of digital technologies ranging from smart factories to additive manufacturing to enable mass customization of products. Second, the garment industry in the Association of Southeast Asian Nations (ASEAN) can diversify beyond the current markets of the European Union and the United States, while exploring options to pursue product differentiation and produce higher value-added garments. Third, improving productivity and adopting better production technologies can strengthen the sector's resilience to future demand shocks, while placing more emphasis on shorter supply chains, local alternative supplies, and local markets. Finally, it may also be crucial for the industry to adopt more flexible production and business models, like enabling garment factories to switch across production types to meet changing consumer demand.

Electronics

Electronics manufacturing is important for the region, but the diversity of products produced differs significantly by country, ranging from capital-intensive products like digital storage devices to more labor-intensive products such as electrical components. The industry faced several structural challenges even before COVID-19. For instance, the industry generally has inadequate industrial systems and lacks the complete upstream and downstream portions of value chains. The industry also generally focuses on low value-added products and processes, such as the assembly and testing stages of the industry value chain rather than upstream stages (research and development and product design) that generate higher economic value. Furthermore, the growing interconnectedness of global supply chains, the need for more complex designs and shorter delivery times, and a rising focus on the reliability of production systems require electronics manufacturing companies in the region to adapt to new disruptive technologies, including the Internet of Things, artificial intelligence, and machine-learning technologies. The pandemic has accelerated a global digital transformation while at the same time introducing new challenges. Many regional electronics manufacturers face delays in production due to supply chain interruptions, resulting in the failure to meet the rising demand for some consumer electronics during the pandemic. Interruptions in manufacturing and shipping also trigger a domino effect on transportation, sales, prototyping, and the launch of new products. As new lifestyle paradigms birthed by the pandemic could alter electronics demand, the challenge will be to understand and keep pace with these structural shifts.

To address these challenges and improve the competitiveness of the electronics industry post-COVID-19, Southeast Asia countries could consider responses in two policy areas. The first is to upgrade special economic zones (SEZs) by improving the clustering of firms to maximize industry linkages, leading to more collaboration and pooling of resources while promoting competition. SEZs could also be supported by industry-specific policies such as promoting electronics exports in free trade agreements, benefitting the region's manufacturers. Improved collaboration between government and industry, and between local players and foreign investors within the SEZs, may facilitate the transition toward high-value activities within the electronics supply chain. The second area is actively developing human capital to attract foreign direct investment, remain competitive, and transit to manufacturing electronics with high added value.

Digital Trade

Digital trade is relatively new. While the contributions to gross domestic product of digital products (software), digitally enabled services (business process outsourcing, online advertising, export of data processing services), and indirect digital services are not yet captured well in national statistics across Southeast Asia, their importance is likely to grow tremendously as more activities shift online. Much of the region's digital trade currently concentrates on information technology and business process outsourcing (IT-BPO). Software application (app) development has also been picking up in some countries. To harness the growth potential of the region's digital trade sector, addressing the following key challenges is vital: risk from automation; limited connectivity; low level digitalization of micro, small, and medium-sized enterprises (MSMEs); tax base erosion; and a restrictive regulatory framework. For instance, many MSMEs lack the resources to research international sales opportunities, to build a global business network, and to market their products overseas. Digital technologies can help, but many MSMEs lack understanding of available digital solutions, available software or business platforms, and related trade opportunities. Some may consider the (further) digitalization of their business model and information technology infrastructure as too risky, disruptive, or costly.

To address the challenges identified and support an enabling environment for digital trade, Southeast Asian countries could develop an IT-BPO road map, enhance connectivity, support skills development, enable MSMEs to go digital, and rethink digital regulation. For example, to enable MSMEs to go digital, a range of initiatives is needed to support digital skills development. Greater industry involvement in curriculum development can help ensure that key skills like English language fluency, critical thinking, and complex problem solving are covered. This needs to be accompanied by support and financial incentives for employers to ensure more and higher quality training in the workplace.

Introduction

The coronavirus disease (COVID-19) has had devastating health, social, economic, and financial impacts. Governments have introduced measures ranging from accommodative monetary policies to expansionary fiscal policies to manage the pandemic's short-term impacts. However, the impacts and assistance differ by sectors and demographic groups. As the policy discussions move toward the recovery phase (with a 3-year timeline), it is important to have a sector approach to develop targeted recommendations for medium-term growth. This report shows five sectors of common relevance to COVID-19 recovery in Cambodia, Indonesia, Myanmar, the Philippines, and Thailand. In each sector, there are unique challenges created by COVID-19 as well as differences in their growth prospects and opportunities. Policy interventions are outlined which could help address some of the current challenges and seize the available growth opportunities.

The report begins by prioritizing the sectors important for medium-term recovery. It then analyzes sector-specific challenges, growth opportunities, and potential policy interventions to help policy makers develop targeted strategies for the next three years.

▶ Prioritizing Sectors

The COVID-19 pandemic has impacted a wide range of sectors. Social distancing measures and border closures have decimated both domestic and external demand for consumer-driven sectors such as retail and accommodation. Depressed demand and disrupted supply chains also directly contributed to the rapid decelerations across manufacturing industries. The socioeconomic impacts across the focus countries have been damaging and broad, where sharp economic contractions and record unemployment rates have raised poverty rates and widened inequalities. More positively, this pandemic has increased the urgency and incentives for governments to introduce structural reforms to support sustainable economic recovery. Taking a sector approach to recovery is critical to identify reforms and strategies that can address fundamental, sector-specific challenges including economic imbalances, productivity and value addition, and employee welfare especially given the finite financial and administrative resources of governments. This regional study aims to identify and prioritize five sectors important across most or all the focus countries and to have a common set of challenges. Box 1 summarizes the approach taken to prioritize sectors.

Box 1: Approach to Prioritize Sectors in the Focus Countries

The following approach was taken to prioritize the sectors:

1. **Develop a set of criteria to evaluate the sectors of the five focus countries**
   The following five criteria were selected:
   a) **Contribution to Gross Domestic Product (GDP) pre-pandemic:** Measures the sector's share in GDP before the pandemic, using data from the Asian Development Bank (ADB) or the respective national statistics offices.[a]
   b) **Contribution to employment pre-pandemic:** Measures the sector's employment figures using official labor statistics from ADB and International Labour Organization (ILO) databases.
   c) **Impact of COVID-19:** Measures the economic impact on the sectors using national accounts data from national statistics offices. For countries with a high reporting lag (Cambodia and Myanmar), the impact was informed through available assessments by ADB and ILO.
   d) **Competitive advantage:** Measures the sector's competitiveness in each country. For tradeable sectors, the World Bank's Revealed Comparative Advantage (RCA) index was used. For non-tradeable sectors, a wider range of competitiveness factors (e.g., demographics and capacity of the labor force, unit labor costs, size of the domestic market, and others) were assessed.
   e) **Alignment with future growth drivers:** Measures a sector's relevance to future trends like urbanization and a growing consuming class and alignment with national development plans.

2. **Identify and prioritize a set of common sectors**
   Based on the methodology, five sectors were prioritized for further assessments:
   a) **Tourism.** This industry covers two critical sectors: wholesale and retail trade, and accommodation and food service activities. In July 2020, the United Nations Conference on Trade and Development (UNCTAD) estimated that in the most pessimistic scenario, a 12-month break in international tourism would cost $3.3 trillion or 4.2% of global GDP, while major tourist destinations like Thailand would face the steepest declines in employment and wages.[b] Tourism has been an important driver of job creation in the focus countries. In the Philippines and Indonesia, 2.5 million and 1.9 million travel and tourism jobs were created between 2015 to 2019, respectively.[c] Air transport restrictions and the sudden decline in tourist arrivals resulted in significant losses in the five countries.[d]
   b) **Agro-processing.** The agriculture, forestry, and fishing sectors represent the most important contributor to GDP and employment in many of the focus countries. For example, in 2019, Myanmar had 21% and Cambodia had 22% of their GDP in this sector. While there are opportunities to enhance productivity and resilience (e.g., adopting precision agriculture), focus must be shifted to higher value-added activities in the supply chain.[e] One such subsector is agro-processing, expected to continue its growth given the abundance of arable land and agricultural products, large domestic market, low cost of labor, and increased government focus across the five countries. For instance, the industry has been absorbing laid-off employees due to COVID-19.
   c) **Garments.** Garment manufacturing, a subsector of labor-intensive manufacturing, is significant in many of the focus countries. COVID-19 led to apparel order cancellations, production line conversion to manufacture personal protection equipment, factory closures, and worker retrenchment.[f] The industry is particularly important for Cambodia where it contributed over 18% to GDP in 2018[g] and employs over half a million people.[h] The garment industry is also an important source of female employment, accounting for close to 20% of female employment in Cambodia in 2019.[i] Many Southeast Asian countries have competitive advantages in garment manufacturing due to the relatively low labor costs, strategic location, preferential market access, and supportive government policies.
   d) **Electronics.** The electronics manufacturing industry is a particularly significant driver of economic activity in Indonesia, Thailand, and the Philippines, contributing close to 2% of GDP in these countries and accounting for 9% to 15% of gross value added in manufacturing.[j] The industry also increased the countries' roles in the global value chains, playing a role in generating export sales and attracting foreign investment.[k] The production structure of the industry differs considerably across Southeast Asia. Thailand's production is typically capital intensive, focusing on electronic hardware components like hard-disk drives (HDDs) and semiconductor integrated circuits. Conversely, Cambodia is

continued on next page

Box 1 *continued*

currently focused on more labor-intensive production of electrical components like wires, cables, and transformers.

e) **Digital trade.** Digital exports include digitally enabled products (e.g., apps and e-commerce), digitally enabled services (e.g., online advertising and business process outsourcing), and indirect digital services. Traditional economic metrics have failed to keep pace with the rapid growth of the digital economy and there is currently a lack of robust data to measure the importance of digital trade for exports. Recent estimates suggest digital exports are already very important to the focus countries (e.g., it already ranks as the 6th largest export sector in the Philippines and the 11th in Indonesia) and could grow as much as nine times in these countries by 2030. The source of this digital trade value varies significantly by country. In the Philippines, digital exports are dominated by its information technology and business process outsourcing (IT-BPO) sector. According to the IT & Business Process Association of the Philippines (IBPAP), the industry contributed 2.7% to total employment in the Philippines in 2016 and accounted for 10% to 15% of the global IT-BPO market share.

It is important to stress that while these five sectors are prioritized, the integrated nature of supply chains implies that sector reforms will also require cross-cutting policies. For example, it is difficult to target improved manufacturing productivity without addressing infrastructure development (e.g., transport and storage, information and communication systems, and construction). Furthermore, policy measures need to address issues in the relevant upstream sectors supplying raw materials to be effective. For instance, while agro-processing was selected as a focus sector, policies targeting the agriculture, forestry, and fishing sector are also important, and its implications must be explored. These five priority sectors serve as a baseline to also discuss improvements in ancillary sectors.

[a] ADB. 2020. *Key Indicators Database*. Manila. https://kidb.adb.org/kidb/.
[b] Thailand Business News. 2020. "Thailand's tourism sector to lose over $47 billion (UN report)." https://www.thailand-business-news.com/tourism/79806-thailands-tourism-sector-to-lose-over-47-billion-un-report.html.
[c] WTTC. 2020. *Travel & Tourism: Global Economic Impact & Trends 2020*. London. https://wttc.org/Research/Economic-Impact.
[d] ADB. 2020. *Reviving Tourism amid the COVID-19 Pandemic*. Manila. https://www.adb.org/sites/default/files/publication/633726/reviving-tourism-amid-covid-19-pandemic.pdf.
[e] S. Boettiger, N. Denis, and S. Sanghvi. 2017. Successful agricultural transformations: Six core elements of planning and delivery. *McKinsey & Company*. 1 December. https://www.mckinsey.com/industries/chemicals/our-insights/successful-agricultural-transformations-six-core-elements-of-planning-and-delivery.
[f] International Labour Organization (ILO). 2020. *Recommendations for garment manufacturers on how to address the COVID-19 pandemic*. Geneva. https://www.ilo.org/wcmsp5/groups/public/---asia/---ro-bangkok/documents/briefingnote/wcms_741642.pdf.
[g] National Institute for Statistics. 2020. *National accounts*. Phnom Penh. https://www.nis.gov.kh/nis/NA/NA2018_Tab_files/TAB1-2.htm.
[h] Vasundhara Rastogi. 2018. Cambodia's Garment Manufacturing Industry. *ASEAN Briefing*. 1 November. https://www.aseanbriefing.com/news/cambodias-garment-manufacturing-industry/.
[i] ILO. 2020. The supply chain ripple effect: How COVID-19 is affecting garment workers and factories in Asia and the Pacific. Geneva. o.
[j] The data was sourced from national statistics from the three countries.
[k] ILO. 2019. *The electronics industry in Indonesia and its integration into global supply chains*. Geneva. https://www.ilo.org/wcmsp5/groups/public/---ed_dialogue/---sector/documents/publication/wcms_732119.pdf.

TOURISM INDUSTRY

Sharp declines in international arrivals in 2020 across focus countries

Cambodia: 80%

Indonesia: 75%

Myanmar: 75%

Philippines: 84%

Thailand: 83%

Four major challenges pre-COVID-19

Structural imbalances

Infrastructure gaps

Large share of informal employment

Low average spend per tourist

Three major shifts from COVID-19

Increased emphasis on health and hygiene factors

Preference for proximity tourism

Demand for environmentally sustainable tourism

Four areas of policy action

Restoring demand

- Improve coordination to reduce information gaps
- Develop domestic marketing campaigns

Building new channels of demand

- Develop more tourism destinations
- Develop policies to regulate halal tourism

Building capacities to support future demand

- Provide digital and nondigital skills development
- Identify the current status of digitalization

Increasing resilience of the industry

- Improve communication channels between the private sector and the government
- Create a permanent crisis management task force

SECTION II

Tourism

▶ **Tourism accounts for over 20% of GDP and employment in some focus countries.**

Tourism is a significant driver of two major sectors—wholesale and retail trade, and accommodation and food service activities—and has been a key contributor to economic growth in the five countries. Apart from Southeast Asia's history, culture, and endowment of natural landscapes, developments in low-cost air transport, rising incomes, and targeted tourism investment have led to rapidly growing tourism industries. For example, the number of visitor arrivals to Southeast Asia increased significantly from 2005 to 2019, growing from 37 million in 2005 to nearly 144 million in 2019.[1] Before COVID-19, the World Travel & Tourism Council estimated there could be over $780 billion worth of travel and tourism investment in the region between 2016 to 2026.[2] Southeast Asian countries also introduced regional initiatives such as the "ASEAN Tourism Strategic Plan, 2016–2025" to further develop the industry, which includes reforms such as visa liberalization.[3]

The tourism industry witnessed significant growth in the focus countries over the last decade. Figure 1 shows the increase in international tourists across the region in the last decade, where the total number of international visitor arrivals more than doubled from around 66 million in 2009 to 144 million in 2019. Thailand alone accounted for almost 30% of total arrivals in Southeast Asia in 2019. Unsurprisingly, tourism plays a significant economic role across Southeast Asian countries.

Table 1 summarizes the industry's economic significance across the region. It shows that tourism is particularly critical for Cambodia, the Philippines, and Thailand, where it accounted for at least 20% of GDP, employment, and total exports in 2019. Such trends have led to a sharp rise in hospitality assets and infrastructure across the focus countries. For example, the supply of beds in classified hotels in Indonesia increased from 124,789 in 2010 to 314,051 in 2018.[4]

To cater to the further expected increase in tourist arrivals, the countries had plans before COVID-19 to upgrade their infrastructure. For instance, Indonesia had plans to expand Jakarta's Soekarno-Hatta International Airport and build a new greenfield airport in the city.[5] The Government of Thailand announced expansion plans for Bangkok's Suvarnabhumi airport.[6] Reviving the tourism industry in the focus countries could generate positive spillover effects in the region due to the significant interdependence between the Southeast Asian countries in the tourism sector. Thailand receives 51% of international visitors coming to the Greater Mekong Subregion (GMS).[7] Many visitors to Thailand are likely to visit other countries in the region,

[1]   ASEAN Stats. 2021. *ASEAN Visitor Arrivals Dashboard*. Jakarta. https://data.aseanstats.org/dashboard/tourism.
[2]   WTTC. 2016. *Travel & Tourism Investment In ASEAN*. London. http://asean.psu.ac.th/Data/topic/1/t000072.pdf.
[3]   ASEAN Secretariat. 2015. *ASEAN Tourism Strategic Plan 2016–2025*. Jakarta. https://www.asean.org/storage/2012/05/ATSP-2016-2025.pdf.
[4]   BPS. 2019. *Number of Accommodations, Rooms, and Beds Available in Classified Hotel 2009-2011*. Jakarta. https://www.bps.go.id/indicator/16/307/3/number-of-accommodations-rooms-and-beds-available-in-classified-hotel.html.
[5]   F. Dahrul. 2019. Travel Boom Drives Multi-Billion Indonesian Airports Expansion. *Bloomberg*. 13 February.
[6]   T. Hongtong. 2018. AoT gives airport expansion okay. *Bangkok Post*. 21 November. https://www.bangkokpost.com/business/1798589/aot-gives-airport-expansion-okay.
[7]   ADB. 2020. *Impact of COVID-19 on Thailand's tourism sector*. Manila. https://www.adb.org/sites/default/files/linked-documents/54177-001-sd-12.pdf.

Figure 1: Rapid Rise in International Tourists across Southeast Asia

International visitor arrivals increased significantly across Southeast Asia in the last decade

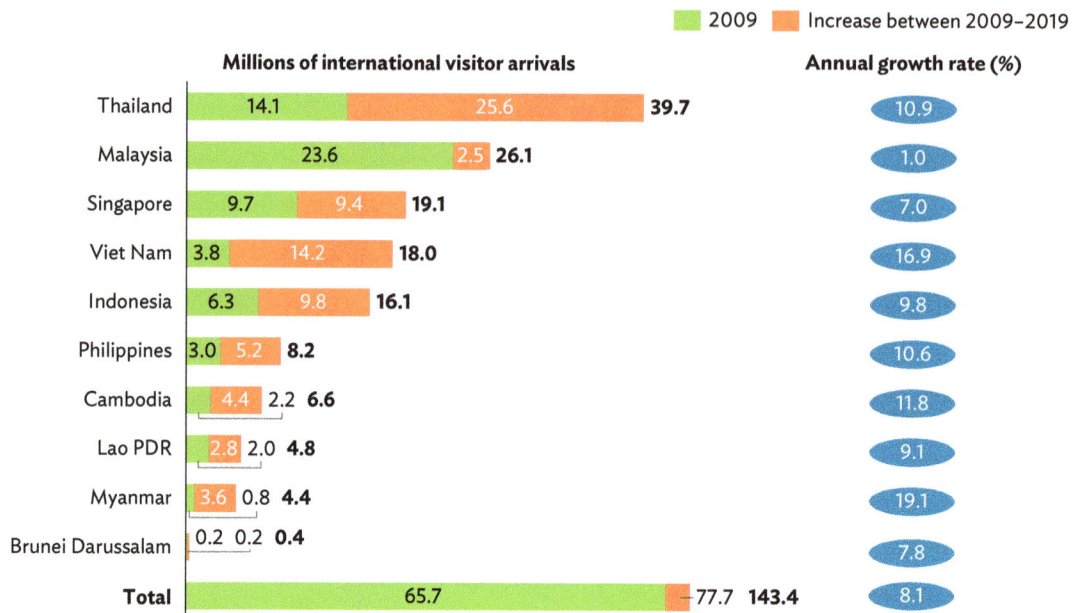

Legend: 2009 ■ | Increase between 2009–2019 ■

Millions of international visitor arrivals | **Annual growth rate (%)**

Country	2009	Increase	Total	Annual growth rate (%)
Thailand	14.1	25.6	39.7	10.9
Malaysia	23.6	2.5	26.1	1.0
Singapore	9.7	9.4	19.1	7.0
Viet Nam	3.8	14.2	18.0	16.9
Indonesia	6.3	9.8	16.1	9.8
Philippines	3.0	5.2	8.2	10.6
Cambodia	4.4	2.2	6.6	11.8
Lao PDR	2.8	2.0	4.8	9.1
Myanmar	3.6	0.8	4.4	19.1
Brunei Darussalam	0.2	0.2	0.4	7.8
Total	65.7	77.7	143.4	8.1

Lao PDR = Lao People's Democratic Republic.
Note: Data for Timor-Leste are unavailable.
Sources: Association of Southeast Asian Nations Secretariat Statistics; AlphaBeta analysis.

Table 1: Tourism as an Employment Driver

The tourism industry is a significant driver of jobs and economic growth across Southeast Asia

	Contribution of travel and tourism to Gross Domestic Product %	Contribution of travel and tourism to employment %	International Visitor Impact –Visitor spend as a share of total exports %
Brunei Darussalam	5.9	7.9	3.3
Cambodia	26.4	26.4	32.9
Indonesia	5.7	9.7	7.7
Lao PDR	9.1	9.6	12.6
Malaysia	11.5	14.7	9.4
Myanmar	4.6	4.8	10.3
Philippines	25.3	24.1	10.7
Singapore	11.1	14.1	4.2
Thailand	19.7	21.4	21.1
Viet Nam	8.8	9.1	4.4

Lao PDR = Lao People's Democratic Republic.
Note: Data for Timor-Leste are unavailable.
Sources: World Travel & Tourism Council; AlphaBeta analysis.

with up to 30% of long-haul market visitors estimated to visit multiple countries in the GMS.[8] Recognizing this collaborative potential, Myanmar and Thailand signed a "two countries, one destination" cooperative scheme in 2017[9] and a deal to promote tourism routes connecting ancient cities of the two countries in 2019.[10]

It is also crucial to note the importance of domestic tourism. The total value of domestic tourism expenditure in the region increased from $70 billion in 2010 to $145 billion in 2019, at an annual rate of about 8.5%.[11] This is comparable to international tourism spending in Southeast Asia which grew from $69 billion in 2010 to $148 billion in 2019, at an annual rate of 8.9%.[12] Domestic tourism is especially significant in the Philippines, where the total inbound tourism (2019 expenditure of foreign visitors and nationals permanently residing abroad) amounted to ₱548.8 billion, while domestic tourism (resident visitors) expenditure was at ₱3.1 trillion—implying that expenditures from domestic tourism accounted for over 85% of total tourism spend in the country.[13] Domestic air passenger traffic has also been increasing at a rapid pace. For instance, in Myanmar, the number of air passengers traveling between two local airports surged from 826,000 in 2008 to over 2.8 million in 2017 (or at a 15% yearly increase).[14] In some countries such as Indonesia, Malaysia, the Philippines, and Viet Nam, the number of domestic air passengers even exceeded international visitor arrivals in 2017.[15]

▶ **There were four structural challenges in the tourism industry prior to COVID-19, including imbalances such as overreliance on tourism sources.**

There were several challenges affecting the tourism industry even before COVID-19:

- **Structural imbalances weaken industry resilience.** Three main imbalances could be observed across the five focus countries. First, international tourism accounts for much of the industry's activity. For example, international tourists accounted for more than 60% of tourism spending in Thailand in 2019.[16] In popular destinations like Phuket, revenue from foreign visitors contributed almost 90% of the island's total tourism revenue (footnote 16). Likewise, in Myanmar and Cambodia, international tourists accounted for around 60%[17] and 80% of all tourist receipts, respectively.[18] Second, there is a strong reliance on a few key sources of foreign tourists, most notably the People's Republic of China (PRC); close to a quarter of all inbound tourist arrivals in Thailand, Cambodia, and Myanmar were from the PRC.[19] Figure 2 shows the share of the

---

8   Mekong Tourism Coordinating Office. 2017. *Greater Mekong Subregion Tourism Sector Strategy 2016–2025*. Bangkok. https://www.adb.org/sites/default/files/linked-documents/54177-001-sd-12.pdf.

9   *Bangkok Post*. 2017. Myanmar, Thailand push 'one destination'. 7 February. https://www.bangkokpost.com/business/1194041/myanmar-thailand-push-one-destination.

10 *Bangkok Post*. 2019. Thailand, Myanmar agree to cooperate. 19 April. https://www.bangkokpost.com/business/1663652/thailand-myanmar-agree-to-cooperate.

11 M. Moore. 2020. Value of domestic tourism expenditure Southeast Asia 2010–2019. *Statista*. 11 March. https://www.statista.com/statistics/1102321/southeast-asia-domestic-tourism-expenditure/.

12 M. Moore. 2020. International tourism receipts in Asia Pacific from 2010 to 2019, by region. *Statista*. 9 December. https://www.statista.com/statistics/261711/international-tourism-receipts-of-the-asia-pacific-region/#:~:text=In%202019%2C%20the%20North%2DEast,billion%20U.S.%20dollars%20in%202019.

13 Philippine Statistic Authority. 2020. *2019 Philippine Tourism Satellite Accounts (PTSA) Report*. https://psa.gov.ph/sites/default/files/2019%20Philippine%20Tourism%20Satellite%20Accounts%20%28PTSA%29%20Report_1_0.pdf.

14 ASEAN Secretariat Statistics. 2021. Domestic air passenger traffic (in Thousand person) (database). https://data.aseanstats.org/indicator/ASE.TRP.AIR.C.305.

15 ASEAN Secretariat Statistics. 2021. Domestic air passenger traffic (in Thousand person) (database). https://data.aseanstats.org/indicator/ASE.TRP.AIR.C.305 and ASEAN Secretariat Statistics. 2021. Visitor Arrival to ASEAN Member States by Origin Countries (in person) (database). https://data.aseanstats.org/visitors.

16 National Economic and Social Development Council (NESDC). 2020. *NESDC Economic Report – Thai Economic Performance in Q2 and Outlook for 2020*. Bangkok. https://www.nesdc.go.th/nesdb_en/article_attach/article_file_20200827153114.pdf.

17 World Travel & Tourism Council. 2020. *Myanmar: 2020 Annual research: Key highlights*. London. https://wttc.org/Research/Economic-Impact.

18 World Travel & Tourism Council. 2020. *Cambodia: 2020 Annual research: Key highlights*. London. https://wttc.org/Research/Economic-Impact.

19 The estimates were taken from individual country reports. World Travel & Tourism Council. 2020. London. https://wttc.org/Research/Economic-Impact.

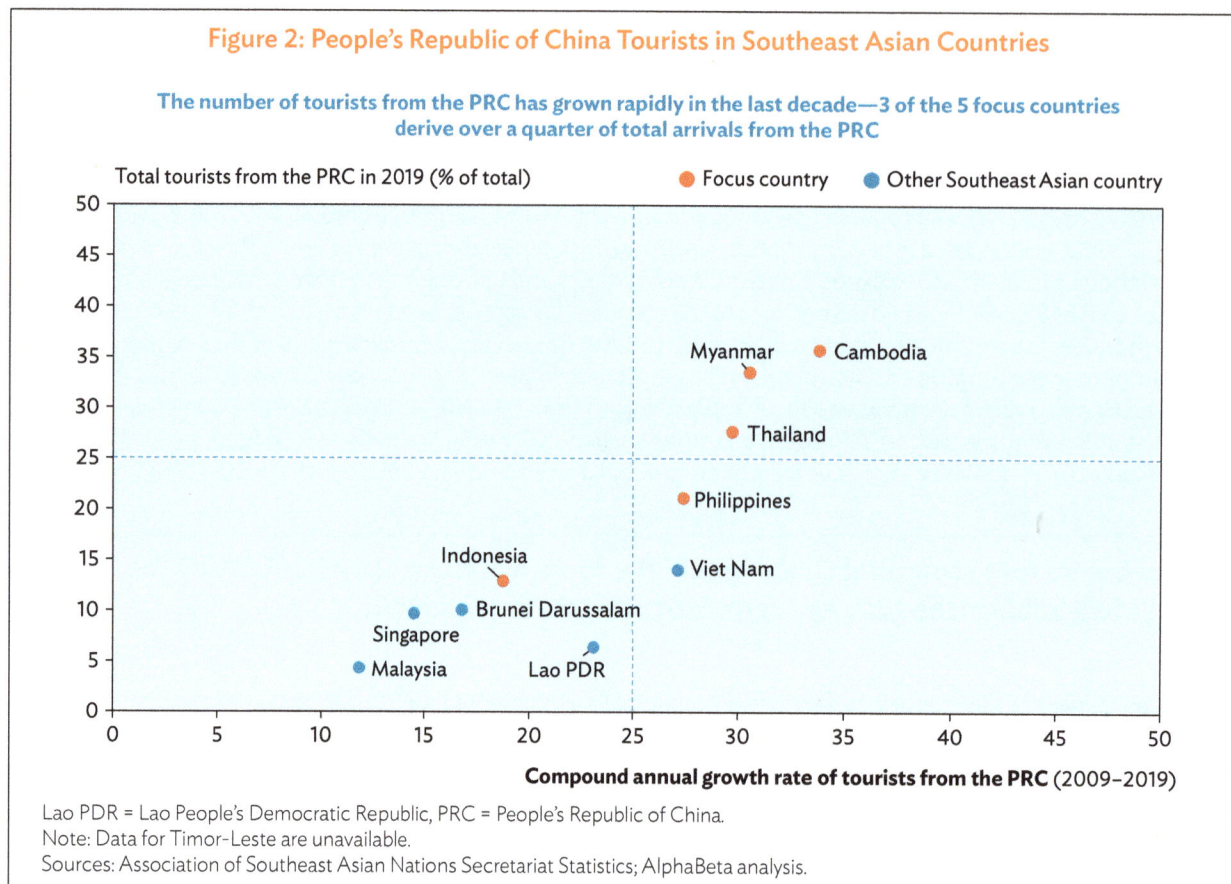

Figure 2: People's Republic of China Tourists in Southeast Asian Countries

The number of tourists from the PRC has grown rapidly in the last decade—3 of the 5 focus countries derive over a quarter of total arrivals from the PRC

Lao PDR = Lao People's Democratic Republic, PRC = People's Republic of China.
Note: Data for Timor-Leste are unavailable.
Sources: Association of Southeast Asian Nations Secretariat Statistics; AlphaBeta analysis.

extent of reliance on tourists from the PRC. Consequently, this has led to an overdependence on Chinese tourist spending, accounting for almost 30% of Thailand's international tourism receipts in 2019.[20] Third, tourism activities in the five countries were unsustainably concentrated in a limited number of destinations, resulting in pressures negatively impacting the environmental and social landscapes of popular tourist destinations. For example, Jakarta and Bali accounted for almost 40% of all hotel stays in Indonesia in 2016.[21] Similarly, 40% of all tourism revenue in Thailand came from Bangkok in 2019.[22] In 2017, Bali had to declare a "garbage emergency" after plastic waste inundated its beaches.[23] Likewise, tourist overloads and its negative environmental impacts led to temporary closures of Maya Bay, Thailand and parts of Boracay Island, Philippines to allow nature to recover.[24]

- **Infrastructure gaps limit diversification in tourism destinations.** Infrastructure gaps in the five countries limit these countries from diversifying beyond a few primary tourist hotspots. Myanmar has the weakest tourism infrastructure across Southeast Asia, with infrastructure investment failing to keep up with the sharp

---

[20] Ministry of Tourism & Sports. 2020. *International Tourist Arrivals to Thailand 2020*. Bangkok. https://www.mots.go.th/more_news_new.php?cid=599.

[21] BPS. 2019. *Number Of Accommodation, Average Worker, And Visitor Per Day By Province, 2018 (Classified Hotel)*. Jakarta. https://www.bps.go.id/statictable/2009/04/06/1373/jumlah-akomodasi-rata-rata-pekerja-dan-jumlah-tamu-per-hari-menurut-provinsi-2009-2018-hotel-bintang-.html.

[22] *Tat News*. 2019. Tourism revenue grows in Thailand's emerging destinations in Jan-June 2019. Bangkok. https://www.tatnews.org/2019/09/tourism-revenue-grows-in-thailands-emerging-destinations-in-jan-june-2019.

[23] R. Oliphant. 2017. Bali declares rubbish emergency as rising tide of plastic buries beaches. *The Telegraph*. https://www.telegraph.co.uk/news/2017/12/28/bali-declares-rubbish-emergency-rising-tide-plastic-buries-beaches/.

[24] South China Morning Post. 2018. *Famous Southeast Asian beaches will close due to environmental concerns and tourism overload*. https://www.scmp.com/news/asia/southeast-asia/article/2139181/famous-southeast-asian-beaches-close-due-environmental.

rise in tourism demand.[25] Indonesia continues to lag behind its regional peers in foreign tourist arrivals due to the infrastructure deficit though the country has some of the world's best diving spots, cultural heritage sites, and natural wonders. In 2019, it received nearly 16 million international tourists,[26] less than half of Thailand's 40 million international arrivals.[27] Limited tourist service infrastructure is one of the key reasons behind this gap.[28] The lack of consistent water supply and sanitation facilities contributed to the erosion of natural assets in some tourist destinations, making it harder for Indonesia to attract tourists (footnote 28). According to the World Economic Forum's Travel & Competitiveness Report in 2019, Indonesia's score on tourist service infrastructure is lower than the Southeast Asia average.[29]

- **Informal employment.** Informal employment represents most employment in the five countries' tourism sector. For example, in Myanmar and Cambodia, informal employment makes up nearly 70% and over 90% of all tourism employment, respectively.[30] A large share of informal workers in the tourism industry could present several challenges. First, it could make achieving and maintaining high-quality standards more difficult. In Myanmar, deficiencies in service qualifications among potential employees is a persistent challenge for business owners.[31] Second, it could make meeting regional objectives difficult. The "ASEAN Tourism Strategy Plan 2016–2025" lists the regional tourism standard certification system as one means to enhance Southeast Asia's competitiveness as a single tourism destination, which could be difficult to implement without formalizing the industry (footnote 3). Third, the informal tourism industry could make recovering from future economic crises more challenging since workers and businesses are difficult to identify and because informal workers are typically the hardest hit. Informal workers typically lack access to basic protection, including social protection coverage, and are often disadvantaged in accessing health care services (footnote 30). The lack of vocational schools is also a significant barrier to formalizing employment. For instance, in Myanmar, most vocational centers for the hospitality industry are in Yangon or Mandalay, several hours away from the rest of the country, making it hard for workers from other areas to receive certification (footnote 31).

- **Low average spending per tourist.** Catering to low-value tourists, like backpackers, and limited destination and product diversification has meant that average spending per tourist is far below the Southeast Asian target for many countries. In Thailand, an average tourist from the PRC spent nearly $958 in 2018.[32] In Cambodia, an average international tourist spent $705 in 2018.[33] The "ASEAN Tourism Strategy Plan 2016–2025" plans to increase per capita spending by international tourists from $877 in 2013 to $1,500 in 2025 (footnote 3). In Cambodia, the average daily spending of tourists declined by about 18% from 2013 to 2018 due to low tourism destination and product diversification.[34] Figure 3 shows international tourist's average spending in the focus countries in 2018. While Thailand has already met the target, the remaining countries are still behind—in particular, Cambodia needs to grow average spending by 9.8% annually and Indonesia

[25] World Travel and Tourism Council. 2016. *Travel and tourism investment in ASEAN*. London. http://asean.psu.ac.th/Data/topic/1/t000072.pdf.
[26] BPS. 2020. Number of Foreign Tourist Visits to Indonesia by Nationality (People), 2018–2019. Jakarta https://www.bps.go.id/indicator/16/1821/1/number-of-foreign-tourist-visits-to-indonesia-by-nationality.html.
[27] National Statistical Office. 2020. *International Tourist Arrivals to Thailand by Nationality: 2010–2019.* http://statbbi.nso.go.th/staticreport/page/sector/en/17.aspx.
[28] World Bank. 2016. Program-for-results Information Document (PID) Concept stage. Bangkok. https://ewsdata.rightsindevelopment.org/files/documents/99/WB-P157599_MdQqQ2z.pdf.
[29] WEF. 2019. *The Travel & Tourism Competitiveness Report 2019.* Cologny. http://www3.weforum.org/docs/WEF_TTCR_2019.pdf.
[30] ILO. 2020. *COVID-19 and employment in the tourism sector: Impact and response in Asia and the Pacific.* Bangkok. https://www.ilo.org/wcmsp5/groups/public/---asia/---ro-bangkok/documents/briefingnote/wcms_742664.pdf.
[31] K. Schregenberger. 2018. Tourism sector still desperate for talent. *Frontier Myanmar.* 23 March. https://www.frontiermyanmar.net/en/tourism-sector-still-desperate-for-talent/.
[32] National Statistical Office. 2020. *Number of Tourists, Length of Stay, Per Capita Spending and Tourism Receipts from International Tourist Arrivals to Thailand by Country of Residence: 2010–2019.* Bangkok. http://statbbi.nso.go.th/staticreport/page/sector/en/17.aspx.
[33] Ministry of Tourism. 2018. *Tourism Statistics Report 2018.* Phnom Penh. https://amchamcambodia.net/wp-content/uploads/2019/04/Year_2018.pdf.
[34] World Bank. 2020. *Enabling ecotourism development in Cambodia.* Washington, DC. https://blogs.worldbank.org/eastasiapacific/enabling-ecotourism-development-cambodia.

Figure 3: Per Capita Spending by International Tourists

Cambodia, Indonesia, and the Philippines will need to raise per capita spending by international tourists to meet the ASEAN target

Per capita spending by international tourists in 2018, ($)

	ASEAN target	Cambodia	Indonesia	Philippines	Thailand
Per capita spending	1,500	779	987	1,357	1,709
Annual growth required to meet 2025 target (%)		9.8	6.2	1.4	-

ASEAN = Association of Southeast Asian Nations.
Note: Based on the target set in the ASEAN Tourism Strategy Plan 2016–2025 to increase average international tourist spending to $1,500 by 2025. Data for Myanmar are unavailable.
Sources: Association of Southeast Asian Nations Secretariat Statistics; World Bank Group; AlphaBeta analysis.

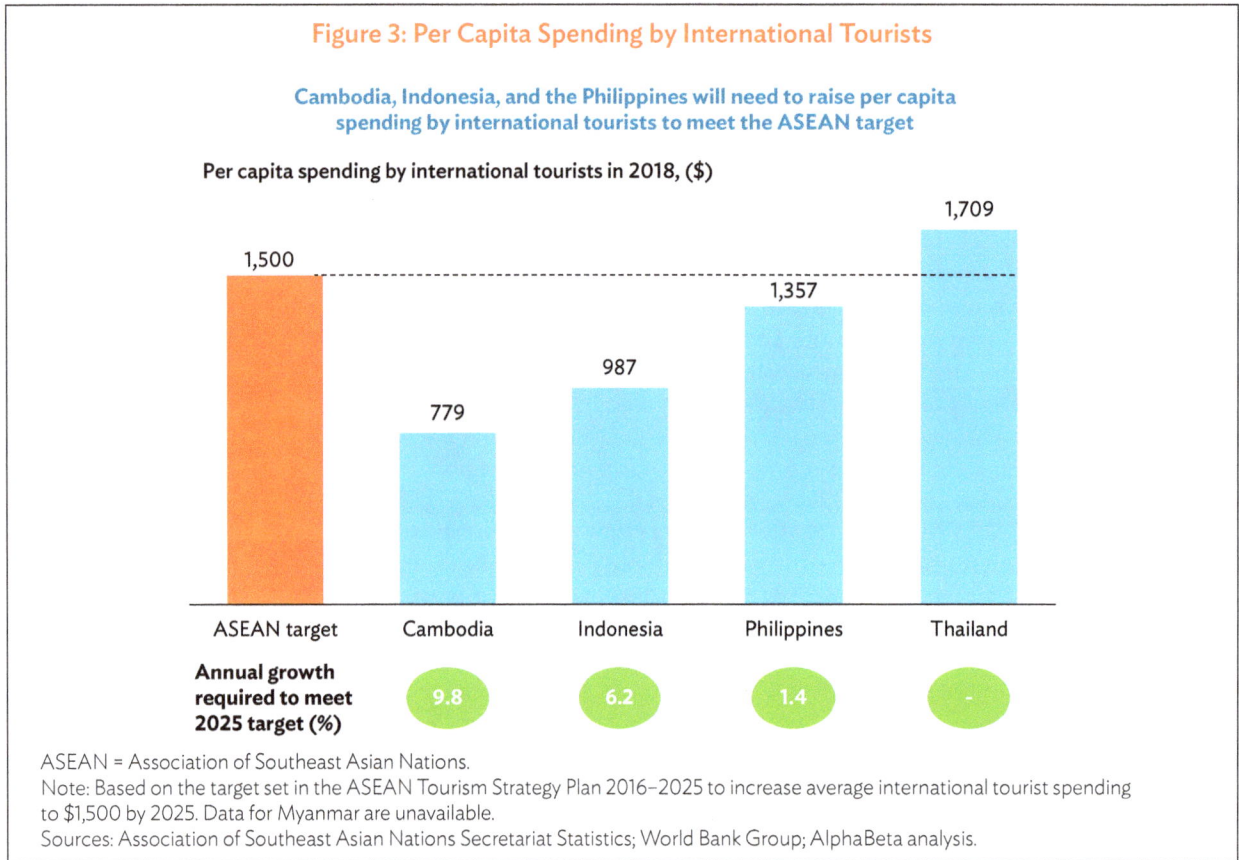

by 6.2% to meet the 2025 target. By developing more tourist destinations, countries could make tourists stay longer. Cambodia increased the average length of stay of an international tourist from 5.2 days in 1998 to 7 days in 2018 (footnote 33). However, this is still lower than the 9.3 days that an average international tourist spent in Thailand in 2018 (footnote 32).

▶ COVID-19 created three major shifts to the nature of tourism, beyond reducing overall demand.

Travel restrictions globally devastated the tourism industry across Southeast Asia. For instance, Cambodia's Ministry of Tourism revealed an 80% decline in foreign visitor arrivals in 2020,[35] Indonesia reported a 75% year-on-year drop,[36] Thailand's arrivals fell by 83% in 2020,[37] the Philippines experienced an 84% decline in foreign visitors in the same year,[38] while Myanmar recorded a 75% fall.[39]

---

[35] Xinhua Net. 2021. *Int'l tourist arrivals to Cambodia down 80 pct in 2020 due to COVID-19: minister.* http://www.xinhuanet.com/english/2021-01/27/c_139701642.htm.

[36] Statistics Indonesia. 2021. *Number of foreign tourist visits per month to Indonesia according to the entrance, 2017 - now (Visit), 2021.* https://www.bps.go.id/indicator/16/1150/1/number-of-foreign-tourist-visits-per-month-to-indonesia-according-to-the-entrance-2017---now.html.

[37] *Travel Daily.* 2021. Foreign tourist arrivals in Thailand fall to decade low. https://www.traveldailymedia.com/foreign-tourist-arrivals-in-thailand-fall-to-decade-low/#:~:text=Tourist%20arrivals%20slumped%20to%206.7,according%20to%20the%20ministry%20data.

[38] CNN Philippines. 2021. *Foreign tourist arrivals drop by 83.7% in 2020 — DOT.* https://cnnphilippines.com/news/2021/1/12/ph-foreign-tourist-arrivals-drop-2020.html#:~:text=In%20its%20year%2Dend%20report,8.2%20million%20arrivals%20in%202019.

[39] *Myanmar Times.* 2021. Myanmar sees 75% drop in tourist arrivals. https://www.mmtimes.com/news/myanmar-sees-75-drop-tourist-arrivals.html (accessed 19 January 2021).

The pre-pandemic challenges were exacerbated by COVID-19, leading to three additional challenges:

- **Increased emphasis on health and hygiene.** Health and hygiene have always been key factors in global tourism competitiveness, and the World Economic Forum Travel and Tourism Competitiveness Index has indicators to track health and hygiene levels.[40] The pandemic made tourists much more aware of the importance of health precautions, making these considerations crucial in selecting travel destinations. A recent study revealed that future travelers are likely to choose destinations perceived to be clean and have managed the pandemic relatively well.[41] For example, 72% of tourists polled indicated that they would consider the destination's social responsibility toward preventing the spread of COVID-19 before deciding to travel.[42] Consequently, there should be increased dialogue between health department policy makers and tourism operators to ensure they address travelers' concerns.

- **Preference for proximity tourism.** There are suggestions that COVID-19 could lead to a fundamental decline in long-haul, international tourism, a structural decline in total distance traveled per tourist per trip. Concerns on the threats of unrestricted travel remain and, nervous consumers may not wish to travel beyond their comfort zone,[43] leading to a shift in tourism patterns toward proximity or short-haul domestic and international tourism.[44] Other trends could also support proximity tourism. First, the post-COVID recovery could see the re-emergence of patriotic consumption (like in post-World War 2), where citizens support local businesses as an act of communitarian commitment (footnote 44). Second, a fall in household incomes could make domestic tourism more economically feasible. According to the International Air Transport Association, airfares could be lower in the short-term, but could rise in the future, due to constraints on aircraft capacity.[45] Third, adopting digital tools to conduct virtual meetings could lessen the demand for long-haul meetings, incentives, conferences, and exhibitions tourism.[46]

- **Demand for environmentally sustainable tourism.** COVID-19 will likely lead governments to promote environmentally sustainable tourism, and though it is not new, demand is rising. Governments can use the pandemic to develop new marketing narratives and initiatives. Indonesian public officials highlighted the value of using COVID-19 as an opportunity to make tourism more environmentally sustainable.[47] According to the World Economic Forum's Travel & Competitiveness Report in 2019, Indonesia was placed in the bottom 20% on environmental sustainability in the world (footnote 29). Thailand will close all its national parks for an annual average of 3 months beginning in 2021 to help them recover from tourism-related stress.[48] Cambodia's Ministry of Tourism released the Roadmap for Recovery of Cambodia Tourism During and Post COVID-19, focusing on ecotourism as one of the four pillars to revive Cambodia's tourism.[49]

[40] T. Weltman, M. Soshkin, and J. A. Bell. 2020. These could be the most popular travel destinations after COVID-19. *WEF*. 5 November. https://www.weforum.org/agenda/2020/11/these-could-be-the-most-popular-travel-destinations-after-covid-19/.

[41] PATA. 2020. *The Impact of Health and Hygiene on Post COVID-19 Destination Competitiveness*. Bangkok. https://crc.pata.org/health-hygiene-post-covid-19-destination-competitiveness/.

[42] K. Soni. 2020. COVID-19 could change travel – but not in the way you think. *WEF*. 25 September. https://www.weforum.org/discom?bobulate=G2CKD5eAVWn%2B9LldBniEE0te9zSebv%2B%2FiyrJiHBWVRAobPq0Q5ik1pS0GRS%2B%0A%2Fcu9BrtVmhQ%2BJDiWaCCiGaEcfw%3D%3D%0A.

[43] D. Loannides and S. Gyimothy. 2020. The COVID-19 crisis as an opportunity for escaping the unsustainable global tourism path. *Tourism Geographies*, 22:3, 624-632. https://www.tandfonline.com/doi/full/10.1080/14616688.2020.1763445.

[44] F. Romagosa. 2020. The COVID-19 crisis: Opportunities for sustainable and proximity tourism. *Tourism Geographies*. https://www.tandfonline.com/doi/full/10.1080/14616688.2020.1763447.

[45] B. Pearce (IATA). 2020. *COVID-19: Cost of air travel once restrictions start to life*. https://www.iata.org/en/iata-repository/publications/economic-reports/covid-19-cost-of-air-travel-once-restrictions-start-to-lift/.

[46] OECD. 2020. *Rebuilding tourism for the future: COVID-19 policy response and recovery*. Paris. https://read.oecd-ilibrary.org/view/?ref=137_137392-qsvjt75vnh&title=Rebuilding-tourism-for-the-future-COVID-19-policy-response-and-recovery.

[47] J. Winterflood. 2020. Post-Pandemic, Will Bali Rethink Tourism? *The Diplomat*. 10 June. https://thediplomat.com/2020/06/post-pandemic-will-bali-rethink-tourism/.

[48] R. Thanthong-Knight. Thailand to Close National Parks Every Year to Help Environment. *Bloomberg*. 4 September. https://www.bloomberg.com/news/articles/2020-09-04/thailand-learns-from-pandemic-to-close-parks-for-nature-recovery.

[49] Hin Pisei. 2020. Tourism recovery roadmap drafted. *The Phnom Penh Post*. 28 December. https://www.phnompenhpost.com/business/tourism-recovery-roadmap-drafted and Ministry of Tourism (2021). *Roadmap For Recovery of Cambodia Tourism During and Post COVID-19*. Phnom Penh. https://ibccambodia.com/wp-content/uploads/2021/05/Eng_Roadmap_Translation-Final-1.pdf.

▶ **Four areas need policy response to strengthen the tourism sector in the focus countries.**

Figure 4: Intra-Association of Southeast Asian Nations and Extra-ASEAN Visitor Arrivals

The number of extra-ASEAN visitors to ASEAN has grown by almost five times that of intra-ASEAN visitors

% compound annual growth rate

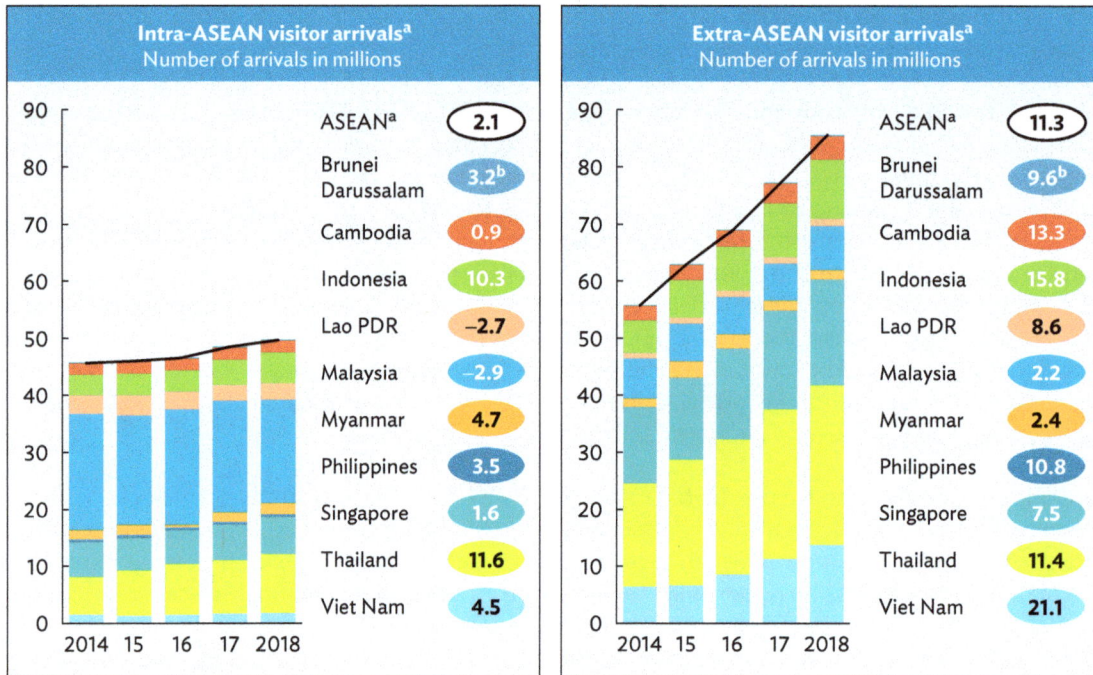

	Intra-ASEAN visitor arrivals[a] Number of arrivals in millions		Extra-ASEAN visitor arrivals[a] Number of arrivals in millions
ASEAN[a]	2.1	ASEAN[a]	11.3
Brunei Darussalam	3.2[b]	Brunei Darussalam	9.6[b]
Cambodia	0.9	Cambodia	13.3
Indonesia	10.3	Indonesia	15.8
Lao PDR	−2.7	Lao PDR	8.6
Malaysia	−2.9	Malaysia	2.2
Myanmar	4.7	Myanmar	2.4
Philippines	3.5	Philippines	10.8
Singapore	1.6	Singapore	7.5
Thailand	11.6	Thailand	11.4
Viet Nam	4.5	Viet Nam	21.1

(Left panel: stacked bar chart, years 2014, 15, 16, 17, 2018, vertical axis 0–90. Right panel: stacked bar chart, years 2014, 15, 16, 17, 2018, vertical axis 0–90.)

ASEAN = Association of Southeast Asian Nations, Lao PDR = Lao People's Democratic Republic.
Notes:
a   Does not include Timor-Leste.
b   Data for Brunei Darussalam only cover visitor arrivals by air transport.
Source: ASEAN Statistics.

The long-term potential of tourism in Southeast Asia remains strong with many growth opportunities, but appropriate policy responses are needed to harness this potential. For instance, tourism could tap the growth of the consuming class. The size of the middle class in Asia and the Pacific could grow by over 700 million people between 2020–2025.[50] However, intra-ASEAN travel is not growing at the same rate as extra-ASEAN travel (Figure 4). About 37% of visitor arrivals in Southeast Asia in 2018 were from other countries in the region compared to 45% in 2014. The number of extra-ASEAN visitor arrivals has been growing at 11% per annum from 2014 to 2018, almost five times the growth of intra-ASEAN visitor arrivals. If the growth of intra-ASEAN travelers is increased to even half the growth experienced in extra-ASEAN travelers (through policies such as simplified visa processing), this could result in an additional 15.5 million annual visitor arrivals by 2025

---

50   The middle class is defined as those households with per capita incomes between $10 and $100 per person per day (pppd) in 2005 PPP terms. For further details, see Brookings Institution. 2017. *The unprecedented expansion of the global middle class: An update.* Washington, DC. https://www.brookings.edu/wp-content/uploads/2017/02/global_20170228_global-middle-class.pdf.

compared to a business-as-usual scenario.[51] Furthermore, the enforced stoppage of the industry presents a timely window for countries to address existing imbalances (e.g., environmental damage), and to set the stage for a more sustainable future.

There are policy responses addressing the identified challenges and supporting the tourism industry in the short term, effecting structural changes for more sustainable growth in the longer term. The following policy responses could help the focus countries in four ways: (i) restoring demand, (ii) building new demand, (iii) developing capacities to support new demand, and (iv) building industry resilience.

(i)   Restoring Demand

To restore demand, countries could create enabling conditions to help the industry operate during the pandemic and help businesses adjust to take advantage of economic opportunities, like domestic tourism.

1. **Restoring tourist confidence.** Given the continued uncertainties over virus management, it is important to ensure that steps are in place to restore the confidence of international and domestic travelers. These may include:

   a. **Improving coordination to reduce information gaps.** Health and hygiene will be a top traveler concern. Policy makers must ensure the industry is updated on the latest guidance provided by health care leaders and work together to develop solutions like contact tracing to help maintain health and safety standards.[52] Enhanced communication for consumers and businesses is crucial. The Philippines' Department of Tourism published updated health and safety guidelines on the operations of accommodation establishments in the "*Bayanihan* to Heal as One" Act. Cambodia's Ministry of Tourism has been working closely with the private sector to implement epidemic preventive measures for tourism safety following the Ministry of Health's guidelines.[53] Improved information flows and cooperation will also help countries plan reopening strategies. For instance, countries would be better able to negotiate special travel visas and implement reopening plans.

   b. **Creating safety standards and certificates.** To assuage travel concerns, countries could certify businesses, and even cities, on safety and health protocols. Thailand announced plans to introduce a post-COVID health and safety certification for tourism establishments to help restore traveler confidence.[54] The Amazing Thailand Security and Health Administration (SHA) certification focuses on 10 tourism industry business types to ensure they commit to strict safety measures like ensuring sufficient ventilation and standards of cleanliness. These are the restaurants and cafes; accommodation providers; amusement and recreation parks; transport operators; travel agents and tour operators; spas, wellness resorts, and retreats; department stores and shops; golf courses and driving ranges; theatres and cinemas; and souvenir shops. Other focus countries currently have no existing plans to adopt such a policy, but can create similar standards and certifications for businesses. To boost the confidence of tourists, Southeast Asian countries could collaborate and agree on minimum international standards on health and hygiene in airports, transport, and accommodations. As the pandemic comes under control, countries could issue certificates for areas that adhered to safety and health protocols to attract both domestic and international travelers.

   c. **Promoting ways to help travelers minimize risk.** As countries attempt to reopen borders, tourism continues to be hurt by lockdown and quarantine uncertainties. Most countries addressed health concerns to reduce the risks of traveling. Authorities could explore other risk minimizing activities like offering special insurance packages and working with suppliers (e.g., flag carriers) to promote flexibility.

---

[51] ASEAN Secretariat. 2020. *Mid-Term Review (MTR) of the Master Plan on ASEAN Connectivity (MPAC) 2025.* Jakarta. http://aadcp2.org/6275-2/.

[52] D. Fenton. 2020. These 6 strategies can help tourism recover in Latin America. *WEF.* 15 October. https://www.weforum.org/agenda/2020/10/these-6-strategies-can-help-tourism-recover-in-latin-america-df689974cd/.

[53] *Viet Nam Plus.* 2020. Cambodia promotes domestic tourism. https://en.vietnamplus.vn/cambodia-promotes-domestic-tourism/174160.vnp.

[54] B. Ireland. 2020. Thailand to introduce post-Covid health and safety certification. *Travel Weekly.* 21 April. https://www.travelweekly.co.uk/articles/368532/thailand-to-introduce-post-covid-health-and-safety-certification.

The Singapore Tourism Board partnered with insurance companies to provide inbound travel insurance coverage for COVID-19 related expenses incurred in Singapore.[55] Travel operators like airlines and hotels could work with authorities to adopt more flexible booking and payment approaches to reduce tourists' risks. For example, Qatar Airlines offers a "travel with confidence" program with no change fees and ticket extensions of up to 2 years.[56] The governments of focus countries can coordinate with tourism industry players to provide these benefits.

   d. **Planning for gradual and targeted reopening.** Given the evolving and uncertain COVID-19 situation (e.g., variant strains and subsequent waves in several countries), recovery in tourism is likely to be uneven across countries and could face several "start-stops" though there is momentum in vaccine administration and the establishment of health screening protocols and air travel bubbles. Therefore, countries should plan for the gradual and targeted reopening of their borders, developing key enablers (e.g., clear protocols, proof of vaccination) and identifying specific tourist segments. For instance, Singapore led efforts to establish travel lanes for business, official, and high economic value travelers.[57] They can enter Singapore without quarantine for short-term visits and stay in a dedicated facility near the airport. New Zealand created an air travel bubble with neighboring Cook Islands allowing people to travel without quarantine.[58] Among the focus countries, Thailand allowed foreign golfers to visit six resorts with advance arrangements, and these visitors can move around the resorts.[59] Given the increased preferences for proximity tourism, Southeast Asian countries could focus more on visitors from neighboring Northeast Asia (e.g., Republic of Korea) instead of traditional long-haul markets of Europe. Another opportunity is attracting longer-term tourists who might want to move around several countries due to increasingly common work-from-home arrangements. These people could have plans to travel, but are uncertain about the travel, health, and hygiene protocols. Countries in the region could launch a portal where tourists outside Southeast Asia can access "safe spots" within the region along with accredited accommodations following regional standards.

2. **Promoting domestic tourism.** Promoting higher levels of domestic tourism can help offset some of the lost aggregate demand while international travel is still halted. Even as vaccines become widely available, domestic tourism is estimated to recover 1 to 2 years earlier than outbound foreign travel.[60] There are opportunities to redirect outbound travelers' spending to domestic tourism spending while borders remain closed. In addition, increasing domestic tourism is also a step toward a more resilient and sustainable tourism industry, especially with the possibility of consumer preferences shifting from long-haul international tourism toward proximity tourism. With rising incomes across Southeast Asia, the promotion of domestic tourism applies to all focus countries. While they all have some plans to strengthen domestic tourism, the scope and degree of initiatives differ. Thailand's push appears to be the strongest, with the government approving a budget of more than B20 billion to incentivize Thai nationals to travel domestically.[61] Myanmar's Ministry of Hotels and Tourism launched a domestic tourism campaign to offset the loss in international tourism revenues, which includes lifting quarantine measures between states and regions and gradually reopening tourism destinations with physical distancing and destination management guidelines.[62] While domestic tourism could be viable, it

[55]   STB. 2020. New insurance coverage for inbound travellers to cover Covid-19 related costs in Singapore. 18 November. https://www.stb.gov. sg/content/stb/en/media-centre/media-releases/New-insurance-coverage-for-inbound-travellers-to-cover-Covid-19-related-costs-in-Singapore.html.

[56]   Qatar Airways. Book today and travel when you need. https://www.qatarairways.com/en/travel-with-confidence.html.

[57]   *SCMP.* 2020. Coronavirus: Singapore to open business travel bubble; half of its migrant workers were infected. https://www.scmp.com/news/asia/southeast-asia/article/3113983/coronavirus-singapore-open-business-travel-bubble.

[58]   *Channel News Asia.* 2020. New Zealand creates its first 'travel bubble' with Cook Islands. 12 December. https://www.channelnewsasia.com/news/world/new-zealand-cook-islands-travel-bubble-covid-19-quarantine-13756124.

[59]   *BBC.* 2021. Thailand allows visitors to play golf in quarantine. 15 January. https://www.bbc.com/news/business-55672347.

[60]   U. Binggeli, M. Constantin, and E. Pollack. 2020. COVID-19 tourism spend recovery in numbers. *McKinsey & Company.* https://www.mckinsey.com/industries/travel-logistics-and-transport-infrastructure/our-insights/covid-19-tourism-spend-recovery-in-numbers.

[61]   *TTG Asia.* 2020. Thailand throws US$718m into domestic tourism push. https://www.ttgasia.com/2020/06/18/thailand-throws-us718m-into-domestic-tourism-push/.

[62]   *Myanmar Times.* 2020. Myanmar rolls out plans to boost domestic tourism. https://www.mmtimes.com/news/myanmar-rolls-out-plans-boost-domestic-tourism.html.

might not be enough to offset the decline in international travel (and the average spend per international tourist) in the short to medium term, especially for less developed countries like Cambodia and Myanmar.

Some specific policies to promote domestic tourism include:

a. **Developing domestic marketing campaigns.** While Southeast Asian countries all have some plans to boost domestic tourism, not many have comprehensive marketing campaigns (i.e., slogans, use of local influencers, dedicated websites, social media use, advertising partnerships with the private sector, and others) to attract local travelers. Focus country governments need to develop coherent marketing drives, bringing together industry stakeholders onto an integrated platform to promote domestic tourism. For example, Indonesia has a substantial marketing movement that includes social media campaigns and promotional programs (e.g., Bali Rebound), and its Ministry of Tourism also maintains the "Wonderful Indonesia" website, curating information on localized cultural activities like hand weaving, pottery, and painting to attract tourists to villages.[63] Furthermore, the campaign contains virtual tours for potential tourists.[64] Other campaigns include Singapore's $33 million "SingapoRediscovers" campaign[65] and Brunei Darussalam's "A Taste of Brunei" campaign urging locals to visit local attractions and spending on locally-made products.[66]

b. **Providing targeted financial incentives to citizens.** Governments could consider providing travel vouchers and discounts to incentivize their citizens to travel domestically. As part of its B19 billion ($641 million) "We Travel Together" campaign, Thailand plans to cover subsidies on accommodation, domestic flights, and e-vouchers that could be used for food and other services.[67] Indonesia's Ministry of Tourism and Creative Economy rolled out an incentive program dubbed Big Promo, where up to 50,000 vouchers are set aside for domestic travelers to redeem discounts on staycations, tours and attractions, meals, and shopping.[68]

(ii)   Building New Channels of Demand

Diversifying tourism offerings is critical in addressing some of the challenges (e.g., over-reliance on the source of inbound tourists, the low average spend of tourists, overly concentrated destinations) that have been particularly exposed by COVID-19. Some options for the focus countries are:

1. **Developing more tourism destinations.** There is a concentration of visitors in key destinations despite growing interests from tourists to visit less crowded places. Dispersing visitors has many benefits like lowering stress on infrastructure and increasing local employment, aside from its positive impacts on local economies and a fairer overall distribution of wealth from tourism. The concentration of tourism in a few key destinations occurs despite the resources available. Table 2 shows the latest results of the Travel and Competitiveness Index, showing that Cambodia, Indonesia, the Philippines, and Thailand all have "Natural and Cultural Resources" rankings that are above their overall industry competitiveness rankings. This implies a strong potential for focus countries to develop new tourism hotspots, relying in part on improving infrastructure and other enabling conditions highlighted by the index.[69] While some focus countries had diversification plans underway before the pandemic, such as Indonesia's

---

63   *Wonderful Indonesia.* 2020. Discover the Art of Hand-Weaving At These Indonesian Villages. 8 October. https://www.indonesia.travel/gb/en/trip-ideas/discover-the-art-of-hand-weaving-at-these-indonesian-villages.

64   *Wonderful Indonesia.* 2020. The Ultimate Virtual Holiday: Look Around Indonesia in 360 degrees. https://www.indonesia.travel/gb/en/video-360.

65   C. Min. 2020. *S$45 million tourism campaign launched urging locals to explore Singapore. Channel News Asia.* 22 July. https://www.channelnewsasia.com/news/singapore/singaporediscovers-45-million-tourism-campaign-stb-singapoliday-12952932.

66   R. A. Bakar. 2020. Domestic tourism campaign kicks off with over 50 activities. *The Scoop.* 4 November. https://thescoop.co/2020/11/04/domestic-tourism-campaign-kicks-off-with-over-50-activities/.

67   V. Vichit-Vadakan. 2020. Thailand launches US$641 million scheme to boost domestic tourism in pandemic's wake. *SCMP.* 10 July. https://www.scmp.com/week-asia/economics/article/3092568/thailand-launches-us641-million-scheme-boost-domestic-tourism.

68   TTG Asia. 2020. Tourism vouchers rolled out in Indonesia to encourage local spending. https://www.ttgasia.com/2020/11/24/tourism-vouchers-rolled-out-in-indonesia-to-encourage-local-spending/.

69   WEF. 2020. Infrastructure subindex (database). https://reports.weforum.org/travel-and-tourism-competitiveness-report-2019/rankings/#series=TTCI.C.

Table 2: Travel and Tourism Competitive Index 2019

The focus countries rank relatively strongly on natural and cultural resources

Travel and Tourism (T&T) Competitive Index (2019)[a]

Country[b]	Overall	Enabling Environment	T&T Policy and Enabling Conditions	Infrastructure	Natural and Cultural Resources
Cambodia	98	106	78	101	72
Indonesia	40	72	4	71	18
Philippines	75	93	53	80	46
Thailand	31	63	42	32	21

[a] Out of a total sample of 140 countries. "Enabling Environment" captures the general conditions necessary for operating in a country; "T&T Policy and Enabling Conditions" captures specific policies or strategic aspects that impact the T&T industry more directly; the "Infrastructure" captures the availability and quality of physical infrastructure of each economy; and "Natural and Cultural Resources" the principal "reasons to travel." The "Overall" ranking is calculated through the aggregation of subindices scores under each of the four pillars.

[b] Myanmar was not included in the study.

Sources: World Economic Forum; AlphaBeta analysis.

"10 new Balis" plan[70] and Thailand's plans to boost the tourism competitiveness of its second-tier provinces, there is now a greater urgency to do so.[71] Cambodia's Four-Strategic Plan for Tourism Development has a strong emphasis to diversify tourism destinations beyond Angkor Archaeological Park and the Preah Vihear temple complex by designating the Tonle Sap Lake area, Kulen Mountain, Siem Reap town and surrounding areas as zones for new tourism product development.[72] In Cambodia and Lao PDR, ADB supports the transformation of secondary towns in the central and southern corridors of the GMS through its Second GMS Tourism Infrastructure for Inclusive Growth Project.[73] This includes funding assistance to help upgrade selected national, provincial, and rural roads.

Beyond the identification and marketing of new destinations, a lot more planning (e.g., land, financial, private-public partnerships) is needed to improve access, like upgrading provincial airports, improving road infrastructure, and developing tourism service infrastructure (e.g., sanitation facilities).

2. **Catering to different types of tourists.** Focus countries could strongly consider a push into other forms of tourism aligned with their core competencies and competitive advantages to broaden their tourism base. Accessing new tourism segments could help expand the number of tourist sources, enhance environmental

[70] *SCMP*. 2019. Indonesia beyond Bali: the tourism development plans to create new hubs and diversify the economy. 15 August. https://www.scmp.com/lifestyle/travel-leisure/article/3022863/theres-more-indonesia-bali-president-joko-widodo-plans.

[71] *Bangkok Post*. 2019. Tourism agencies focus on second-tier provinces. 4 July. https://www.bangkokpost.com/business/1706510/tourism-agencies-focus-on-second-tier-provinces.

[72] *The Phnom Penh Post*. 2019. Government unveils tourism masterplan to increase visitors. https://www.phnompenhpost.com/business/government-unveils-tourism-masterplan-increase-visitors.

[73] ADB. 2018. *Proposed Loan and Grant Kingdom of Cambodia and Lao People's Democratic Republic: Second Greater Mekong Subregion Tourism Infrastructure for Inclusive Growth Project*. Manila. https://www.adb.org/sites/default/files/project-documents/49387/49387-002-rrp-en.pdf.

sustainability, and help increase the average spend per international tourist. For instance, Thailand is already considering this strategy by targeting higher-spending visitors seeking privacy and social distancing in the COVID-19 era. The Thai Tourism Minister announced plans to initiate marketing efforts toward wealthier European and American customers to invite them to luxury resorts in the islands of Phuket, Samui, Phangan, and Phi Phi.[74] Some channels of tourism with particularly high potential are discussed below.

a. **Ecotourism.** Ecotourism offers two key benefits. First, it can help create jobs, especially for disadvantaged communities and regions. Second, it can help preserve and replenish natural resources facing severe risks. Reductions in natural capital since 2000 have been decreasing Indonesia's gross national income by 7.2% each year.[75] The governments of the five focus countries have long been aware of the ecotourism's potential. Indonesia has worked with multilateral organizations such as the ILO to develop a strategic plan for sustainable tourism and green jobs.[76] Initiatives include "Indonesia Incorporated" which aims to attract 1.5 million foreign and 20 million domestic tourists to potential ecotourism hotspots like Bromo Tengger Natural Park, Komodo National Park, Kawah Ijen Banyuwangi Natural Park, and Tanjung Puting National Park.[77] The World Bank currently supports Cambodia in developing its ecotourism sector through the Cambodia Sustainable Landscape and Ecotourism Project, and an advisory report showed that much needs to be done in strengthening regulatory frameworks and key institutions, ecotourism destination planning and marketing, as well as private sector participation (footnote 34). The Philippines' National Ecotourism Strategy and the National Ecotourism Strategy and Action Plan 2013–2022 were designed to develop a globally competitive ecotourism destination. Likewise, Thailand's Second National Tourism Development Plan is dedicated to developing quality tourist segments such as ecotourism.[78] Despite these plans, there are numerous implementation gaps, particularly in the following areas:

- **Infrastructure development.** Infrastructure gaps remain an issue, particularly in the development of efficient transport and delivery networks, especially outside the first-tier destinations across the focus countries. In Cambodia, the World Bank identified several priority investments in infrastructure development, like providing suitable access to roads and boat docks, solid waste management facilities, and nature-based lodging and toilet facilities (footnote 34). The Green Recovery report (the third in this series of four reports) expands on the opportunities for governments to reorient fiscal spending to support economic recovery while ensuring that the longer-term benefits of environmental sustainability and economic diversification (e.g., promoting ecotourism) can be enjoyed. Furthermore, there are several ADB programs to help focus countries upgrade infrastructure for ecotourism development. ADB is currently working with the Government of Indonesia to mobilize investments for waste management and waste-to-energy developments to develop ecotourism.[79] In the Philippines, ADB initiated investment support to ensure the resilience, viability, and sustainability of key tourism cities.[80] Strategic investments being prepared will ensure access to adequate urban and tourism services with improved infrastructure and nature-based solutions, enhance planning and operation capacities of local government and facility personnel, and introduce market-driven interventions to enhance the skills of tourism workers.

---

[74] P. Chuwrich. 2020. Thailand Aims to Turn Away from Mass Tourism and Target the Wealthy. *Bloomberg.* 19 June. https://www.bloomberg.com/news/articles/2020-06-19/thailand-aims-to-turn-away-from-mass-tourism-target-the-wealthy.

[75] Bappenas. 2019. *Low carbon development: A paradigm shift towards a green economy in Indonesia.* Jakarta https://drive.bappenas.go.id/owncloud/index.php/s/ZgL7fHeVguMi8rG#pdfviewer.

[76] Ministry of Tourism and Creative Economy of the Republic of Indonesia. 2012. *Strategy Plan. Sustainable Tourism and Green Jobs for Indonesia.* https://www.cbd.int/financial/greenmarkets/indonesia-greentourism-ilo.pdf.

[77] Invest Islands. 2019. *Indonesia Ecotourism Features At The Centre Of The New Tourism Strategy Devised By The Government.* https://invest-islands.com/indonesia-ecotourism-centre-tourism-strategy-government/.

[78] The Ministry of Tourism and Sports Thailand. 2017. The Second National Tourism Development Plan. (2017–2021).

[79] ADB. 2020. *Country Partnership Strategy: Indonesia, 2020–2024, Emerging Stronger.* Manila. https://www.adb.org/sites/default/files/institutional-document/640096/cps-ino-2020-2024.pdf.

[80] ADB. 2019. *Country Operations Business Plan: Philippines (2020–2022).* Manila. https://www.adb.org/sites/default/files/institutional-document/533741/cobp-phi-2020-2022.pdf.

- **Legal frameworks to safeguard the environment.** There is still a lack of clear guidelines for the private sector on the regulatory landscape for ecotourism. Governments not only need to accelerate the development of legal frameworks, but also ensure these regulations are enforceable.
- **Innovative financing mechanisms to fund development.** Apart from traditional financing mechanisms, countries could look at alternative sources to fill their financing gaps. For example, ADB helps Indonesia explore coral reef insurance and blue bonds to develop marine aquaculture, artificial reefs, renewable energy, and ecotourism (footnote 79).

b. **Health and wellness tourism.** The health and wellness tourism segment consists of two categories: The health component refers to medical procedures like consultations and surgeries while the wellness component includes spas and yoga. Thailand and the Philippines can accelerate their current plans to expand the health tourism component. Due to the high quality of their medical services, the two countries are well-placed to become hubs for this segment in the region. This type of tourism could also play an important role in helping the tourism industries in these two countries recover. The Philippines' Department of Tourism announced plans to attract health and wellness tourists after the pandemic.[81] In Thailand, health and wellness tourists were one of the first tourists to be allowed to enter the country during the pandemic.[82] Thailand also announced plans to attract medical tourists to Phuket's luxury resorts in a bid to shift toward high-value tourism.[83] Countries could also develop strategies to attract tourists seeking wellness activities, as requirements are lower compared to the specific advanced skills and facilities typically needed for health tourism. To expand the health and wellness segment, countries could consider the following:

- **Develop talent for this segment.** Both Thailand and the Philippines face challenges due to a "brain drain" of their medical talent. Thailand has eight and the Philippines has six physicians per 10,000 people, far lower than the 22 physicians per 10,000 people in Singapore.[84] To cater to the domestic and international market effectively, the two countries need to invest in talent development and retention. Without such policies, health tourism could further the inequality in access to medical services in these countries. Apart from developing medical talent, countries also need to develop support staff. Lack of English language skills is considered a significant barrier to Thailand's medical industry, and the country must invest in language training for its nurses, receptionists, and other relevant staff to build this segment.[85] For wellness tourism, studies indicate that the lack of staff training is a key impediment to the industry's development. Much can also be learned from countries outside Southeast Asia. In Sri Lanka, the Export Development Board established the Sri Lanka Wellness Tourism Association in 2020 to provide coordinated and certified training programs, with over 50 stakeholders including indigenous Ayurveda practitioners.[86]
- **Improve connectivity with target markets.** Inadequate direct flights from North America, Europe, and Northeast Asia to the Philippines is considered a significant barrier in attracting health and wellness tourists. The Cebu Health and Wellness Council acknowledged the inability of this Philippine city to compete with Thailand and Singapore due to direct access issues.[87] The Philippines could improve air connectivity to boost this segment. There are opportunities for other prioritized countries to enhance air connectivity to negotiate with airlines and target countries, given the results of the

[81] *Balikbayan.* 2020. In post-COVID-19 world, Philippine health tourism primed for significant growth. 22 May. https://balikbayanmagazine.com/lifestyle/health/in-post-covid-19-world-philippine-health-tourism-primed-for-significant-growth/.

[82] *IMTJ.* 2020. Green shoots for medical tourism to Thailand. 5 August. https://www.imtj.com/news/green-shoots-medical-tourism-thailand/.

[83] A. Somanas. 2020. Hoteliers push back at Thailand's shift to target high-end tourists. *TTG Asia.* 22 June. https://www.ttgasia.com/2020/06/22/hoteliers-push-back-at-thailands-shift-to-target-high-end-tourists/.

[84] World Bank. 2020. Physicians (per 1,000 people). https://data.worldbank.org/indicator/SH.MED.PHYS.ZS.

[85] W. Pattharapinyophong. 2017. *The Opportunities and Challenges for Thailand in Becoming the Medical Tourism Hub of the ASEAN Region.*

[86] ADB. 2020. *Analysis of the Global and Asian Wellness Tourism Sector.* Manila. https://www.adb.org/sites/default/files/institutional-document/633886/adou2020bp-global-asian-wellness-tourism.pdf.

[87] *IMTJ.* 2018. Why medical tourism is not taking off in the Philippines. 6 April. https://www.imtj.com/news/why-medical-tourism-not-taking-philippines/.

International Air Transport Association Air Connectivity Index.[88] In the 2019 Index, Cambodia ranked 53rd and Myanmar ranked 67th globally, pointing to a need to enhance areas like air transport regulations and infrastructure.

c. **Government support in marketing.** In some prioritized countries, medical service providers have been unable to create a coordinated marketing campaign to attract tourists and relied on word-of-mouth to win business.[89] To achieve scale and to target the untapped international markets, governments could help the industry create more effective and coordinated marketing campaigns, and some have dedicated significant support to promote this segment. For instance, India introduced the National Medical and Wellness Tourism Promotion Board and the Ministry of Ayurveda, Yoga & Naturopathy, Unani, Siddha, Sowa Rigpa and Homoeopathy (AYUSH) to market the segment (footnote 86). The Government of India also released the "Incredible India" mobile app designed to aid in trip planning and features wellness experiences such as yoga prominently.

d. **Halal tourism.** Halal tourism is growing fast, catering to the faith-based needs of Muslim travelers (Figure 5). According to the Global Muslim Travel Index, rapid growth is expected, with total expenditure rising from $155 billion in 2016 to $300 billion in 2026 (driven by a rise in Muslim travelers from 121 million to around 185 million). Indonesia can take advantage of the opportunities from Halal tourism during a post-COVID-19 recovery phase. The Halal International Tourism Organization Secretary-General said operators and customers of Halal tourism understand the need for privacy, which implies that this tourist segment could recover faster than others, given current social distancing requirements and capacity limits.[90] Along with Malaysia, Indonesia got top rank on the Global Muslim Travel Index in 2018 among member countries of the Organization of Islamic Cooperation.[91] Indonesia has existing plans to expand this segment[92] and identified Aceh and West Sumatra to become Halal tourist destinations.[93] Halal tourism can also help target Middle East high-value tourists. In 2016, the average Saudi Arabian tourist spent more than $2,200, almost twice spent by average international tourists that year.[94] Halal tourism is not limited to countries whose faith is predominantly Islam. For example, Japan is constantly enhancing its hospitality for Muslim travelers to the country, with more Japanese hotels offering facilities and services for Muslim visitors.[95] However, apart from Indonesia, this segment has largely been downplayed in other focus countries.

To tap this segment, countries could consider two policy initiatives:

- **Strengthen Sharia certification for hotels.** Only Indonesia has built Sharia-compliant hotels classified through the Hotel Sharia business certification.[96] Despite certification, customers have complained of inconsistencies in Sharia-compliance.[97] Strengthening the certification process and monitoring compliance is critical in gaining and retaining consumer trust in this segment.

88 IATA. 2020. *Air Connectivity: Measuring the connections that drive economic growth.* Montreal. https://www.iata.org/en/iata-repository/publications/economic-reports/economic-reports/air-connectivity-measuring-the-connections-that-drive-economic-growth/.
89 A. Hyder et al. 2019. *Medical tourism in emerging markets: The role of trust, networks, and word-of-mouth.* Volume 36 (Number 3).
90 A. Yldiz. 2020. Halal tourism to make strides amid pandemic: Expert. *AA.* 10 August. https://www.aa.com.tr/en/life/halal-tourism-to-make-strides-amid-pandemic-expert/1937236.
91 Mastercard-Crescent Rating. 2019. *Global Muslim Travel Index 2019.* https://www.crescentrating.com/download/thankyou.html?file=hJGfOCBy_20190406_MC-CR_GMTI_2019_Interactive.pdf.
92 L. Afifa. 2019. Jokowi Sets Target to Complete Halal District in 2 Years. *Tempo.* 16 April. https://en.tempo.co/read/1196334/jokowi-sets-target-to-complete-halal-district-in-2-years.
93 *The National News.* 2016. Indonesia pushes for Muslim travelers to boost sector. 29 August. https://www.thenationalnews.com/business/travel-and-tourism/indonesia-pushes-for-muslim-travellers-to-boost-sector-1.146669.
94 BPS. 2019. Average Expenditure of International Visitor per Visit by Country of Residence (US $), 2015–2018. Jakarta. https://www.bps.go.id/indicator/16/272/1/average-expenditure-of-international-visitor-per-visit-by-country-of-residence-.html.
95 Japan National Tourism Organization. *Halal tourism is on the increase in Japan.* https://www.japan.travel/en/plan/muslim-travelers/.
96 S. Nurhidiyati et al. 2017. The prospects of Sharia hotel business in Indonesia. *Asia Pacific Journal of Advanced Business and Social Studies.* Volume 3 (Issue 2). https://apiar.org.au/wp-content/uploads/2017/07/11_APJABSS_v3i2_Bus-121-130.pdf.
97 I. Tisnadibrata. 2020. Indonesia taps into Muslim tourist market with Shariah hotels. *Arab News.* 18 November. https://www.arabnews.com/node/1585606/lifestyle.

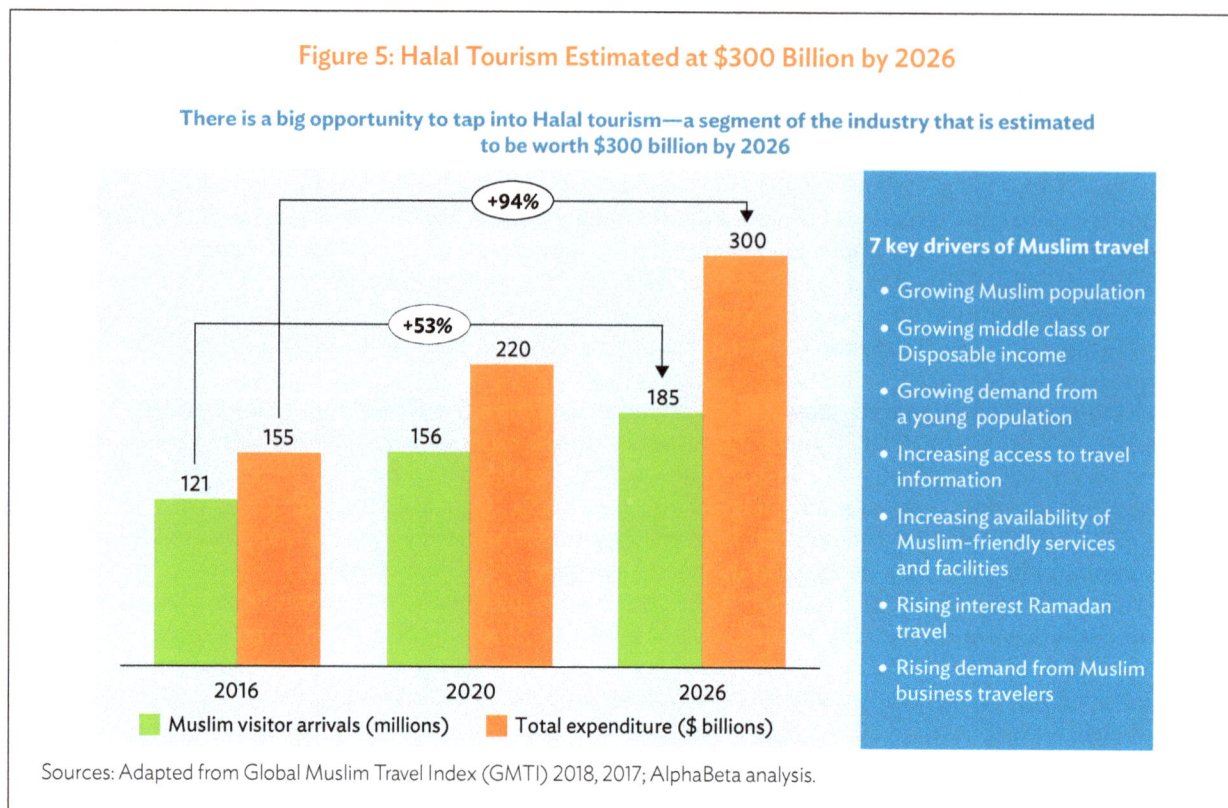

Figure 5: Halal Tourism Estimated at $300 Billion by 2026

There is a big opportunity to tap into Halal tourism—a segment of the industry that is estimated to be worth $300 billion by 2026

+94%

+53%

300

220

185

155

156

121

2016   2020   2026

Muslim visitor arrivals (millions)   Total expenditure ($ billions)

7 key drivers of Muslim travel

- Growing Muslim population
- Growing middle class or Disposable income
- Growing demand from a young population
- Increasing access to travel information
- Increasing availability of Muslim-friendly services and facilities
- Rising interest Ramadan travel
- Rising demand from Muslim business travelers

Sources: Adapted from Global Muslim Travel Index (GMTI) 2018, 2017; AlphaBeta analysis.

- **Develop policies to regulate halal tourism.** Currently, there is no specific regulation on halal tourism in Indonesia.[98] Hence, policies to regulate standards related to Halal-compliant hotels, spas, saunas and massages, and travel agencies must be created.

(iii)   Building Capacities to Support Future Demand

Much has been written about emergency measures to maintain capacities in tourism to ensure demand can be met when it eventually returns. State support for airlines, as well as businesses and workers in the tourism-related sectors (e.g., postponement of fees and taxes, credit guarantees, or cash aid), is common across Southeast Asian countries. ADB supports programs like $1.5 billion loans to Thailand and $250 million loans to Cambodia.[99] Beyond these, the emphasis should shift to developing higher capacities and more advanced capabilities to address future trends, support new priorities (e.g., diversification of tourism offerings), and spread and encourage this shift across the tourism global value chains. To do this, there is a need to invest in upskilling programs. Informal workers contribute significantly to the industry's employment in the focus countries (footnote 30). As governments consider diversifying toward new markets (e.g., high-end tourists) and segments (e.g., ecotourism), the need to train workers and businesses will increase. Building new and stronger capacities is crucial for MSMEs who are the hardest hit by the pandemic; even those which survived

---

98   A. Rasyid. 2019. *Sustainable Development of Halal Tourism in Indonesia: Opportunities and Challenges.* https://eudl.eu/pdf/10.4108/eai.26-1-2019.2283271. The Regulation of the Minister of Tourism and Creative Economy No. 2 of 2014 on Guidelines for the Implementation of Sharia Hotel Business was revoked by the Minister of Tourism Regulation No. 11 of 2016.

99   *ADB.* 2020. $1.5 Billion ADB Loan to Support Thailand's COVID-19 Response. 4 August. https://www.adb.org/news/1-5-billion-adb-loan-support-thailands-covid-19-response and *ADB.*2020. ADB Approves $250 Million Loan to Support Cambodia's COVID-19 Response. 8 July. https://www.adb.org/news/adb-approves-250-million-loan-support-cambodias-covid-19-response.

so far will find it difficult to stay relevant without significant capacity upgrades. These programs need to focus on raising core nondigital skills:

1. **Provide nondigital skills development.** This includes the following:
   a. **Undertake skilling programs.** Governments could directly undertake skilling programs for industry workers to increase their competitiveness and develop a strong service culture. Another area for improvement pertains to crowd control measures (i.e., queue management systems, capacity planning over the calendar year, and others), important in more sustainable forms of tourism. The focus countries generally have programs to upskill tourism workers. The Tourism Authority of Thailand organized Spanish and Portuguese language training courses online for tourism staff, targeting European travelers; however, the scope is small relative to the country's tourism potential.[100] The overall skills gap is quite pronounced in most of the focus countries. Cambodia's tourism ministry signed a memorandum with Swisscontact Cambodia to provide tourism and hospitality vocational skills training for Cambodian youth in five provinces of Kratie, Stung Treng, Rattanakiri, Mondulkiri, and Preah Vihear.[101] The agreement also sought to build the capacity of government officials to become trainers, facilitators, and evaluators of Cambodia's tourism human resources. Myanmar, with support from Luxembourg Development Cooperation Agency, established the Myanmar Institute of Tourism and Hospitality focused on training and developing supervisors, managers, and trainers in the hotel and tourism industries. Despite these programs, much more needs to be done because a large share of the industry's labor force works informally and does not have access to these programs, limiting their reach and effectiveness. Consequently, policies to include informal workers and more collaboration between industry stakeholders and vocational institutes is needed.
   b. **Build the management capability of businesses.** National governments could collaborate directly with businesses to improve the capabilities of their leadership and management. The Tourism Authority of Thailand has created a training program to help local operators improve efficiency, overcome challenging factors, and come up with efficient risk management against uncertainty.[102]

2. **Enable digital transformation in the tourism industry**
   Tourism is already at the forefront of digital change, and COVID-19 could encourage governments to accelerate digital transformation, especially for MSMEs. For example, 82% of travel bookings in 2018 were completed online or via mobile devices, without human interaction.[103] Fourth Industrial Revolution (4IR) technologies could potentially broaden the impact beyond online or mobile transactions to transform the entire tourism value chain. This includes technologies that, for example, provide a more seamless customer experience in booking trips (particularly in remote locations) or allow service providers to hire qualified staff. Added to this is being able to market more effectively through social media with the youth's growing usage and presence in varying platforms across ASEAN. This is a demographic segment with high spending potential, providing tourism options in fostering and strengthening an emotional connection between visitors and destinations and their local communities. For example, #MekongMoments was a marketing campaign initiated by the Mekong Tourism Coordination Office where businesses encouraged their customers to share their experiences via their social media accounts and tagging #MekongMoments.[104] The user-generated content was shown on MekongMoments.com, directing traffic to the respective websites of the tourism businesses. Box 2 has a list of global examples of digital technology utilization to support tourism.

---

[100] *Pattaya Mail.* 2020. TAT language training prepares Thai tourism personnel for post-COVID-19 era. 22 May. https://www.pattayamail.com/coronavirus/tat-language-training-prepares-thai-tourism-personnel-for-post-covid-19-era-301037.

[101] *Khmer Times.* 2020. Re-skilling and Up-skilling tourism workers in Cambodia. https://www.khmertimeskh.com/50753068/re-skilling-and-up-skilling-tourismwworkers-in-cambodia/.

[102] D. Worraachaddejchai. 2020. Tourism Authority of Thailand rethinks strategy as 2020 doubts grow. *Bangkok Post.* https://www.bangkokpost.com/business/1844554/tourism-authority-of-thailand-rethinks-strategy-as-2020-doubts-grow.

[103] TrekkSoft. 2019. *Travel Trends Report 2019.* https://www.trekksoft.com/en/resources/ebooks/travel-trends-report-2019.

[104] Destination Mekong. Be in the Moment - Travel Responsibly. https://www.destinationmekong.com/initiatives/mekong-moments/.

Box 2: Digital Applications to Support Tourism

- **Singapore.** The Singapore Tourism Board partnered with the American augment reality technology company, Niantic, to showcase tourism offerings and encourage residents to discover hidden gems in the country using the popular smartphone game Pokémon GO.[a] This was part of the country's SingapoRediscover campaign to support local businesses.
- **Viet Nam.** The Mekong Tourism Coordinating Office created the Experience Mekong Collection website to help build the capacity of responsible and sustainable tourism businesses in the Greater Mekong Subregion while showcasing them to help tourists discover these small and medium businesses.[b]
- **Finland.** The country's tourism promotion agency, Visit Finland, launched the "Rent a Finn" campaign to give potential tourists an opportunity to discover the Finnish ways of living and market the country as a tourist destination.[c] It had a live stream series showcasing different areas of the Finnish lifestyle (e.g., "Eat with a Finn" or "Relax with a Finn").
- **Scotland.** Since 2019, the National Trust for Scotland has sought to uplift tourism experiences using augmented reality.[d] For example, at Brodie Castle, a "Bunnies below!" sign prompts visitors to download an app, which launches an augmented reality experience by bringing a bunny to life.
- **Faroe Islands.** A remote tourism project was launched, where a "virtual tourist" with a mobile phone, tablet, or personal computer can view sights remotely guided by a local.[e] The local has a video camera and the "tourist" uses a keypad to get the local to move accordingly, perhaps moving closer to a scene, giving the "tourist" an interactive remote experience.
- **Wales.** Visit Wales, responsible for promoting the country's tourism, partnered with digital agency iCrossing to adopt a data-first approach to understand tourists' demands and tailor products and service offerings accordingly.[f] For example, it used search data from social media to understand tourists' concerns and how they could be addressed.[g]

[a] Singapore Tourism Board. 2020. Gotta explore 'em all! Singapore Tourism Board teams up with Niantic to promote tourism offerings through Pokémon GO. https://www.stb.gov.sg/content/stb/en/media-centre/media-releases/Gotta-explore-em-all-Singapore-Tourism-Board-teams-up-with-Niantic-to-promote-tourism-offerings-through-Pokemon-GO.html.
[b] Experience Mekong collection. http://www.experiencemekong.com/about-us-3/.
[c] *Forbes*. 2020. Finland's Tourism Board Launches Virtual 'Rent A Finn' Campaign. https://www.forbes.com/sites/micheleherrmann/2020/05/14/finlands-tourism-board-launches-virtual-rent-a-finn-campaign/?sh=25a02d6d55b0.
[d] *Engine Creative*. Augmented reality tourism experience developed for the cultural heritage sector. https://www.enginecreative.co.uk/blog/family-friendly-augmented-reality-tourism-experience-developed-for-the-cultural-heritage-sector/.
[e] Remote Tourism. 2020. https://www.remote-tourism.com/.
[f] *The Drum*. 2017. Location, location, location: iCrossing and Visit Wales on putting the country on the tourism map. https://www.thedrum.com/opinion/2017/06/23/location-location-location-icrossing-and-visit-wales-putting-the-country-the.
[g] Based on remarks shared by Jens Thraenhart, CEO, Mekong Tourism Coordinating Office (MTCO).

Enabling tourism's digital transformation is important in all the focus countries as the level of information and communications technology (ICT) readiness is very low. Table 3 summarizes the "ICT Readiness" subindex under the Enabling Environment pillar of the Travel & Tourism Competitiveness Index. Thailand is best placed to accelerate the digital transformation of its tourism industry with its high score on fixed-broadband connections, mobile phone subscriptions, and quality of electricity supply, among other indicators. With the declining cost of smartphones and increasing internet penetration, the other focus countries can expect ICT readiness to improve and should also start planning for digital transformation.

Providing digital skills training is crucial in digital transformation. The focus countries could:
  a. **Identify the status of digitalization.** Before they initiate digital transformation plans, the countries need to gain a better understanding of the industry's current capabilities. Singapore launched a Tourism Transformation Index, a self-diagnostic tool for companies to assess their strengths, identify areas of opportunity, and provide recommendations on the next steps to take in their digital transformation journeys.[105]
  b. **Create a skilling program to address skills gaps.** Once the status is identified, governments need to develop programs to address specific digital skills gaps. Thailand's Digital Economy Promotion Agency plans to provide digital marketing training for local operators (footnote 102). In Singapore, the tourism board helped develop the SME Leadership Academy, an online training program focusing on MSMEs in retail and

---

[105] M. Sagar. 2020. Singapore Tourism Board launches digital initiatives to support businesses during COVID-19 outbreak. *OpenGovAsia*. 27 April. https://opengovasia.com/singapore-tourism-board-launches-digital-initiatives-to-support-businesses-during-covid-19-outbreak/.

Table 3: Information and Communications Technology Readiness Sub-Index

Thailand is best placed to accelerate the digital transformation of its tourism industry

Score on 8 sub-indicators on ICT readiness[a,b]
WEF's Travel & Tourism Competitiveness Index, 2019

No.	Indicators	Cambodia	Indonesia	The Philippines	Thailand
1	ICT use for B2B transactions (1–7)	4.5	5.1	5.1	5.1
2	Internet use for B2C transactions (1–7)	4.6	5.6	5.1	5.5
3	Internet users (% of population)	34	32.3	60.1	52.9
4	Fixed-broadband internet subscriptions (per 100 population)	0.8	2.4	3.2	11.9
5	Mobile-cellular telephone subscriptions (per 100 population)	116	164.9	110.4	176
6	Active mobile-broadband subscriptions (per 100 population)	66.9	98.3	68.6	99
7	Coverage by mobile network signal (% of population)	99	98.6	95	98
8	Quality of electricity supply (1–7)	3.6	4.6	4.9	5.3
	Overall score on ICT readiness index (1–7)	**3.9**	**4.7**	**4.4**	**5.2**

ICT = information and communications technology, WEF = World Economic Forum.
Notes:
a   There is no data for Myanmar.
b   The first, second, and eighth indicators are measures on a scale of 1–7, where 7 is best among all studied countries.
Source: World Economic Forum.

tourism. The program covers digital marketing and provides online collaboration tools to support remote working. Programs could include courses on utilizing social media platforms for cost-effective marketing, accessing the sharing economy, and using digital contactless payment systems.

c. **Provide financial incentives.** Governments could consider financial incentives to encourage the industry's adoption of digital technologies. In Germany, tourism MSMEs can benefit from the Digital Now program (Digital Jetzt), which provides MSMEs with financial subsidies to invest in digital technologies (footnote 46).

The application of new technologies to the industry could result in labor productivity increasing by an average of 26% in the next five years.[106]

(iv)   Increasing Industry Resilience

COVID-19 demonstrated that global tourism is particularly vulnerable to sudden demand shocks. It also showed that tourism can be resilient by being flexible, adapting, and finding creative ways to survive. For instance,

---

106   ADB. 2021. *Reaping the Benefits of Industry 4.0 Through Skills Development in High-Growth Industries in Southeast Asia: Insights from Cambodia, Indonesia, the Philippines, and Viet Nam.* Manila. https://www.adb.org/publications/benefits-industry-skills-development-southeast-asia.

Singapore hotels have been used as quarantine facilities for people entering the country.[107] In the United Kingdom, hospitality businesses such as the Cairn Group have redeployed their hotel staff to nursing homes given transferable service skills.[108] However, there is a strong need to develop initiatives and enact reforms to strengthen the industry's resiliency. To increase resiliency, countries could:

1. **Improve data collection and availability for faster crisis response.** The crisis showed the lack of available timely data to support policy and business decision-making in crises (footnote 46). The time lag of official data's publication and the lack of granular data (e.g., monthly data) have been exposed in recent months. For example, while Indonesia and Cambodia publish monthly reports on tourism statistics,[109] Myanmar does not. Several Indonesian experts argued that the lack of real-time economic indicators made it challenging for businesses to plan for varying scenarios during the pandemic.[110] Better data made easily available could help the industry reach target customers better. For example, Thailand announced plans to identify and invite repeat customers to luxury resorts, focusing on high-end tourism (footnote 74). Countries also need to pay attention to data security. Cyberattacks on Myanmar's COVID-19 QR pass system reportedly left the private data of its residents exposed.[111] To improve data collection and availability, countries could:
   a. **Simplify the worker and business registration processes.** To improve data collection, countries need to expand their ability to identify workers and businesses operating in the industry, especially with the significant number of informal workers in tourism. They need to simplify worker registration and business and worker licensing. They could consider setting up digital portals to ease the processes.[112] For instance, Estonia launched the e-Business digital platform so entrepreneurs can register their companies without going to any government agency, reducing the process from five days to a few hours.[113] In Peru, the Tax Authority and the Ministry of Labor introduced a mandatary electronic payroll system in 2007 for firms with three or more workers.[114] The system allows businesses to easily register employees resulting in almost 70,000 workers being formalized from 2007 to 2019.[115]
   b. **Create tourism-specific publicly available platforms.** The focus countries could launch tourism-specific products like data dashboards to improve industry transparency and help businesses forecast demand. Singapore launched the Singapore Tourism Analytics Network, a data analytics platform to analyze tourism-related data for actionable insights about the industry.[116] Countries could also use third-party data produced by technology companies and telecommunications providers to supplement their existing data and gain more understanding. For example, disease researchers in the US used mobile location data shared by Facebook to assess the compliance with social distancing orders.[117]

---

[107] NTU. 2020. Responding, Reopening and Repositioning: The Hospitality Industry in the COVID-19 Crisis. 22 July. https://nbs.ntu.edu.sg/NewsnEvents/Pages/News-Details.aspx?news=0ce2450d-a758-4ad5-a49e-21c98763de48.

[108] *Hospitality and Catering News*. 2020. Cairn Group redeploy hotel teams to help care homes. 27 March. https://www.hospitalityandcateringnews.com/2020/03/cairn-group-redeploy-hotel-teams-help-care-homes/.

[109] BPS. 2020. Tourist Visits Abroad by month (Visit), 2020. https://www.bps.go.id/indicator/16/1470/1/tourist-visits-abroad-by-month.html; and Ministry of Tourism. 2019. *Tourism Statistics Report: Year 2018*. Phnom Penh. https://www.tourismcambodia.com/img/resources/cambodia_tourism_statistics_2018.pdf.

[110] *The Jakarta Post*. 2020. High frequency data key to better mitigating COVID-19 crisis, researcher says. 15 October. https://www.thejakartapost.com/news/2020/10/15/high-frequency-data-key-to-better-mitigating-covid-19-crisis-researcher-says.html.

[111] S. Li. 2020. Cyberattacks hobble Myanmar's COVID-19 QR pass system, expose massive security flaws. *Kr-asia*. 1 October. https://kr-asia.com/cyberattacks-hobble-myanmars-covid-19-information-website-expose-massive-security-flaws.

[112] ILO. 2018. *New technologies and the transition to formality: The trend towards e-formality*. Geneva. https://www.ilo.org/wcmsp5/groups/public/---ed_emp/---emp_policy/documents/publication/wcms_635996.pdf.

[113] e-Estonia. 2020. e-business register. https://e-estonia.com/solutions/business-and-finance/e-business-register/.

[114] IZA Institute of Labor Economics. 2018. *Pathways to Formalization: Going beyond the Formality Dichotomy*. Bonn. http://ftp.iza.org/dp11750.pdf

[115] ILO. 2019. Electronic Payroll in Peru. 12 July. https://www.ilo.org/employment/Informationresources/Publicinformation/Videos/WCMS_716702/lang--en/index.htm.

[116] Singapore Tourism Analysis Network. https://stan.stb.gov.sg/portal/home.html.

[117] K. Paul, J. Menn, and P. Dave. 2020. In coronavirus fight, oft-criticized Facebook data aids U.S. cities, states. *Reuters*. 3 April. https://www.reuters.com/article/health-coronavirus-facebook-location/in-coronavirus-fight-oft-criticized-facebook-data-aids-u-s-cities-states-idUSKBN21K3BJ.

Google Mobility Reports could also help countries gain a granular understanding of the tourism industry by publishing mobility data on visits to cafes, theme parks, museums, and public beaches.[118] Online search data can help in real-time surveillance and provide more reliable forecasts of tourism activities.[119] In Germany, telecommunications provider Deutsche Telekom has been sharing anonymized data to trace population movement flows with the Robert Koch Institute, a government agency responsible for disease control and prevention.[120] Such information sharing could be extended to government tourism agencies to aid in their reopening plans.

2. **Improve coordination and cooperation among tourism stakeholders.** Tourism's cross-cutting nature means that an effective response to a tourism crisis requires coordination across several policy areas (e.g., food and beverage, accommodation, health, environment, immigration, foreign affairs). Formulating policies to help the industry recover, rebuild, and become resilient would require close coordination among the private sector, the government, and other countries in the region. To strengthen intra-country and regional coordination, countries can:
   a. **Improve communication between the government and private sector.** Governments can open new means of communication to enable faster response during crises. For example, Greece established an open communication line to enable tourism operators, businesses, and market representatives to contact the Ministry of Tourism to address emerging issues.[121]
   b. **Include industry associations in policy decisions.** The tourism industry is often fragmented because of differing interests. To improve coordination, governments should work closely with tourism associations to inform policy, and tourism businesses in several countries took steps to raise their concerns and propose solutions to governments. The US Travel Association worked closely with medical experts to prepare guidelines for COVID-safe operations (footnote 74).
   c. **Strengthen coordination among Southeast Asian countries.** Given the regional nature of tourism in Southeast Asia, coordination also needs to be strengthened among countries. In May 2020, Southeast Asian countries agreed to cooperate on seven efforts during the pandemic. One of the agreed-upon efforts was to "intensify collaboration of Southeast Asian National Tourism Organizations (NTOs) with other relevant sectors in the region, especially in the sectors of health, information, transportation, immigration."[122] To make this collaboration more effective for future crises, the focus countries can establish a regional multisector body that helps overcome the challenges created by tourism's cross-cutting nature.

3. **Develop a crisis management strategy.** To safeguard the tourism industry from future crises, countries can develop more effective crisis management strategies by:
   a. **Creating a permanent crisis management task force.** While many countries have created task forces to coordinate their crisis response to the pandemic, some look beyond COVID-19 in putting a crisis management system in place. For instance, Greece said that its Committee for Crisis Management will remain in place beyond COVID-19. Such task forces could be activated when required. For example, Australia activated its National Tourism Incident Communications Plan (NTICP) in January 2020 in

[118]   C. Newton. 2020. Google uses location data to show which places are complying with stay-at-home orders — and which are not. *The Verge.* 3 April. https://www.theverge.com/2020/4/3/21206318/google-location-data-mobility-reports-covid-19-privacy.

[119]   S. Civik. 2020. *Where Should We Go? Internet Searches and Tourist Arrivals.* IMF. Washington, DC. https://www.imf.org/en/Publications/WP/Issues/2020/01/31/Where-Should-We-Go-Internet-Searches-and-Tourist-Arrivals-48949.

[120]   OECD. 2020. Tracking and tracing COVID: Protecting privacy and data while using apps and biometrics. 23 April. http://www.oecd.org/coronavirus/policy-responses/tracking-and-tracing-covid-protecting-privacy-and-data-while-using-apps-and-biometrics-8f394636/.

[121]   OECD. 2020. *Tourism Policy Responses to the coronavirus (COVID-19)*. Paris. https://www.oecd.org/coronavirus/policy-responses/tourism-policy-responses-to-the-coronavirus-covid-19-6466aa20/.

[122]   *PRS Newswire.* 2020. ASEAN Agrees Seven Tourism Cooperation Efforts Amidst the COVID-19 Pandemic. 2 May. https://en.prnasia.com/releases/apac/asean-agrees-seven-tourism-cooperation-efforts-amidst-the-covid-19-pandemic-279097.shtml.

response to the bushfire crisis, extending it to cover COVID-19. The NTICP committee distributes consistent and reliable information on crises.[123]

b. **Developing a risk management system.** Countries could develop risk management systems to help them calibrate their responses even in a still evolving situation. Colombia, for example, plans to develop a Risk Management System for its Tourism Sector Reactivation Plan (footnote 46).

Many of these policy recommendations apply to the five focus countries. However, some of these recommendations can benefit from increased regional cooperation with the other Southeast Asian countries. Accurate data on movement restrictions in the region could enhance risk management and aid the implementation of reopening plans.

Table 4 summarizes the key policy recommendations and their relevance to each focus country.[124]

Table 4: Summary of Recommendations for Tourism

Key recommendations and their relevance to focus countries

Degree of relevance: High (blue) | Medium (green) | Low (orange)

Category	Recommendation	Cambodia	Indonesia	Myanmar	Philippines	Thailand
Restoring demand	Restoring confidence in tourists	High	High	High	High	High
	• Improve coordination to reduce information gaps	Medium	Medium	Medium	Medium	Medium
	• Create safety standards and certificates	High	High	High	High	High
	• Promote ways to help travelers de-risk	High	High	High	High	High
	• Plan for gradual and targeted reopening	High	High	High	High	High
	Promote domestic tourism	High	Medium	Medium	Medium	Low
	• Develop domestic marketing campaigns	High	Medium	Medium	Medium	Low
	• Provide targeted financial incentives to citizens	High	Medium	Medium	Medium	Low
Building new channels of demand	Develop more tourism destinations	High	High	High	High	High
	Cater to different types of tourists	Medium	Medium	High	High	High
	• Ecotourism	Medium	High	High	High	High
	• Health and wellness tourism	Medium	High	Medium	High	High
	• Halal tourism	Medium	High	Medium	Medium	High
Building capacities	Nondigital skills development	High	High	High	High	High
	Digital transformation of the tourism industry	High	High	High	Medium	High
Strengthening industry resilience	Improve data collection and availability for faster crisis response	Medium	High	High	High	Medium
	Improve coordination and cooperation between tourism stakeholders	High	High	High	High	High
	Develop a crisis management strategy	High	High	High	High	High

Note: This exercise is based on a broad assessment of the observed gaps and what countries have done (i.e., current responses in terms of presence and scope of policy measures).
Source: AlphaBeta analysis.

---

[123]   OCED. 2020. *Tourism Policy Responses to the coronavirus (COVID-19)*. Paris. https://www.oecd.org/coronavirus/policy-responses/tourism-policy-responses-to-the-coronavirus-covid-19-6466aa20/.

[124]   This exercise is based on a broad assessment of the observed gaps and what countries have done (i.e., current responses in terms of presence and scope of policy measures)

Box 3 provides an overview of some of the relevant country plans and ADB programs by country.

Box 3: Examples of ADB Country Programs on Tourism

The Asian Development Bank (ADB) has several lending and non-lending products and services related to tourism and the policy recommendations in the five focus countries:[a]

- **Relief packages.** ADB supports COVID-19 response in the focus countries by providing loans. For example, ADB provided a $1.5 billion loan to Thailand, a part of which would be used to support MSMEs in industries affected by the outbreak, such as tourism.[b]
- **Coastal tourism and ecotourism.** ADB currently supports Cambodia in developing coastal tourism and improving the resilience, competitiveness, and sustainability of coastal cities.[c] In Indonesia, ADB helps mobilize public and private sector investments to improve ocean health and develop ecotourism. Similarly, ADB is preparing a Sustainable Tourism Development Project in the Palawan province of the Philippines to support sustainable ocean-based tourism.[d]
- **Regional integration.** Through its regional programs in the GMS and as well as other subregional economic cooperation programs, ADB helped Myanmar build a sustainable and inclusive tourism industry, with emphasis on transportation, environmental protection, climate change, and human resource development including employment creation. In Cambodia and Lao People's Democratic Republic, ADB supports the transformation of secondary towns in the central and southern corridors of the GMS through its Second Greater Mekong Subregion Tourism Infrastructure for Inclusive Growth Project.[e] With its Country Partnership Strategy 2013–2016, ADB supported Thailand in the promotion of regional tourism.
- **Diversification in the industry.** To help Cambodia economically diversify, ADB focuses on comprehensively developing a few priority secondary cities with the potential to become tourism centers, like Kampot and Battambang, while helping the country upgrade selected national, provincial, and rural roads. ADB also supports the development of community-based tourism to help the economy recover from the pandemic by strengthening local capacity for community-based tourism development and promotion, supporting new and existing tourism and livelihood activities, and enhancing community-based public facilities and services.[f]

ADB = Asian Development Bank, COVID-19 = coronavirus disease 2019, GMS = Greater Mekong Subregion, MSMEs = micro, small, and medium-sized enterprises.

[a]   The Country Operations Business Plans include:
- ADB. 2019. *Country Operations Business Plan: Cambodia (2020–2022)*. Manila. https://www.adb.org/documents/cambodia-country-operations-business-plan-2020-2022.
- ADB. 2019. *Country Operations Business Plan: Indonesia (2020–2022)*. Manila. https://www.adb.org/sites/default/files/institutional-document/526266/cobp-ino-2020-2022.pdf.
- ADB. 2019. *Country Operations Business Plan: Myanmar (2020–2022)*. Manila. https://www.adb.org/sites/default/files/institutional-document/541976/cobp-mya-2020-2022.pdf.
- ADB. 2019. *Country Operations Business Plan: Philippines (2020–2022)*. Manila. https://www.adb.org/sites/default/files/institutional-document/384671/cobp-phi-2018-2020.pdf.
- ADB. 2019. *Country Operations Business Plan: Thailand (2020–2022)*. Manila. https://www.adb.org/sites/default/files/institutional-document/541811/cobp-tha-2020-2022.pdf.

The Country Partnership Strategies include:
- ADB. 2019. *Country Partnership Strategy: Cambodia, 2019–2023, Inclusive pathways to a competitive economy*. Manila. https://www.adb.org/sites/default/files/institutional-document/534691/cps-cam-2019-2023.pdf.
- ADB. 2020. *Country Partnership Strategy: Indonesia, 2020–2024, Emerging Stronger*. Manila. https://www.adb.org/sites/default/files/institutional-document/640096/cps-ino-2020-2024.pdf.
- ADB. 2017. *Country Partnership Strategy: Myanmar, 2017–2021, Building the foundations for inclusive growth*. Manila. https://www.adb.org/sites/default/files/institutional-document/640096/cps-ino-2020-2024.pdf.
- ADB. 2018. *Country Partnership Strategy: Philippines, 2018–2023, High and inclusive growth*. Manila. https://www.adb.org/sites/default/files/institutional-document/456476/cps-phi-2018-2023.pdf.
- ADB. 2013. *Country Partnership Strategy: Thailand, 2013–2016*. Manila. https://www.adb.org/sites/default/files/institutional-document/33990/files/cps-tha-2013-2016.pdf.

[b]   ADB. 2020. *$1.5 Billion ADB Loan to Support Thailand's COVID-19 Response*. Manila. https://www.adb.org/news/1-5-billion-adb-loan-support-thailands-covid-19-response.

continued on next page

Box 3 *continued*

c ADB. 2019. *Resilient coastal cities for enhancing tourism economy: Integrated planning approaches.* https://www.adb.org/sites/default/files/publication/541031/adbi-wp1043.pdf.
d ADB. 2019. *Country Operations Business Plan: Philippines (2020–2022).* Manila.https://www.adb.org/sites/default/files/institutional-document/533741/cobp-phi-2020-2022.pdf.
e ADB. 2018. *Proposed Loan and Grant Kingdom of Cambodia and Lao People's Democratic Republic: Second Greater Mekong Subregion Tourism Infrastructure for Inclusive Growth Project.* Manila. https://www.adb.org/sites/default/files/project-documents/49387/49387-002-rrp-en.pdf.
f ADB. 2020. *Cambodia: Community-Based Tourism COVID-19 Recovery Project.* Manila. https://www.adb.org/projects/53243-001/main#project-pds.

AGRO-PROCESSING INDUSTRY

Five major challenges pre-COVID-19

- Inconsistent supply of raw materials
- Low level of automation and technological adoption
- Infrastructure gaps
- Lack of access to key enablers such as financing, technologies, and skilled labor
- Lack of environmental sustainability and shifting consumer purchasing behaviors

Three major shifts from COVID-19

- Shifts in demand for food and beverage products
- Breakdown in the supply of production inputs
- Increased food protectionism policies

Four areas of policy action

Enhancing the efficiency and transparency of supply chains
- Invest in reliable data management systems
- Harmonize standards for food products

Increasing the value-add of the industry
- Expand food product range
- Attract investments and companies

Pursuing steps to raise productivity rates
- Focus on research and enabling policies to ensure a more consistent supply of raw materials

Building industry resilience
- Streamline regulatory functions
- Strengthen the local agro-processing ecosystem
- Pursue food-related circularity policies

SECTION III

Agro-Processing

▶ **Southeast Asia's agro-processing industry represents almost 4.6% of the region's GDP.**

Agriculture, forestry, and fishing remain a primary sector across the five focus countries, contributing considerably to GDP and employment. In 2019, more than 20% of Myanmar and Cambodia GDP came from this sector. Though Indonesia and Thailand focused more on manufacturing and services, they remained major exporters of agricultural products, with Thailand continuing to be an important rice exporter.[125] Studies also show that developing agriculture systems contribute to significant poverty reduction.[126]

While there are opportunities to enhance the productivity and resilience of primary agriculture (e.g., adopting digital technologies and focusing on higher-value crops), there is a need to diversify and shift to higher value-added activities across the agriculture and food value chain. One such industry is agro-processing which involves transforming agricultural raw materials into higher-value forms such as food and beverages.[127] Examples include milling grain into flour and pressing oil from vegetable seeds. This is part of the industrialization strategy of developed countries.[128] For instance, Australia developed its post-farmgate sector over the years and became a major global food processor.[129] As a result, the value added to the productivity and profitability of agro-processing increased, and leading global food companies now have a presence in Australia.[130]

Agro-processing is already an important economic contributor to some focus countries. Figure 6 summarizes the industry's contribution to GDP while Figure 7 shows its employment contribution. In Indonesia, the industry contributed over 6% to GDP and hired more than 3.6 million workers in 2018. The industry is a key priority in Indonesia's 2015–2035 National Industrial Development Master Plan and one of the five priority industries under Making Indonesia 4.0–Indonesia's Industry 4.0 development strategy. In the Philippines, agro-processing accounts for almost half of the manufacturing sector's total output.[131] While most of the roughly 500 food and beverage processors registered under the Philippine Food and Drug Administration are micro to medium-sized businesses,

---

[125] M. Hamid and M. Aslam. 2017. The Competitiveness and Complementarities of Agriculture Trade among ASEAN-5 Countries: An Empirical Analysis. *International Journal of Economics and Finance*; Vol. 9, No. 8; 2017. https://www.researchgate.net/publication/318364183_The_Competitiveness_and_Complementarities_of_Agriculture_Trade_among_ASEAN-5_Countries_An_Empirical_Analysis.

[126] OECD. 2011. *Agricultural Progress and Poverty Reduction.* Paris. https://www.oecd-ilibrary.org/docserver/5kg6v1vk8zr2-en.pdf?expires=1610522674&id=id&accname=guest&checksum=4136FDCCE803E67E19B1F1C5D84B3A60.

[127] Agro-processing is a subset of manufacturing that processes raw materials and intermediate products derived from agriculture. The agro-processing industry encompasses early stages in the production value chain for the manufacture of food products, beverages, tobacco products, textiles, leather and related products, wood and products of wood and cork, excluding furniture, and paper and paper products.

[128] ADB. 2013. *Agriculture and Structural Transformation in Developing Asia: Review and Outlook.* Manila. https://www.adb.org/sites/default/files/publication/30380/ewp-363.pdf.

[129] Agribusiness Australia. 2020. *2020 State of the Industry Implications for the Australian Agriculture Sector.* Adelaide. https://www.agribusiness.asn.au/documents/item/575.

[130] Australian Government Australian Trade and Investment Commission. 2020. *Australian industry capabilities.* Canberra. https://www.austrade.gov.au/International/Buy/Australian-industry-capabilities/food-and-beverage.

[131] Flanders Investment and Trade. 2019. *Philippines Food Industry 2018–2019.* Manila. https://www.flandersinvestmentandtrade.com/export/sites/trade/files/market_studies/Philippines%20Food%20Industry.pdf.

Figure 6: Agro-Processing Contribution to Gross Domestic Product

Southeast Asia's agro-processing industry represents almost $130 billion of GDP (or 4.6% of Southeast Asia's total GDP)

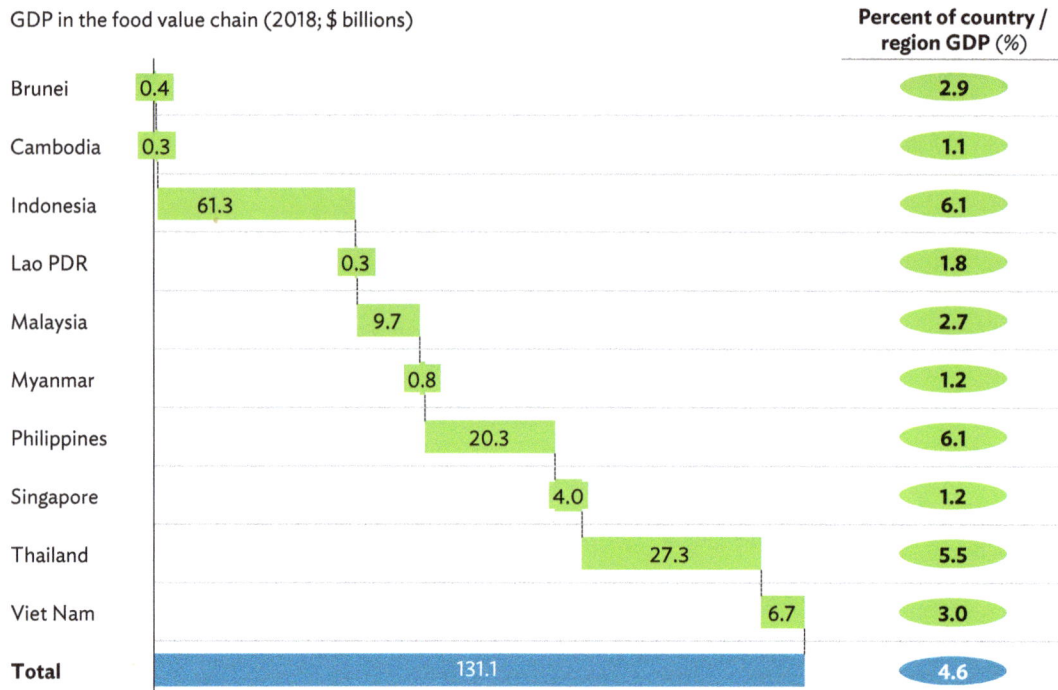

GDP in the food value chain (2018; $ billions)

Percent of country / region GDP (%)

Country	GDP in the food value chain (2018; $ billions)	Percent of country / region GDP (%)
Brunei	0.4	2.9
Cambodia	0.3	1.1
Indonesia	61.3	6.1
Lao PDR	0.3	1.8
Malaysia	9.7	2.7
Myanmar	0.8	1.2
Philippines	20.3	6.1
Singapore	4.0	1.2
Thailand	27.3	5.5
Viet Nam	6.7	3.0
Total	131.1	4.6

GDP = gross domestic product, Lao PDR = Lao People's Democratic Republic.
Note: Excluding Timor-Leste.
Sources: National statistics offices; AlphaBeta analysis.

some of these food and beverage processors were also among the largest corporations in the Philippines.[132] In Thailand, approximately 9,000 agro-processing companies employ over 1.6 million workers.[133] For Cambodia and Myanmar, the focus was still on primary agricultural production, although there are plans to emphasize agro-processing. For instance, the Government of Cambodia began prioritizing the agro-processing industry to diversify the country's industrial base while promoting higher value-added exports and strengthening food security.[134]

Agro-processing is expected to continue growing with the abundance of arable land and agricultural products, large domestic market, low labor cost, and increased government focus across the five countries. In 2020, the industries in Cambodia and the Philippines absorbed workers from other sectors displaced by COVID-19 as governments encouraged laid-off employees to return to their home provinces and start small-scale farming and production.[135]

[132] Food Export Association. 2020. *Philippines Country Profile*. https://www.foodexport.org/get-started/country-market-profiles/southeast-asia/philippines-country-profile#foodprocessing.

[133] Thailand Board of Investment. 2016. *Thailand: Food Industry*. Bangkok. https://www.boi.go.th/upload/content/Food%20industry_5aa7b40bd758b.pdf.

[134] GIZ. 2020. *Partnership Ready Cambodia: Agriculture and Food Processing*. Eschborn. https://www.giz.de/en/downloads/GBN_Sector%20Brief_Kambodscha_Agriculture_en.pdf.

[135] M. Leitner. 2020. COVID-19 is sending millions of overseas workers back into Southeast Asia's rural areas. *Asian Development Blog*. 21 October. https://blogs.adb.org/blog/covid-19-sending-millions-overseas-workers-back-southeast-asia-s-rural-areas.

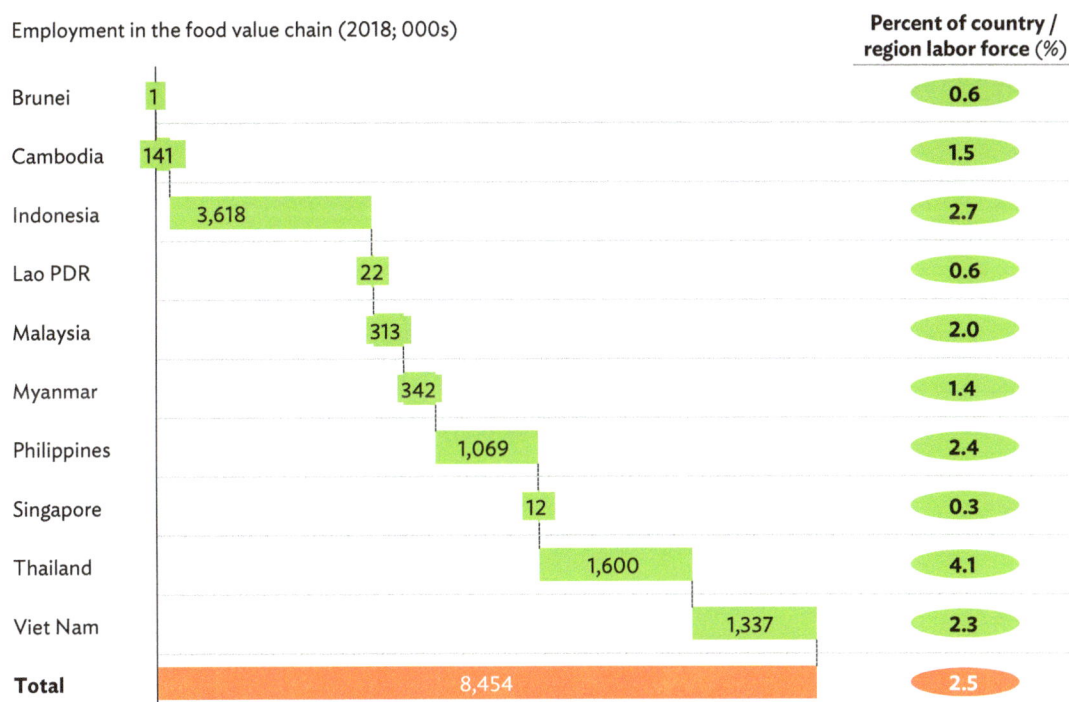

Figure 7: Agro-Processing Contribution to Employment

Southeast Asia's agro-processing industry represents around 8.5 million jobs (2.5% of Southeast Asia's labor force)

Employment in the food value chain (2018; 000s)

Country	Employment	Percent of country / region labor force (%)
Brunei	1	0.6
Cambodia	141	1.5
Indonesia	3,618	2.7
Lao PDR	22	0.6
Malaysia	313	2.0
Myanmar	342	1.4
Philippines	1,069	2.4
Singapore	12	0.3
Thailand	1,600	4.1
Viet Nam	1,337	2.3
Total	8,454	2.5

Lao PDR = Lao People's Democratic Republic.
Note: Excluding Timor-Leste.
Sources: International Labour Organization; National statistics offices; AlphaBeta analysis.

▶ **Challenges across the agro-processing value chain have hindered industry growth.**

Five challenges were affecting the agro-processing industry even before the COVID-19 pandemic:

- **Inconsistent supply of raw materials.** The agro-processing industry is a key purchaser of agricultural inputs, and volatilities in the supply of these raw materials led to production uncertainties. Factors affecting the supply of raw materials include adverse weather conditions exacerbated by climate change, diseases, fluctuations in global market prices and exchange rates, limitations on cultivation areas, and significant post-harvest food waste. For example, a sharp decline in the supply of raw materials could result in higher prices and subsequently lower agro-processing outputs. In the Philippines, crop yields and fish production are expected to decrease due to climate change.[136] A recent study found the gross production value of Philippine agriculture decreases with increases in temperature and precipitation.[137] In Cambodia, over the last 5 years, agriculture showed decelerating growth mainly attributed to extreme weather conditions.[138] Post-harvest food losses are

[136] K. Bermejo. 2017. Climate change will impact Philippines' ability to feed its people. *Eco-Business*. 17 October. https://www.eco-business.com/news/climate-change-will-impact-philippines-ability-to-feed-its-people/.

[137] J. Dait. 2020. Effect of Climate Change on Philippine Agriculture. *International Journal of Science and Research (IJSR)* ISSN (Online): 2319-7064. Effect of Climate Change on Philippine Agriculture (ijsr.net).

[138] NBC. 2019. *Cambodia's Agriculture Productivity: Challenges and Policy Direction*. Phnom Penh. https://www.nbc.org.kh/download_files/research_papers/english/3.1.1.Report_of_Cambodia's_Agriculture.pdf.

prevalent in developing countries. Between 20% and 30% of food is wasted along the value chain, even before food waste during consumption.[139] In Myanmar, a study by the United Nations Development Programme found post-harvest losses at around 20%.[140] Food losses and other factors like the lack of irrigation systems led to rice prices rising by 40% from 2009 to 2013, potentially also affecting rice-related agro-processing products like flour.[141] Seasonality in raw material availability is another issue, preventing efficient year-round operations of agro-processing companies. These difficulties in securing more consistent material supplies are worsened by the lack of robust market linkages. Many smallholder farmers lack access to formal markets and businesses, reducing available raw materials for the agro-processing industry.[142]

- **Low level of automation and technological adoption.** Agro-processing is largely labor-intensive in most focus countries, relying on rudimentary processing methods. In Indonesia, more than 30% of workers in manufacturing handle food and beverages, and up to 85% of food manufacturing companies lag in digitalization.[143] In Cambodia, agro-processing is still in a developing stage facing a lack of processing facilities and technology, and case studies of food manufacturers found the lack of sophisticated production technology limited production capacity.[144] Furthermore, due to cost constraints, manufacturers have to use inefficient and high maintenance secondhand machinery. In Myanmar, most mills operate with obsolete processing systems, resulting in about 20% quality and quantity losses during milling.[145] The failure to adopt more productive processing methods constrained production volumes and the ability to add value to output, thus limiting the capability to charge higher prices.

- **Infrastructure gaps hindered the industry's development.** Underdeveloped utility, transport, and logistics infrastructure hindered the development of agro-processing, especially in the rural areas of the focus countries. In Indonesia, inadequate transportation and storage infrastructure outside Java island, including ports and cold storage facilities, restrict the growth of more agro-processing factories and activities.[146] In Cambodia and Myanmar, poor utility infrastructure networks result in an unreliable supply of critical production factors like water and electricity, raising the cost of food and beverage production.[147] Table 5 shows the World Bank's Logistics Performance Index which includes trade-related infrastructure.[148]

- **Lack of access to key enablers has impeded the growth of the industry.** Many operators in the agro-processing industry face several access challenges restricting their ability to scale. This is a catch-22 situation as many of these access challenges exist due to the size of the operators, in an industry where most firms are MSMEs. These enablers include:
  a) **Financing.** Financing institutions typically think it risky to loan funds to MSMEs given factors like the lack of business credentials, informal status, and the inability to assess risks. As a result, many MSMEs in agro-processing lack the working capital to diversify sources of raw materials and scale up. In Thailand, while

[139] UNDP. 2018. *Enhancing Food Security through Improved Post-Harvest Practice in the Dry Zone of Myanmar.* Yangon. https://www.mm.undp.org/content/myanmar/en/home/presscenter/pressreleases/2018/enhancing-food-security-through-improved-post-harvest-practice-i.html.

[140] Temasek. 2018. *Better Together: Business, Government, Society and Our Sustainable Future.* Singapore. https://alphabeta.com/wp-content/uploads/2018/07/better-together.pdf.

[141] World Bank. 2014. *Myanmar: Farmers' Profits Lost Due to Volatile Rice Prices.* Washington, DC. https://www.worldbank.org/en/news/feature/2014/11/24/myanmar-farmers-profits-lost-due-to-volatile-rice-prices.

[142] Deloitte. 2019. *Cultivating Southeast Asia for the Future of Food.* Singapore. https://www2.deloitte.com/content/dam/Deloitte/sg/Documents/innovation/sea-inno-converge-cultivating-sea-for-the-future-of-food.pdf.

[143] ADB. 2020. *Innovate Indonesia Unlocking Growth Through Technological Transformation.* Manila. https://www.adb.org/sites/default/files/publication/575806/innovate-indonesia-unlocking-growth.pdf.

[144] ADB. 2011. *Impediments to Growth of the Garment and Food Industries in Cambodia: Exploring Potential Benefits of the ASEAN-PRC FTA.* Manila. https://www.adb.org/sites/default/files/publication/29156/wp86-chhoang-hamanaka-impediments-growth.pdf.

[145] IFC. 2020. *Creating Markets in Myanmar.* Washington, DC. https://www.ifc.org/wps/wcm/connect/45d30b3c-5b78-437e-be6f-92171f4d209d/cpsd-myanmar.pdf?MOD=AJPERES&CVID=n9MWw4m.

[146] USDA Foreign Agricultural Service. 2019. *Indonesia: Food Processing Ingredients Report Update.* Jakarta. https://apps.fas.usda.gov/newgainapi/api/report/downloadreportbyfilename?filename=Food%20Processing%20Ingredients_Jakarta_Indonesia_4-8-2019.pdf.

[147] EuroCham. 2017. *Agriculture and Agro-Processing Sector in Cambodia.* London. http://www.ukabc.org.uk/wp-content/uploads/2017/04/AgriProject_Reporting_FINAL-VERSION-copy.pdf.

[148] World Bank. 2020. *Global Rankings 2018.* Washington, DC. https://lpi.worldbank.org/international/global?sort=asc&order=Infrastructure#datatable.

Table 5: Logistics Performance Index 2018 Scores and Rankings

World Bank's Logistics Performance Index 2018, selected countries

Focus countries

Country	LPI Rank	LPI Score	Customs	Infrastructure	Inter-National Shipments	Logistics Competence	Tracking and Tracing	Timeliness
Germany	1	4.20	4.09	4.37	3.86	4.31	4.24	4.39
Sweden	2	4.05	4.05	4.24	3.92	3.98	3.88	4.28
Belgium	3	4.04	3.66	3.98	3.99	4.13	4.05	4.41
Austria	4	4.03	3.71	4.18	3.88	4.08	4.09	4.25
Japan	5	4.03	3.99	4.25	3.59	4.09	4.05	4.25
Netherlands	6	4.02	3.92	4.21	3.68	4.09	4.02	4.25
Singapore	7	4.00	3.89	4.06	3.58	4.10	4.08	4.32
Denmark	8	3.99	3.92	3.96	3.53	4.01	4.18	4.41
United Kingdom	9	3.99	3.77	4.03	3.67	4.05	4.11	4.33
Finland	10	3.97	3.82	4.00	3.56	3.89	4.32	4.28
Thailand	32	3.41	3.14	3.14	3.46	3.41	3.47	3.81
Viet Nam	39	3.27	2.95	3.01	3.16	3.40	3.45	3.67
Malaysia	41	3.22	2.90	3.15	3.35	3.30	3.15	3.46
Indonesia	46	3.15	2.67	2.89	3.23	3.10	3.30	3.67
Philippines	60	2.90	2.53	2.73	3.29	2.78	3.06	2.98
Brunei	80	2.71	2.62	2.46	2.51	2.71	2.75	3.17
Lao PDR	82	2.70	2.61	2.44	2.72	2.65	2.91	2.84
Cambodia	98	2.58	2.37	2.14	2.79	2.41	2.52	3.16
Myanmar	137	2.30	2.17	1.99	2.20	2.28	2.20	2.91

Lao PDR = Lao People's Democratic Republic, LPI = logistics performance index.
Note: Each sub-indicator has been given a score between 1 (worst) to 5 (best). The LPI Score is a simple average across the six sub-indicators. There are 160 countries in the LPI 2018 version. There is no data for Timor-Leste.
Source: World Bank LPI.

there are various government financial support measures, only about 40% of Thai manufacturing firms gain access to credit.[149] In Indonesia, over 50% of MSMEs indicated that they lack access to financial institutions.[150]

b) **Technologies.** Many MSMEs in agro-processing could be unaware of the opportunities and potential benefits of advanced processing equipment and digital tools. There could be resistance to adopting new technologies with high capital costs. A survey of MSMEs in Myanmar revealed that 34% of these firms cited the lack of information and awareness on how to access business services including the understanding of new technologies and tools (footnote 144).

c) **Skilled labor.** Another challenge facing MSMEs in many focus countries is the access to skilled employees due to reasons like the limitations of the education systems, resulting in lower productivities. In Myanmar, workers in MSMEs were generally underperforming across skillsets as over 50% of employers identified skill gaps in technical, computer, critical thinking, and management skills (footnote 144).

d) **Markets.** Even if agro-processing companies had access to financing, technologies, and skilled labor, many have limited access to stable and high-value markets to expand their operations and commercialize.[151] Barriers include poor physical infrastructure to reach marketplaces, the lack of

---

[149] C. Punyasavatsut. 2011. SMEs *Access to Finance in Thailand.* ERIA. https://www.eria.org/uploads/media/Research-Project-Report/RPR_FY2010_14_Chapter_7.pdf.

[150] Deloitte. 2015. *Digital banking for small and medium-sized enterprises: Improving access to finance for the underserved.* Singapore. https://www2.deloitte.com/content/dam/Deloitte/sg/Documents/financial-services/sea-fsi-digital-banking-small-medium-enterprises-noexp.pdf.

[151] Oxfam International. 2014. *Small and Medium Enterprises in Agriculture Value Chain.* Oxford. https://iixfoundation.org/wp-content/uploads/2011/08/OXFAM-SME-Report-November-2014_FINAL.pdf.

information about pricing and demand, the inability to meet domestic and international quality and distribution standards, and limited marketing resources. For instance, Philippine processed food manufacturers often face the risk of product recalls for their exports due to food safety concerns.[152] Some manufactured goods exporters (including processed foods) indicated that the lack of information on new markets hindered them from utilizing free trade agreements (FTAs) in the region.[153]

    e) **Business support.** There are also several gaps in the supporting services for businesses. Companies in agro-processing identified the lack of certification schemes and clear regulations as barriers. Agro-processing operators in Cambodia cited complex regulations and licensing processes as constraints, contributing to increased consumer prices and business compliance costs.[154] There is also a lack of programs to support entrepreneurial activities and innovation. For example, Indonesia does not have sufficient innovation hubs to cultivate entrepreneurship (though some are emerging in Jakarta).[155] In addition, the lack of an enabling regulatory environment, was identified as one of the impediments to the creation of agro-processing public-private partnerships (PPPs).[156]

- **The lack of environmental sustainability of the industry and shifting consumer purchasing behaviors.** The agro-processing industry contributes to food loss and waste generation across the production value chain. This includes waste during processing, packaging, distribution to food markets, and spoilage at wholesale and retail markets. Due to high urbanization rates in many focus countries, the food value chains have been extended, exacerbating waste concerns. Thus, a lack of infrastructure, such as roads, storage, cooling, and market logistics, can cause food products to expire or spoil while on the way to distribution channels.[157] For instance, the Indonesian Cooling Chain Association, reported that the country's cold storage capacity only covers just over half of fishery production.[158] Since the fish or processed fish products need to be transported to markets, this lack of a cold chain can lead to spoilage. Almost 40% of seafood caught by local fishers in Indonesia are wasted because of poor fishery management (including the lack of cold supply chains), translating to over $7 billion loss of fish products every year.[159] Other factors contributing to unsustainable agro-processing practices include the lack of capacity for the adoption of Good Manufacturing Practices and the limited adoption of technologies for the sustainable management of wastes (e.g., animal waste and wastewater from meat processors). Industrial waste can lead to water pollution if it is directly discharged into water bodies. In Myanmar, inspections found that most factories in industrial zones had no systematic waste disposal systems.[160] There are also shifts in consumer preferences toward environmentally sustainable products. Over the years, consumers have become more aware

---

[152] P. Neo. 2020. Boosting international trade: Philippines seeks food safety gains for exports to reduce recalls. *Food Navigator Asia.* 2 March. https://www.foodnavigator-asia.com/Article/2020/03/02/Boosting-international-trade-Philippines-seeks-food-safety-gains-for-exports-to-reduce-recalls.

[153] ADBI. 2010. *FTAs and Philippine Business: Evidence from Transport, Food, and Electronics Firms.* Tokyo. https://www.econstor.eu/bitstream/10419/53566/1/618027203.pdf.

[154] ERIA. 2018. *A Case Study of Cambodia's Agro-Industry.* Jakarta. https://www.eria.org/uploads/media/RURB_2018_Chapter_5_Agro-Industy_Cambodia.pdf.

[155] Asia Pacific Foundation of Canada. 2018. *2018 Survey of Entrepreneurs and MSMEs In Indonesia.* Vancouver. https://apfcanada-msme.ca/sites/default/files/2018-10/2018%20Survey%20of%20Entrepreneurs%20and%20MSMEs%20in%20Indonesia_0.pdf and Tulustambunan. 2011. Entrepreneurship Development: SMEs in Indonesia. *Journal of Developmental Entrepreneurship* 12(01). https://www.researchgate.net/publication/263866456_ENTREPRENEURSHIP_DEVELOPMENT_SMES_IN_INDONESIA.

[156] FAO. 2016. *Public–private partnerships for agribusiness development: A review of international experiences.* Rome. https://snrd-asia.org/wp-content/uploads/SNRD-Newsletter/issue-1/Documents/PPP/Public-Private%20Partnerships%20for%20Agribusines%20Development.pdf and A. Balisacan. 2013. The Challenges of Public-Private Partnerships in Agriculture and the Rural Sector. *Public-Private Partnership Center.* 3 April. https://ppp.gov.ph/speeches/statement-of-sec-balisacan-at-the-asia-pacific-agriculture-policy-apap-roundtable-2-april-2013-japan/.

[157] J. Parfitt et al. 2010. Food waste within food supply chains: Quantification and potential for change to 2050. *Philosophical Transactions of the Royal Society* 365. https://royalsocietypublishing.org/doi/pdf/10.1098/rstb.2010.0126.

[158] I. Jumat. 2014. F. Minim - Industri Rantai Pendingin Sulit Berkembang. *Neraca.* 28 February. https://www.neraca.co.id/article/38959/fasilitas-fiskal-minim-industri-rantai-pendingin-sulit-berkembang.

[159] M. Nurhasan. 2019. Poor fishery management costs Indonesia $7 billion per year. Here's how to stop it. *The Conversation.* 13 May. https://theconversation.com/poor-fishery-management-costs-indonesia-7-billion-per-year-heres-how-to-stop-it-109671 and SEAFDEC. 2017. *Fisheries Country Profile: Indonesia.* Bangkok. http://www.seafdec.org/fisheries-country-profile-indonesia/.

[160] Safe Water. 2017. *Industrial Waste.* https://www.safewater.org/fact-sheets-1/2017/1/23/industrial-waste; and Khin Wine Phyu Phyu. 2016. Industrial zone wastewater shows rising pollution. *Myanmar Times.* 4 January. https://www.mmtimes.com/business/18303-industrial-zone-waste-water-shows-rising-pollution.html.

of the environmental sustainability of their purchases, translating to higher demand for sustainable products.[161] Consumers might be more willing to purchase food products if manufacturers minimize single-use plastic packaging or limits food waste. For instance, 71% of consumers in Indonesia and 62% in Thailand said they would consider more environmental-friendly grocery products.[162]

▶ **Demand and supply challenges emerged due to COVID-19.**

These pre-pandemic challenges were exacerbated by COVID-19, mainly in several areas:

- **Shifts in demand for food and beverage products.** While the pandemic led to panic buying and greater online sales, there has been lower overall demand for food and beverage products, resulting in lower revenues for food processors.[163] Figure 8 highlights the projected impact for food and beverage companies in Southeast Asia due to the pandemic.[164] Reasons include the increasing number of employees working from homes, lower purchasing power due to job losses and wage reduction, as well as the switch from processed food products to fresh or homemade substitutes.[165] For instance, according to a Nielsen study,

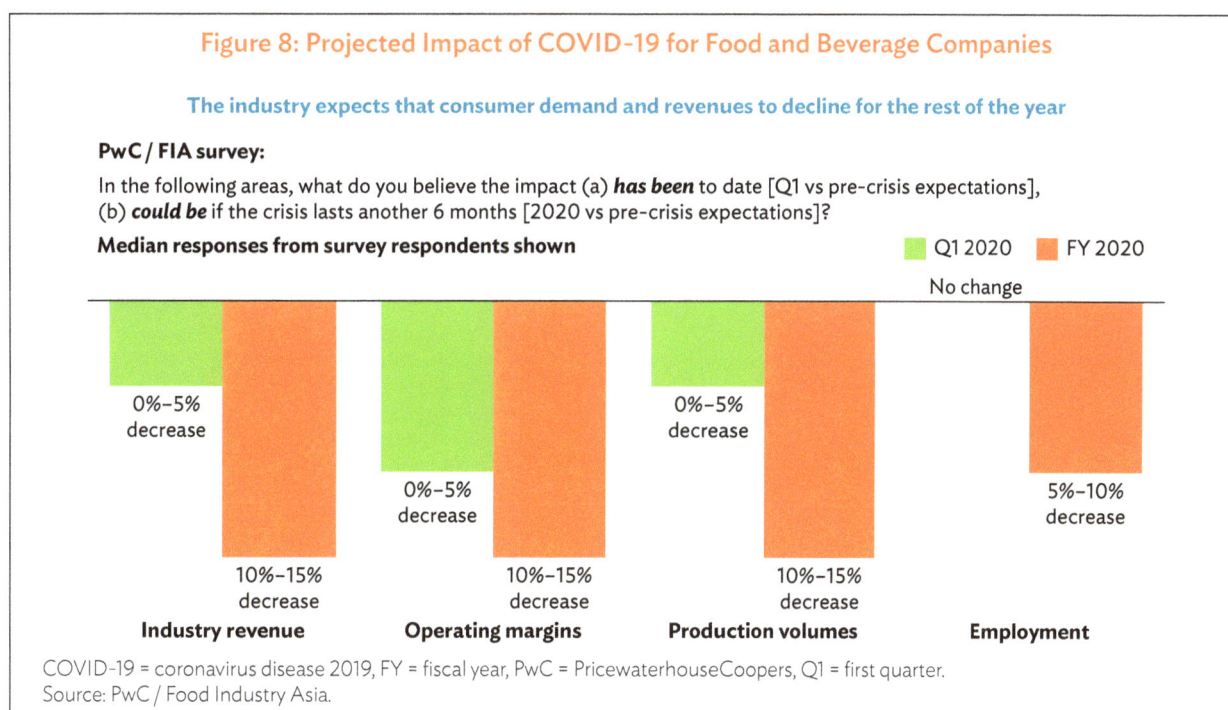

Figure 8: Projected Impact of COVID-19 for Food and Beverage Companies

The industry expects that consumer demand and revenues to decline for the rest of the year

PwC / FIA survey:

In the following areas, what do you believe the impact (a) *has been* to date [Q1 vs pre-crisis expectations], (b) *could be* if the crisis lasts another 6 months [2020 vs pre-crisis expectations]?

Median responses from survey respondents shown   Q1 2020   FY 2020

No change

Industry revenue: 0%–5% decrease (Q1 2020); 10%–15% decrease (FY 2020)
Operating margins: 0%–5% decrease (Q1 2020); 10%–15% decrease (FY 2020)
Production volumes: 0%–5% decrease (Q1 2020); 10%–15% decrease (FY 2020)
Employment: 5%–10% decrease (FY 2020)

COVID-19 = coronavirus disease 2019, FY = fiscal year, PwC = PricewaterhouseCoopers, Q1 = first quarter.
Source: PwC / Food Industry Asia.

[161] J. Devenyms. 2020. Consumers still care about sustainability amid pandemic, report finds. *Food Dive.* 24 April. https://www.fooddive.com/news/consumers-still-care-about-sustainability-amid-pandemic-report-finds/576682/.

[162] McKinsey & Company. 2020. *Survey: Food retail in Indonesia during the COVID-19 pandemic.* New York. https://www.mckinsey.com/industries/retail/our-insights/survey-food-retail-in-indonesia-during-the-covid-19-pandemic; and McKinsey & Company. 2020. *Survey: Food retail in Thailand during the COVID-19 pandemic.* New York. https://www.mckinsey.com/industries/retail/our-insights/survey-food-retail-in-thailand-during-the-covid-19-pandemic.

[163] There has been increased demand for specific agro-processed products such as rubber gloves during the pandemic.

[164] FIA. 2020. *Maintaining food resilience in a time of uncertainty.* Singapore. https://f.hubspotusercontent10.net/hubfs/6055518/Resources/COVID-19/FIA-PwC_Maintaining%20Food%20Resilience%20in%20a%20Time%20of%20Uncertainty.pdf.

[165] G. Lim. 2020. From convenience to conscious: COVID-19 pandemic leads to shift in snacking priorities – experts. *Food Navigator Asia.* 2 July. https://www.foodnavigator-asia.com/Article/2020/07/02/From-convenience-to-conscious-Covid-19-pandemic-leads-to-shift-in-snacking-priorities-experts.

56% of consumers said they ate more often at home.[166] This reduces the demand for eateries that are significant buyers of food products. Rabobank of The Netherlands also estimated that reduced out-of-home consumption and slower economic growth would reduce beef consumption by up to 13% and pork consumption by 17% in Southeast Asia.[167] However, COVID-19 also increased the demand for certain food products, like functional foods, perceived to be healthier and essential for protecting the immune systems.[168]

- **Breakdown in the supply of production inputs.** COVID-19 resulted in greater fluctuations and shortages of production factors like labor and raw materials. Countries have imposed travel restrictions and closed borders, limiting business activities and transportation networks. These led to labor shortages at factories, warehouses, and logistics hubs, causing supply chain disruptions. The pandemic worsened the challenge faced by laborers who must travel from rural homes to urban factories to work. Labor shortages at ports resulted in sizeable backlogs of containers, exacerbated by non-essential industries not being able to collect previously ordered shipments. This issue was worsened by paper-based customs processes and the lack of digital infrastructure. For example, by the end of March 2020, the number of unclaimed import containers at Manila's port had increased by 66% compared with pre-crisis levels, with many containers carrying food products, leading to increased food waste (footnote 164). These border and travel restrictions also had impacts on agro-processing inputs such as machinery and raw materials. Figure 9 shows the main challenges facing food and beverage companies in Southeast Asia because of the pandemic, with the top two challenges being supply disruption for raw materials and labor restrictions.

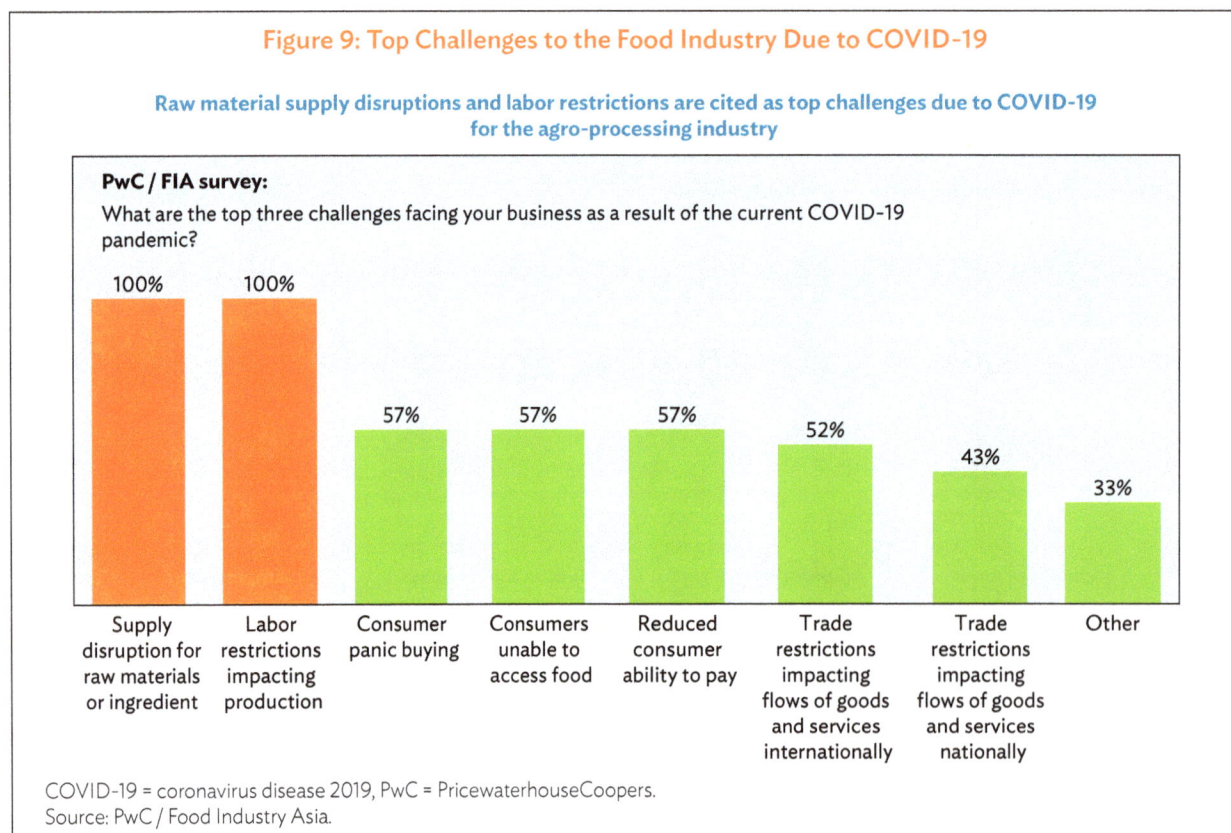

Figure 9: Top Challenges to the Food Industry Due to COVID-19

Raw material supply disruptions and labor restrictions are cited as top challenges due to COVID-19 for the agro-processing industry

PwC / FIA survey:
What are the top three challenges facing your business as a result of the current COVID-19 pandemic?

Supply disruption for raw materials or ingredient	Labor restrictions impacting production	Consumer panic buying	Consumers unable to access food	Reduced consumer ability to pay	Trade restrictions impacting flows of goods and services internationally	Trade restrictions impacting flows of goods and services nationally	Other
100%	100%	57%	57%	57%	52%	43%	33%

COVID-19 = coronavirus disease 2019, PwC = PricewaterhouseCoopers.
Source: PwC / Food Industry Asia.

166 Nielsen. 2020. *Asian Consumers are Rethinking How They Eat Post COVID-19*. New York. https://www.nielsen.com/eu/en/insights/article/2020/asian-consumers-are-rethinking-how-they-eat-post-covid-19/.

167 Rabobank. 2020. *Impact of Coronavirus on Southeast Asian Food & Agribusiness*. April. https://research.rabobank.com/far/en/sectors/regional-food-agri/Coronavirus-Impact-on-SEA-FA.html.

168 S. Aday and M. Aday. 2020. Impact of COVID-19 on the food supply chain. *Food Quality and Safety*, Volume 4, Issue 4, December 2020, pp. 167–180. https://academic.oup.com/fqs/article/4/4/167/5896496.

- **Increased food protectionism policies**. Due to the adverse impact of COVID-19 on food production, some countries imposed trade policies on food product exports and imports to meet domestic needs. Table 6 summarizes the trade and trade-related measures (including food products) by Southeast Asian country. The most common type of trade-restrictive measure was export prohibition.[169] Some of these measures are short term and were removed after a few months.[170] For instance, Cambodia restricted exports of rice for over a month.[171] Countries such as the PRC also introduced more regulations on food imports and tightened cold chain management guidelines.[172] Given that many of the focus countries face infrastructure gaps, there is a risk these countries might not meet these tightened standards and lose access to significant markets. World Bank studies also showed escalating export restrictions could cause the global food export supply to decline by up to 20% and global prices to increase by 6% on average in the quarter following the pandemic outbreak.[173]

Table 6: Number of Trade and Trade-Related Measures Issued by Countries during COVID-19

Restrictive measures account for 39% of trade measures in the region

Types of measures related to COVID-19 by Southeast Asian countries   ■ Focus countries

Countries	Types of Liberalizing Measures					Types of Restrictive Measures								Total
	Tariff / import duties reduction	Trade facilitation	Import ban / restriction / prohibition	Licensing or permit requirements to export	Export liberalisation	Export prohibition	Licensing or permit requirements to export	Import ban / restriction / prohibition	Export quotas	Quarantine requirements	Conformity assessment	Price control	Tariff / import duties increase	
Brunei Darussalam	1													1
Cambodia		1		1		1								3
Indonesia	1	3	1			2								7
Lao PDR	1													1
Malaysia	2					2						1		5
Myanmar	2	1				1								4
Philippines	1	1				1							1	4
Singapore	1	1												2
Thailand	3					2								5
Viet Nam	2					1	1	1	1					6
Total	14	7	1	0	1	10	1	1	1	0	0	1	1	38

Lao PDR = Lao People's Democratic Republic.
Note: Data for Timor-Leste are unavailable.
Sources: Association of Southeast Asian Nations Secretariat; World Trade Organization; and International Trade Centre.

[169] ASEAN Secretariat. 2020. *Trade Measures in the Time of COVID-19: The Case of ASEAN*. Jakarta. ASEAN-Policy-Brief-3_FINAL_.pdf.

[170] ITC. 2021. COVID-19 Temporary Trade Measures (database). https://www.macmap.org/covid19.

[171] P. Neo. 2020. COVID-19 in ASEAN: "Protectionist" measures threaten global supply chains as lockdowns persist. *Food Navigators Asia*. 14 April. https://www.foodnavigator-asia.com/Article/2020/04/14/COVID-19-in-ASEAN-Protectionist-measures-threaten-global-supply-chains-as-lockdowns-persist.

[172] P. Neo. 2020. COVID-19 food inspections: China looks to virtual food import "spot checks" and tightened cold chain guidelines. *Food Navigators Asia*. 25 November. https://www.foodnavigator-asia.com/Article/2020/11/25/COVID-19-food-inspections-China-looks-to-virtual-food-import-spot-checks-and-tightened-cold-chain-guidelines.

[173] World Bank. 2020. *COVID-19 and Food Protectionism: The Impact of the Pandemic and Export Restrictions on World Food Markets*. Washington, DC. https://openknowledge.worldbank.org/bitstream/handle/10986/33800/Covid-19-and-Food-Protectionism-The-Impact-of-the-Pandemic-and-Export-Restrictions-on-World-Food-Markets.pdf?sequence=1&isAllowed=y.

▶ **Four areas of policy response are needed to strengthen the agro-processing industry in the focus countries.**

Governments implemented short-term measures to ensure agro-processing can continue, including recognizing agro-processing as an "essential service" and preserving open borders for trade, with countries like Singapore, Brunei Darussalam, and Myanmar, reaffirming their commitments to keep borders open for goods during the crisis.[174] Moving into the recovery phase, there are policy responses to address the challenges identified earlier, to ensure higher and more sustainable growth. The policy responses suggested below could help: (i) enhance the efficiency and transparency of supply chains, (ii) increase the value-add of the industry, (iii) raise productivity rates, and (iv) build industry resilience.

(i) Enhancing the Efficiency and Transparency of Supply Chains

To enhance existing supply chains, countries could:

1. **Improve information flows and transparency.** There are two areas where better information flows and transparency are required. First, there is a current lack of information on stocks and prices of agro-processing products—a factor behind the panic-buying and restrictive trade policies during the pandemic's onset. The 2007–2008 food price crisis showed how crucial it is to ensure predictability and transparency with timely market information. This can help mitigate panic buying and generate trust in markets, encouraging cooperative solutions and peer learning of experiences.[175] Second, there are opportunities to better understand alternative sources of food production, useful in situations of trade restrictions. Steps to improve information flows and transparency include:
   a. **Investing in reliable data management systems.** Governments can invest in data systems at the local, national, and global levels to provide real-time information for policy makers. For instance, the Group of Twenty (G20) Ministers of Agriculture launched the Agricultural Market Information System, an inter-agency platform to enhance food market transparency and policy response for food security prices, in 2011. This system allows the coordination of policy action in uncertain times and was tested when drought affected southern Europe and North America in 2012. Most of the focus countries already have price monitoring systems and publish the information online.[176] Cambodia maintains the "Agricultural Market Information Service" website with prices for key commodities like cassava and poultry. ADB supported Myanmar's Ministry of Agriculture, Livestock and Irrigation to develop a weather, market, and credit information network.[177] Emerging bottlenecks in the supply chain can also be monitored. The Philippines announced plans to develop a Supply Chain Analysis Dashboard to monitor bottlenecks across the country with support from local government units and the private sector.[178] Southeast Asian countries can explore strategic alliances and develop a platform providing improved information on alternative sources of food production through a mapping of raw material supplier, with closer cooperation and coordination between countries. If an exporting country is affected by disruptions (e.g., disasters,

---

[174] A. Leow. 2020. Singapore, 6 other Pacific countries pledge to keep trade, supply chains going during Covid-19 crisis. *The Business Times.* 25 March. Singapore, 6 other Pacific countries pledge to keep trade, supply chains going during Covid-19 crisis, Government & Economy - THE BUSINESS TIMES.

[175] OECD. 2020. *COVID-19 and the Food and Agriculture Sector: Issues and Policy Responses.* Paris. https://read.oecd-ilibrary.org/view/?ref=130_130816-9uut45lj4q&title=Covid-19-and-the-food-and-agriculture-sector-Issues-and-policy-responses.

[176] AMIS. 2020. Welcome to the Agricultural Market Information Service website. https://amis.org.kh/en; and Department of Agriculture. 2020. Price Monitoring. Quezon City. https://www.da.gov.ph/price-monitoring/.

[177] ADB. 2018. *The Republic of the Union of Myanmar: Climate-Friendly Agribusiness Value Chains Sector Project.* Manila. https://www.adb.org/sites/default/files/project-documents/48409/48409-003-pp-en.pdf.

[178] NEDA. 2021. *Updated Philippine Development Plan.* Manila. http://pdp.neda.gov.ph/wp-content/uploads/2021/02/Pre-publication-copy-Updated-PDP-2017-2022.pdf.

pandemics) and cannot complete a transaction, governments can easily find other sources of raw materials and keep costs down. While countries may already have a list of alternative import sources, a digital platform can enhance the usability and timeliness of such information.

b. **Enabling firms to access information easily.** Though governments can establish data systems, farmers and agro-processing companies also need access to information to manage production, as a lack of information could quickly lead to increased food wastage. For instance, Indonesian farmers are unable to predict market prices, leading to overproduction and occasions where the prices they receive could not even cover their transportation cost.[179] Governments have already begun to address this situation. The European Commission introduced new regulations to improve market transparency in the food supply chain and allow businesses to have access to needed information.[180] Agro-processing companies in Cambodia, Indonesia, the Philippines, and Thailand can access official websites to obtain price and production data. Governments can consider using mobile applications (apps) and push notifications to allow easy access to information. For example, Bank Indonesia and the Pusat Informasi Harga Pangan Strategis Nasional (Information Center for Strategic Food Prices) launched a mobile app that collects pricing information for 10 commodities from traditional markets and allows the public to monitor these prices.[181]

2. **Promote cross-border trade.** Companies in agro-processing, especially MSMEs, face challenges in reaching new markets due to a lack of information and resources to meet international standards. Simplifying trade procedures, harmonizing national with international standards, and mitigating the effects of non-tariff measures will help promote more cross-border trade. Companies can:

a. **Harmonize standards for food products, where possible, to avoid delays and unnecessary compliance costs.** Countries have already issued new non-tariff measures to manage sanitary risks. While such measures can be necessary, these must not significantly increase costs for agro-processing operators, especially if these requirements differ greatly across markets. Countries in Southeast Asia are major exporters. For instance, in 2019, Southeast Asia exported over $1 trillion worth of goods, including food and beverages, to the rest of the world.[182] Meanwhile, intra-ASEAN trade represented more than 20% of the region's total trade.[183] As a result, companies operating across multiple markets globally and across the region may face significant compliance costs if requirements differ significantly. In the Initiative for ASEAN Integration Work Plan IV (2021–2025), there are specific actions that can help countries like Cambodia and Myanmar improve the harmonization and implementation of standards.[184] It is crucial to ensure that these standards should be science-based, transparent, nondiscriminatory, and do not unnecessarily disrupt trade or increase trade costs. Countries in the Greater Mekong Subregion could also use existing tools like the Agriculture Information Network Service to facilitate knowledge sharing (e.g., requirements on food safety standards when exporting into Viet Nam), connect service providers (e.g., freight forwarding services), and enhance trade.[185]

[179]   M. Iswara. 2020. A Land Without Farmers: Indonesia's Agricultural Conundrum. *The Jakarta Post.* 13 August. https://www.thejakartapost.com/longform/2020/08/13/a-land-without-farmers-indonesias-agricultural-conundrum.html.

[180]   European Commission. 2019. Improving market transparency in the agricultural and food supply chain. Brussels. https://ec.europa.eu/info/sites/info/files/food-farming-fisheries/key_policies/documents/market-transparency-faqs_en.pdf.

[181]   S. Ribka. 2017. Central bank to launch app for monitoring food prices. *The Jakarta Post.* 4 April. https://www.thejakartapost.com/news/2017/04/04/central-bank-to-launch-app-for-monitoring-food-prices.html.

[182]   ASEAN Secretariat Statistics. 2020. Trade in Goods (IMTS), Annually, HS 2-digit up to 8-Digit (AHTN), in US$ (database). https://data.aseanstats.org/trade-annually.

[183]   ASEAN Secretariat. 2018. *ASEAN Statistical Highlights 2018.* Jakarta. https://www.aseanstats.org/wp-content/uploads/2018/10/ASEAN-Statistical-Highlights-2018.pdf.

[184]   ASEAN Secretariat. 2020. *Ha Noi Declaration on The Adoption of The Initiative for ASEAN Integration (IAI) Work Plan IV (2021–2025).* Jakarta. https://asean.org/ha-noi-declaration-adoption-initiative-asean-integration-iai-work-plan-iv-2021-2025/.

[185]   AINS. 2021. What is AINS. https://www.gmswga.org/what-is-ains.

b. **Simplify customs regulations for cross-border food trade.** Improving cross-border customs processes for food products and production inputs can reduce food loss related to handling difficulties while easing access to essential raw materials like pesticides. Digital technologies, with appropriate ICT infrastructure, could help reduce export time by 44% in Asia-Pacific.[186] Countries in the region can learn from Chile, the Republic of Korea, and the Netherlands, which have the capacity to generate, issue, and send electronic phytosanitary certificates, needed to ship plants and plant products.[187] Digital tools can help facilitate border procedures by reducing manual inspection times and increase the integrity of the data contained in certificates. An example is the Philippines which transitioned to using electronic phytosanitary certificates.[188] While there have been large-scale initiatives to modernize customs procedures, such as the Transport and Trade Facilitation Action Program in the GMS, much still needs to be done to streamline and simplify customs regulations.[189]

c. **Standardize and support Good Agricultural Practices (GAP).** The Food and Agriculture Organization defines GAP as "a collection of principles to apply for on-farm production and postproduction processes, resulting in safe and healthy food and non-food agriculture products, while taking into account economic, social, and environmental sustainability."[190] GAP methods and certifications aim to improve the safety and sustainability of farmers, animals, consumers, and the environment. In 2006, the ASEAN GAP was developed to enhance the harmonization of national GAP programs within Southeast Asia while facilitating trade regionally and internationally.[191] Countries could incorporate the ASEAN GAP into their national programs or strengthen their existing national GAP programs with regional guidelines and best practices. Though most Southeast Asian countries already have their own national GAP standards and certification schemes, opportunities to increase the implementation and support of GAP remain. For instance, Myanmar launched the GAP Protocol and Guidelines for 15 crops in 2017.[192] However, more recent studies have shown that the application of GAP methods by rice farmers, citing a lack of financing options and knowledge, has been declining.[193] Increasing the share of GAP adoption, in line with regional and international standards, through capacity building programs could attract international buyers and promote greater cross-border trade.

3. **Upgrade infrastructure.** Underdeveloped utility, transport, and logistics infrastructure must be upgraded to facilitate smoother movements among farms, factories, stores, and export hubs. The Government of Cambodia has been developing a Logistics Master Plan (with support from the Japan International Cooperation Agency and the World Bank) to improve transportation. In addition, their Industrial Development Policy 2015–2025 aims to improve agricultural logistics and develop "agro-processing

[186] OECD. 2019. *Digital opportunities for trade in agriculture and food sectors.* Paris. https://www.oecd.org/officialdocuments/publicdisplaydocumentpdf/?cote=TAD/TC/CA/WP(2018)4/FINAL&docLanguage=En.

[187] G. Rosenthal. 2017. *Making Agricultural Trade Flow Smoother, Safer, and Cheaper.* https://www.aphis.usda.gov/aphis/ourfocus/planthealth/ppq-program-overview/plant-protection-today/articles/ephyto-huba

[188] Asia Customs & Trade. 2019. E-application for phytosanitary certificates now a must in PH. 28 August. https://customstrade.asia/e-application-for-phytosanitary-certificates-now-a-must-in-ph/.

[189] ADB. *Transport and Trade Facilitation Action Program (TTF-AP).* Manila. https://www.adb.org/sites/default/files/institutional-document/173415/ttfap-brochure.pdf.

[190] FAO. 2016. *A Scheme and Training Manual on Good Agricultural Practices (GAP) for Fruits and Vegetables Volume 1.* Bangkok. http://www.fao.org/3/a-i6677e.pdf.

[191] FAO. 2016. *A Scheme and Training Manual on Good Agricultural Practices (GAP) for Fruits and Vegetables Volume 2.* Bangkok. http://www.fao.org/3/a-i5739e.pdf; and ASEAN Secretariat. 2020. ASEAN Good Agricultural Practices (GAP) Certification and Control Manuals. http://aadcp2.org/asean-good-agricultural-practices-gap-certification-and-control-manuals/.

[192] DaNa Facility. 2019. *Implementing Good Agricultural Practices in Myanmar.* Yangon. https://www.danafacility.com/wp-content/uploads/2020/09/FINAL-GAP-case-study.pdf.

[193] S. Oo and K. Usami. 2020. Farmers' Perception of Good Agricultural Practices in Rice Production in Myanmar: A Case Study of Myaungmya District, Ayeyarwady Region. *Agriculture* 10(249):249. https://www.researchgate.net/publication/342504191_Farmers'_Perception_of_Good_Agricultural_Practices_in_Rice_Production_in_Myanmar_A_Case_Study_of_Myaungmya_District_Ayeyarwady_Region.

zones" (a form of special economic zones) (footnote 134). In Indonesia, ADB provided support to develop strategic roads to strengthen domestic connectivity in select provinces of East and West Kalimantan, and West, Central, and East Java.[194] In the Philippines, ADB supports the development of the North-South Commuter Railway to help ease chronic road congestion, reduce the cost of logistics, and spur growth in the regions of Luzon.[195]

(ii)   Increasing the Value-Add of the Industry

The agro-processing industry is generally underdeveloped across the five countries due to the limited range of food products, a lack of sales channels, and minimal access to key enablers. It is important to expand the food product range and sales channels and increase access to capital, technology, and supporting services like marketing and research. These countries can:

1. **Expand their food product range.** As incomes increase and consumers become more informed, the demand for healthier food options including organic foods, "free-from" (such as gluten-free) foods, functional foods, and reformulated foods will increase. In Thailand and Malaysia, the health and wellness category is expected to grow by 5% (Thailand) and 9% (Malaysia) annually between 2017 to 2022.[196] For instance, there is a growing demand for functional foods (processed foods containing ingredients like probiotics that aid specific bodily functions and support nutrient intake). Factors involved in expanding the food product range include operational enhancements (e.g., growing of organic produce), sales strategies (e.g., targeting high-end supermarkets for expatriates), as well as technical expertise (e.g., training workers to oversee the processing of reformulated foods). In Australia, the food and agribusiness growth center introduced a plan to increase the value added by the industry through multistakeholder task force formation, worker training, and technology promotion.[197] Across the focus countries, there are some strategies in place which aim to improve industry competitiveness by exploring higher value-added products. Indonesia has a strategic plan to improve the quality of processed food and expand its range of agricultural exports.[198] This plan includes introducing policies that manage the agricultural industry such as issuing and assisting in export documentation of agricultural goods. The other four focus countries also have relevant agribusiness strategies.[199] However, many of these strategies are multiyear plans and the countries may still require considerable support in implementation.

2. **Increase the number of sales channels.** Buying groceries and food products online is a growing trend and there are opportunities for companies to generate value by establishing new direct-to-consumer and e-commerce sales channels (footnote 197). Southeast Asia online sales of packaged food and beverages were estimated to grow from $330 million in 2015 to more than $640 million in 2020, or about 15% annually.[200] Agro-processing businesses that sell directly to the public can benefit from higher sales margins and access to a larger customer base. These local companies will be able to sell beyond their

---

[194] ADB. 2018. *Indonesia: Regional Roads Development II.* Manila. https://www.adb.org/projects/38479-035/main.

[195] ADB. 2019. *Malolos–Clark Railway Project: North-South Commuter Railway, PNR Clark - Phase 2.* https://www.adb.org/news/infographics/malolos-clark-railway-project

[196] KPMG. 2018. *Food for health: Trends and opportunities in health and wellness for the ASEAN region.* Sydney. https://home.kpmg/au/en/home/insights/2018/09/food-for-health-trends-asean-region.html.

[197] FIAL. 2020. *Capturing the prize: The A$200 billion opportunity in 2030 for the Australian food and agribusiness sector.* Sydney. https://workdrive.zohopublic.com.au/file/qx5769e1e310483ee4389b5d9f6cc55e768fe.

[198] I. Rafani and T. Sudaryanto. 2020. *Strategic Plan of the Indonesian Ministry of Agriculture 2020–2024.* Jakarta. https://ap.fftc.org.tw/article/1842.

[199] Department of Trade and Industry. 2020. *Securing The Future of Philippine Industries.* Manila. http://industry.gov.ph/category/agribusiness/; LIFT. 2018. *Myanmar's Agricultural Development Strategy Is Officially Launched.* Yangon. https://www.lift-fund.org/en/news/myanmar%E2%80%99s-agricultural-development-strategy-officially-launched; A. Ponsrihadulchai. 2019. *Thailand Agricultural Policies and Development Strategies.* Bangkok. https://ap.fftc.org.tw/article/1393 and CDRI. 2011. *Cambodia's Agricultural Strategy: Future Development Options for the Rice Sector.* Phnom Penh. https://cdri.org.kh/wp-content/uploads/agriStrategy9e.pdf.

[200] PwC. 2016. *A new delivery Satisfying Southeast Asia's appetite through digital.* Singapore. https://www.pwc.com/gx/en/issues/high-growth-markets/assets/a-new-delivery-satisfying-southeast-asias-appetite-through-digital.pdf.

physical stores or factories, reaching consumers across the country and abroad. However, there are also relatively high transaction costs and challenges in delivery logistics. Situations restricting travel and traditional retail options, including COVID-19, have altered consumer behaviors and generated greater direct-to-consumer sales. For example, since the pandemic outbreak, 23% of consumers in Southeast Asia have started using e-commerce platforms to purchase their products and 28% of consumers indicated they tried using such platforms for the first time.[201] Countries could help businesses expand their sales channels, especially digital ones, and improve digital connectivity (e.g., expanding Internet coverage) and help companies access digital platforms.

3. **Attract investment and companies into the industry.** There is a need to shift the focus to higher value-adding activities further down the food value chain, explore policies to reduce the barriers of entry, and incentivize more companies to enter the industry. Some potential policies include:

   a. **Increasing access to financing options.** More financing options and risk management services for existing companies or those planning to enter the industry must be provided. Agricultural loans and microfinance schemes, often in collaboration with international development organizations, are already available. For instance, Canada's Bank of Montreal introduced a dedicated agriculture and agribusiness banking team to provide specialized technical finance expertise.[202] The Agricultural Bank of China, a dedicated agricultural bank which has expertise in a range of agro-related financial products for farmer households and agro-processing businesses.[203] In Spain, the government partnered with the private sector to develop an agricultural insurance system through risk pooling and subsidies.[204] This helps cover damages caused to agricultural production due to changes in weather conditions, diseases, and forest fires. In 2019, the Dutch Ministry of Foreign Affairs and Rabobank together contributed a total of $80 million to the AGRI3 Fund, a $1 billion sustainable agriculture initiative.[205] The AGRI3 Fund acts as a blended finance vehicle, providing risk minimizing financial instruments for stakeholders in the food value chain, especially farmers. ADB, through its Private Sector Operations Department, provides technical assistance and guaranteed purchases of crops to scale up businesses.[206] However, more needs to be done to increase the coverage levels in the focus countries through measures like localized financing options, matching fund schemes, or programs to link companies with international organizations.

   b. **Providing tax incentives.** Tax incentives have been used to develop new sectors and industries by lowering business costs. For instance, Viet Nam is attractive for foreign and local food processing businesses due to preferential tax policies for investors.[207] In Cambodia, foreign projects can be registered as Qualified Investment Projects to benefit from investment incentives in the form of a 3-year profit tax exemption.

   c. **Developing crucial support services.** To scale operations and increase industry value-add, companies in agro-processing require access to crucial supporting services like research and marketing. In Singapore, FoodInnovate was launched to act as a knowledge center to encourage food innovation efforts.[208] Some initiatives include the High Pressure Processing Resource Sharing Facility and the JTC Food

201 Bain & Company. 2020. *How Covid-19 Is Changing Southeast Asia's Consumers*. Boston. https://www.bain.com/insights/how-covid-19-is-changing-southeast-asias-consumers/.

202 BMO Bank of Montreal. 2020. *BMO Introduces Dedicated Agriculture Banking Team*. Montreal. https://newsroom.bmo.com/2020-10-14-BMO-Introduces-Dedicated-Agriculture-Banking-Team.

203 Agricultural Bank of China. 2020. Agro-related Business. http://www.abchina.com/en/AgroRelated/.

204 Agroseguro. 2013. *Spanish Agricultural Insurance System*. Madrid. https://sustainabledevelopment.un.org/content/documents/386213.%20AGROSEGURO_2.pdf.

205 UNEP. 2020. Dutch government and Rabobank announce anchor investments in AGRI3 Fund. 23 January. https://www.unenvironment.org/news-and-stories/press-release/dutch-government-and-rabobank-announce-anchor-investments-agri3-fund.

206 ADB. 2019. *Scaling-up Investment in Agribusiness is Helping Transform Asia and the Pacific*. 29 August. https://www.adb.org/news/features/scaling-investment-agribusiness-helping-transform-asia-and-pacific.

207 Mazars. 2018. *Food industry players in Vietnam - Notable tax, legal and accounting aspects*. Hanoi. https://www.mazars.vn/Home/Insights/Latest-news/Food-industry-players-in-Vietnam.

208 Enterprise Singapore. 2021. FoodInnovate. https://www.enterprisesg.gov.sg/industries/type/food-manufacturing/boost-capabilities.

Hub @ Senoko, allowing businesses to use advanced food processing technologies with a pay-per-use model.[209] Thailand has also given policy support to agro-processing, creating Food Innopolis, a global food innovation hub focusing on food industry research, development, and innovation.[210] The Philippines will develop a Regional Inclusive Innovation Center to offer MSMEs access to certification for high-value crops like rubber, coffee, and coconuts (footnote 178).

d. **Introducing intellectual protection (IP) rights.** IP rights, such as trademarks, can be important for consumers when making purchasing decisions, as certifications can include information on reputations, ethical stances, food safety standards, and quality.[211] These have become increasingly important over the past years as consumers become better informed and make better purchases. In the Philippines, IP protection has been identified as crucial to the food and beverage industries, and authorities have encouraged companies, especially foreign MSMEs, to register their trademarks.[212]

(iii)   Pursuing Steps to Raise Productivity Rates

The food and agriculture sector, with the agro-processing industry, has had productivity challenges for some time. These are relatively consistent across countries of various sizes, geographical locations, natural conditions, and economic and political environments.[213] In Southeast Asia, farmers rarely achieve over 70% of potential yields due to agronomic and economic limitations.[214] Most of the focus countries have traditional or transitional agricultural value chains characterized by the dominance of MSMEs, local supply chains, labor-intensive operations, and a lack of compliance with contracts and standards.[215] There are areas to further enhance productivity rates to progress to a modern or digital agricultural value chain by using the following measures:

1. **Focusing on research and enabling policies to ensure a more consistent supply of raw materials.** Crops and livestock must become more resilient especially against weather changes and diseases. The Singapore-Massachusetts Institute of Technology Alliance for Research and Technology and the Temasek Life Sciences Laboratory are working on crops that can survive droughts and withstand high temperatures due to climate change.[216] The focus countries also have programs and research institutions like the Cambodian Agricultural Research and Development Institute studying climate-resilient crops.[217] Producers of crops and livestock could provide assurances of acceptable quality of primary materials and in quantities and forms needed by

[209] Enterprise Singapore. 2018. Launch of High Pressure Processing Resource Sharing Facility. 16 April. https://www.enterprisesg.gov.sg/media-centre/media-releases/2018/april/launch-of-high-pressure-processing-resource-sharing-facility; and Enterprise Singapore. 2018. New facility to help food makers test products in small batches. 1 August. https://www.enterprisesg.gov.sg/media-centre/news/2018/august/new-facility-to-help-food-makers-test-products-in-small-batches.

[210] N. Kosal. 2020. Kingdom's agro-processing potential. *The Phnom Penh Post*. 8 June. https://www.phnompenhpost.com/opinion/kingdoms-agro-processing-potential; and Thailand Government Public Relations Department. 2017. *Food Innopolis to Develop Thailand as a Food Research and Innovation Hub*. Bangkok. https://thailand.prd.go.th/ewt_news.php?nid=4850&filename=index.

[211] J. Caplan. 2020. How valuable are food and beverage trademarks? *CITMA*. 10 June. https://www.citma.org.uk/resources/trade-marks-ip/protecting-food-and-drink-brands/how-valuable-are-trade-marks-to-food-and-beverage-manufacturers.html.

[212] ASEAN Briefing. 2018. *IP Protection in the Philippines' Food and Beverage Industry*. https://www.aseanbriefing.com/news/ip-protection-philippines-food-beverage-industry/.

[213] OECD. 2019. *Innovation, Productivity and Sustainability in Food and Agriculture*: Chapter 2 Productivity and sustainability challenges for food and agriculture. Paris. https://www.oecd-ilibrary.org/sites/233203bd-en/index.html?itemId=/content/component/233203bd-en.

[214] BCSD Singapore, PBE, Indonesia BCSD and Viet Nam BCSD. 2016. *Efficient Agriculture, Stronger Economies in ASEAN*. https://www.aprilasia.com/images/pdf_files/BCSD/BCSD_white_paper.pdf.

[215] ERIA. 2018. *Food Value Chain in ASEAN: Case Studies Focusing on Local Producers*. Jakarta. https://www.eria.org/uploads/media/RPR_FY2018_05.pdf.

[216] S. Begum. 2019. Nanotubes transform vegetable genes for more resilient crops. *The Straits Times*. 28 March. https://www.straitstimes.com/singapore/nanotubes-transform-vegetable-genes-for-more-resilient-crops.

[217] GIZ. 2015. *Promotion of Climate Resilience in Rice and Maize: Thailand National Study*. Eschborn. https://snrd-asia.org/download/forest_and_climate_change_for-cc/Thailand-FULL.pdf; Department of Agriculture. 2020. DA pushes for climate-resilient agri-fishery sector. 17 February. https://www.da.gov.ph/da-pushes-for-climate-resilient-agri-fishery-sector/; T. Anderson et al. 2018. Upgrading Agricultural Systems: Opportunities and Challenges for Myanmar. *Cornell Policy Review*. http://www.cornellpolicyreview.com/upgrading-agriculture-myanmar/; and G. Haryono and S. Nurjayanti. 2007. *Agricultural R&D in Indonesia: Policy, Investments and Institutional Profile*. Jakarta. https://www.asti.cgiar.org/pdf/IndonesiaCR.pdf.

processors. For instance, Australian authorities have rolled out quality assurance (QA) schemes for fresh produce to enable producers to review their on-farm practices and meet food safety standards.[218] These schemes motivate producers to invest in research and operations to continue selling their produce. Another possible policy measure could be enhancing business linkages between farmers and agro-processors to improve market access for smallholder farms and diversifying raw material sources for manufacturers. The Cambodian Partnership for Sustainable Agriculture was launched to give smallholder farmers new links with formal markets.[219] In Indonesia, digital agriculture marketplace startups like TaniHub connect farmers directly with different customers including factories (footnote 142).

2. **Promoting the adoption of processing equipment.** Many agro-processing firms rely on rudimentary processing methods in the focus countries even though well-established food processing equipment to improve productivity are already available. Examples include the automated carton erector system (to seal boxes), handheld electric fish scaler (to remove the scales of any fish without damaging the skin), and vacuum packaging machines (to seal products in a plastic wrap). Countries could consider offering financial grants for businesses to encourage adoption. In Singapore, the government introduced the Productivity Solutions Grant and the Enterprise Development Grant to help companies cover 80% of equipment costs to optimize operations.[220] Other than grants, countries could also enhance the awareness of various equipment through tradeshows and conferences. In Cambodia, the local ministries partnered with industry associations to organize a food and agricultural processing business matching forum to give agro-processing companies to have access to processing machinery and potential suppliers.[221] It is important to note that complementary policies like improving utility infrastructure are essential to reap benefits.

3. **Equipping workers with the right nondigital skillsets.** One of the challenges faced by MSMEs in agro-processing is the lack of skilled workers. The following three policy responses may help build nondigital capabilities of the industry:
   a. **Promote skilling programs.** Governments, in partnership with the private sector and civil society, could undertake skilling programs for industry workers. In India, the Ministry of Food Processing Industries collaborates with the Food Industry Capacity and Skill Initiative and the Sector Skill Council to develop courses for food processing workers.[222] Focus countries also currently collaborate with multilateral organizations on various relevant programs. For example, a series of "train the trainer" programs, funded by Thailand, has been conducted in Cambodia and Myanmar since 2018 (as part of the Initiative for ASEAN Integration), covering aspects such as food safety management for the agro-processing industry to meet international standards on Good Manufacturing Practice.[223] However, the participation rates and frequencies of these training programs have been inadequate, particularly considering the size of the industry.
   b. **Enhance the leadership capability of businesses.** Studies on skills shortages and gaps identified a perceived lack of business management and leadership in agro-processing.[224] Governments could work directly with

[218] Government of Western Australia Department of Primary Industries and Regional Development. 2020. *Quality assurance schemes for fresh produce.* Perth. https://www.agric.wa.gov.au/food-safety/quality-assurance-schemes-fresh-produce.

[219] K. Prakash-Mani. 2016. Q&A: How are partnerships changing Asia's food systems? *WEF.* 31 May. https://www.weforum.org/agenda/2016/05/q-and-a-how-are-partnerships-changing-asia-s-food-systems/ and CPSA. 2021. *Cambodian Partnership for Sustainable Agriculture.* https://cpsa-growasia.org/en/.

[220] GoBusiness Gov Assist. 2021. *Pre-scoped Equipment for Food Manufacturing.* https://govassist.gobusiness.gov.sg/productivity-solutions-grant/equipment/foodmanufacturing/.

[221] C. Bunthoeun. 2019. Food processing forum kicks off. *Khmer Times.* 19 August. https://www.khmertimeskh.com/634710/food-processing-forum-kicks-off/.

[222] Ministry of Food Processing Industries. 2020. *Skill Development Initiative.* Delhi. https://mofpi.nic.in/investor-facilitation/skill-development-initiative.

[223] For details, please see: https://asean.org/storage/2017/02/34-Food-Safety-Mng.pdf (accessed 10 January 2021).

[224] ILO. 2013. *Skills shortages and skills gaps in the Cambodian labour market: Evidence from employer skills needs survey.* Geneva. http://ilo.org/wcmsp5/groups/public/---asia/---ro-bangkok/documents/publication/wcms_231862.pdf; and United Nations Economic and Social Commission for Asia and the Pacific (UNESCAP). 2015. *Myanmar Business Survey: Data Analysis and Policy Implications.* Bangkok. https://www.unescap.org/sites/default/files/Web%20Myanmar%20Business%20Survey%20Data%20Analysis_final%20PDF_1.pdf.

businesses to improve the capabilities of industry leadership. There are training programs in Australia, Uganda, and the Philippines which work with businesses and business leaders to upgrade their managerial skills.[225] For example, in Australia, the National Careers Institute has tailored programs for production managers in food processing, covering topics such as leadership and agribusiness management.[226]

   c. **Incentivize the private sector to provide training.** Governments could provide businesses with financial incentives to encourage them to invest in their employees' training. Singapore introduced the Enhanced Training Support Package to subsidize training fees for the food and beverage sector by up to 90%.[227] These courses include training in domain skills such as process innovation, cost management, and quality control.

4. **Facilitating digital transformation.** The food and beverage manufacturing industry could be transformed by the 4IR. The use of big data and the Internet of Things (IoT) can enhance demand forecasting and production planning to improve customer service levels, thus boosting profit margins. Analyzing detailed, real-time data on suppliers' inventory and shipments in transit, to downstream customer demand allows manufacturing companies to tighten inventory control and maximize production capacity.[228] McKinsey & Company estimated that productivity could be increased by up to 50% by adopting relevant technologies in agro-processing in Southeast Asia.[229]

To initiate digital transformation, the focus countries must invest in both hardware (e.g., relevant technologies) and software (e.g., digital skills), ranging from digital technologies enabling smart factories to IoT to improve supply chain monitoring (Box 4). Thailand has already introduced its "Thailand 4.0" strategy to facilitate digital technology adoption in targeted industries including agro-processing.[230]

Digital skills must progress with technology adoption to enable effective implementation. To upskill agro-processing workers with digital skills, governments can:

   a. **Identify the existing state of digitalization.** Before initiating digital transformation plans, countries need to gain a better understanding of the current digital capabilities of the industry and prepare for digital adoption. In New Zealand, AgResearch started a preparation program to create a technology road map to support the industry's transition by identifying barriers, developing pilots, and analyzing data.[231] The Economic Research Institute for ASEAN and East Asia developed an Industry 4.0 Readiness Self-Assessment Tool to guide firms toward digitalization.[232]

   b. **Develop skilling programs.** Once the existing state is assessed, governments need to develop programs that fill gaps in specific digital skills, particularly for managerial employees who would most likely be supervising the use of technologies in farms and factories. In Europe, there are increasingly more courses on implementing digital solutions in the food processing industry.[233] For instance, RISE,

[225] Uganda Ministry of Agriculture, Animal Industry and Fisheries. 2020. *The National Farmer's Leadership Centre*. Entebbe. https://www.agriculture.go.ug/the-national-farmers-leadership-center/; and Philippines Agricultural Training Institute. 2020. Training Programs. Manila. https://ati.da.gov.ph/ati-main/programs/training-programs.

[226] National Careers Institute. 2020. *Agriculture & Food Processing*. Canberra. https://www.myskills.gov.au/industries/agriculture-food-processing.

[227] SkillsFutureSG. 2020. *Enhanced Training Support Package and Enhanced Absentee Payroll to mitigate COVID-19*. Singapore. https://www.ssg.gov.sg/ETSP_EnhancedAP.html.

[228] McKinsey Global Institute. 2014. *Southeast Asia at the crossroads: Three paths to prosperity*. https://www.mckinsey.com/~/media/McKinsey/Featured%20Insights/Asia%20Pacific/Three%20paths%20to%20sustained%20economic%20growth%20in%20Southeast%20Asia/MGI%20SE%20Asia_Executive%20summary_November%202014.ashx.

[229] McKinsey & Company. 2018. *Industry 4.0: Reinvigorating ASEAN Manufacturing for the Future*. Singapore. https://www.mckinsey.com/~/media/mckinsey/business%20functions/operations/our%20insights/industry%204%200%20reinvigorating%20asean%20manufacturing%20for%20the%20future/industry-4-0-reinvigorating-asean-manufacturing-for-the-future.ashx.

[230] Relevant targeted industries include Food for the Future. Thailand Ministry of Industry. *Ministry of Industry's role in Thailand 4.0*. http://www.jtecs.or.jp/wp-content/uploads/hpb-media/PPTTNI.pdf.

[231] AgResearch. 2017. *Preparing NZ for shift to digital agriculture*. Christchurch. https://www.agresearch.co.nz/news/preparing-nz-for-shift-to-digital-agriculture/.

[232] ERIA. 2021. Industry 4.0 and Circular Economy Readiness Self-Assessment Tool. http://www.i4r-eria.org/firm-assessment-sign-up.

[233] EIT. 2020. *Digitalisation and Industry 4.0 in Food Processing*. Brussels. https://professionalschool.eitdigital.eu/professional-courses/digitalisation-and-industry-40-in-food-processing/.

Box 4: Key Technologies to Transform Agro-Processing Productivity

Industry 4.0 includes a range of technologies that could transform productivity in agro-processing. Some examples:

- **Rethinking production approaches through digital innovations.** Process monitoring and control can be automated on the factory floor utilizing a combination of Internet of Things, cloud computing, and Artificial Intelligence (AI). This can enable machines to monitor and analyze manufacturing processes, detect any deviations, and implement necessary adjustments without human intervention. Improvements in technologies such as digital image processing can lead to more accurate food quality inspection, including verification of labeling accuracy, colors, and height or volume.[a] Redesigning manufacturing processes can also take advantage of virtual reality or augmented reality devices, which can enable the simulation of different manufacturing designs immersively.
- **Use of robotics on the production floor.** Though food processing has historically proved challenging for the use of robotics, advancements have now seen robots with "soft grippers" that can quickly, but gently handle even sensitive food products such as fruits and vegetables. Other types of grippers, such as vacuum grippers, are increasingly able to handle delicate or irregularly shaped items, particularly when coupled with imaging technology.[b]
- **Utilization of biotech to support the development of alternative proteins.** Currently, the market base for alternative protein is approximately $2.2 billion compared with a global meat market of approximately $1.7 trillion, but it is growing rapidly, driven by a combination of environmental and health concerns.[c] There is a range of opportunities in agro-processing linked to the development of alternative proteins, including plant proteins, microbial proteins, and cultured meat. This requires using a range of technologies, including big data approaches for protein identification and the development of biotech technologies (such as bioreactors) for high-value, sustainable, and nutritious protein production.
- **Tackling food waste through biotech.** Globally, about 30% of all food produced is wasted, representing $1 trillion in lost economic value annually.[d] Biotech technologies such as irradiation can help reduce post-harvest losses through disinfestations, sprout inhibition, and improving the shelf-life of fresh produce. It can also be effective in reducing food-borne diseases through the destruction of pathogenic organisms.
- **Customized food development through 3D printing.** To meet customers' personalized needs, there is an increasing use of 3D printing. Advancements in 3D printing are seeing the application of edible cement as binding materials, where 3D printers could have applications due to the ability to develop intricate designs, customizable product offerings, and minimize wastage (footnote a). Given the strides in additive manufacturing development or 3D printing, there could be a point where it becomes cost-effective for households to own these, which could create a significant disruption to the food processing sector.
- **The Internet of Things (IoT) to manage supply chains.** IoT refers to networks of sensors and actuators embedded in machines and other physical objects that connect with one another and the Internet. It has a wide range of applications, including data collection, monitoring, decision-making, and process optimization.[e] Radio frequency identification tags on containers can track products as they move from factory to stores, allowing companies to avoid stock-outs and losses. Tighter supply chain management can help significantly minimize food waste and improve product traceability to enhance food safety and reduce food fraud.

3D = three-dimensional.

[a] N. Hasnan and Y. Yusoff. 2018. Application areas of 4IR: Technologies in food processing sector. *Conference paper.* https://www.researchgate.net/publication/333062733_Short_review_Application_Areas_of_Industry_40_Technologies_in_Food_Processing_Sector/link/5d73c97d4585151ee4a5c59d/download.

[b] Robotics Industry Association. 2019. *Robotics in Food Manufacturing and Food Processing.* Michigan. https://www.robotics.org/blog-article.cfm/Robotics-in-Food-Manufacturing-and-Food-Processing/154.

[c] McKinsey & Company. 2019. *Alternative proteins: The race for market share is on.* New York. https://www.mckinsey.com/industries/agriculture/our-insights/alternative-proteins-the-race-for-market-share-is-on.

[d] FAO. 2019. *State of Food and Agriculture 2019. Moving forward on food loss and waste reduction.* Rome. http://www.fao.org/policy-support/resources/resources-details/en/c/1242090/.

[e] McKinsey Global Institute. 2014. *Southeast Asia at the crossroads: Three paths to prosperity.* New York. https://www.mckinsey.com/~/media/McKinsey/Featured%20Insights/Asia%20Pacific/Three%20paths%20to%20sustained%20economic%20growth%20in%20Southeast%20Asia/MGI%20SE%20Asia_Executive%20summary_November%202014.ashx.

Sweden's research institute, developed a "Digitalization and Industry 4.0" course covering multiple technologies.[234]

c. **Incentivize participation.** To encourage the adoption of digital technologies in the industry, governments could consider financial incentives, so workers learn the fundamentals of data analytics or customer experience 4.0. Singapore has provided funding for companies to send their workers for training programs in emerging digital skills (footnote 222).

(iv) Building Industry Resilience

COVID-19 demonstrated that agro-processing is particularly vulnerable to shocks. It is important to learn from this crisis to increase industry preparedness for future pandemics and disruptions. To enhance the industry's resiliency, the government can:

1. **Streamline regulatory functions.** As agro-manufacturing spans the entire agriculture value chain, a comprehensive regulatory system is required (e.g., oversight from ministries including agriculture, health, and trade), with some countries starting to streamline regulatory functions to better support the industry. For instance, in Singapore, the Singapore Food Agency was formed by consolidating the food-related expertise from Agri-food and Veterinary Authority, National Environment Agency, and the Health Sciences Authority.[235] This allows the Singapore Food Agency to recommend more targeted policies, reduce duplication, and oversee communication between the industry and investors. There is a need to systemically review the regulatory structure of the industry and streamline functions as regulations in the focus countries cut across a range of ministries and currently appear fragmented.

2. **Strengthen the local agro-processing ecosystem.** The pandemic showed the importance of maintaining food security and the continuous operation of supply lines. Countries relying heavily on food imports experienced much difficulty with border restrictions. There should be more emphasis on diversification, shorter supply chains, local alternative supplies, and local markets. Brunei Darussalam pursued self-sufficiency and developed its domestic production and agribusiness sector.[236] Measures include government purchase guarantees, technical assistance provisions, joint venture partnerships, schemes to ensure the availability of agricultural inputs to farmers and improvements to land tenure security. Governments could increase the resilience of the industry by preserving seeds important for farmers to restart operations after major disruptions such as disasters. For instance, the Government of Norway maintains the Svalbard Global Seed Vault, a seed bank with over 1 million seed samples from around the world.[237] In Thailand, the ECHO Asia Seed Bank curates seeds that thrive under difficult growing conditions in the tropics.[238] Out of the five focus countries, Myanmar and Thailand are considered self-sufficient, even though food insecurity among households is a serious issue in Myanmar.[239] The other three countries should urgently strengthen their food ecosystems as they work toward self-sufficiency.[240]

[234] RISE. 2020. *Digitalization and Industry 4.0 - Course 1.* Göteborg. https://www.ri.se/en/education/digitalization-and-industry-40-course-1.

[235] SFA. 2020. *Annual Report.* Singapore. https://www.sfa.gov.sg/docs/default-source/publication/annual-report/sfa-ar-2019-2020.pdf.

[236] Oxford Business Group. 2020. *Focus on food security: Self-sufficiency and increased capacity are central aims.* London. https://oxfordbusinessgroup.com/overview/focus-food-security-self-sufficiency-and-increased-capacity-are-central-aims.

[237] U. Ramsey. 2018. Seed Libraries and Food Justice: Cultivating an Effective Legal and Policy Environment. *Georgetown Journal on Poverty Law and Policy* Volume XXV, Number 2, Winter 2018. https://www.law.georgetown.edu/poverty-journal/wp-content/uploads/sites/25/2018/05/25-2-Seed-Libraries-and-Food-Justice.pdf.

[238] Echo Community. 2021. The ECHO Asia Seed Bank. https://www.echocommunity.org/en/pages/echo_asia_seedbank_info.

[239] M. Fader et al. 2013. Spatial decoupling of agricultural production and consumption: quantifying dependences of countries on food imports due to domestic land and water constraints. *Environmental Research Letters*, Volume 8, Number 1. https://iopscience.iop.org/article/10.1088/1748-9326/8/1/014046#erl452631s3; D. Stone. 2014. Is Your Country Food Independent? *National Geographic.* 13 April. https://www.nationalgeographic.com/culture/onward/2014/04/13/is-your-country-food-independent/; and IWMI. 2014. Can Myanmar achieve food security? https://www.iwmi.cgiar.org/2014/12/can-myanmar-achieve-food-security/#:~:text=Myanmar%20is%20self%2Dsufficient%20in,beans%2C%20to%20China%20and%20India.

[240] N. Hamilton-Hart. 2019. Indonesia's Quest for Food Self-sufficiency: A New Agricultural Political Economy? *Journal of Contemporary Asia* Volume 49, 2019 - Issue 5. https://www.tandfonline.com/doi/abs/10.1080/00472336.2019.1617890?journalCode=rjoc20.

3. **Accelerate investments and improve communication policies to guard against risks.** These measures may include:
   a. **Investing in biosecurity capabilities.** Biological outbreaks have been highlighted by experts over the years and COVID-19 exposed the negative impacts of these outbreaks.[241] There is currently little or insufficient effort to enhance biosecurity capabilities in the focus countries. To be resilient against future outbreaks, there is a need to invest in national and international programs to increase adequate biosecurity arrangements to strengthen countries' capacity to manage emergent sanitary and phytosanitary risks.[242] In Queensland, Australia, authorities allocated increased funding to review and strengthen biosecurity capability and capacity, including upgrading disease diagnostic processes.[243]
   b. **Strengthening government communication strategies.** Regular and clear updates will improve consumer trust in the safety and reliability of locally processed food products, helping to prevent panic buying, something seen across many countries as they came under lockdown. Singapore adopted several measures to provide advice, support, and updates on the pandemic regularly.[244] For instance, citizens could subscribe to WhatsApp updates from the Ministry of Health to get very transparent information. In the focus countries, some countries have utilized apps (e.g., Indonesia), dedicated hotlines (e.g., Cambodia), and social media to disseminate information to citizens.[245]

4. **Promote partnerships among agro-processing stakeholders.** Policies to help the industry recover, rebuild, and become resilient require close coordination among the private sector, government, and other countries in the region. Countries could improve partnerships by:
   a. **Improving communication between the private sector and the government.** To enhance partnerships, countries could consider participating in regional and global platforms such as the New Vision for Agriculture Initiative, by the World Economic Forum, or Grow Asia.[246] These platforms allow the discussions of key topics related to agro-processing and the identification of solutions. For instance, policy makers in Tanzania used the Initiative and convened further stakeholder meetings to develop the country's agro-processing industry (footnote 246).
   b. **Encouraging the creation of industry associations.** Industry associations are useful to facilitate communications, consolidate resources, and reduce duplication. For instance, in the United States, the National Association of Manufacturers developed a COVID-19 resource guide to provide round-the-clock support of key information for companies to get through this crisis including best practices of operational activities and a consolidated library of government support measures.[247]

[241] Daniel M. Gerstein. 2020. Biosecurity Is the Lesson We Need to Learn from the Coronavirus Pandemic. *RAND*. 11 May. https://www.rand.org/blog/2020/05/biosecurity-is-the-lesson-we-need-to-learn-from-the.html.

[242] ADB. 2014. *Modernizing Sanitary and Phytosanitary Measures to Expand Trade and Ensure Food Safety*. Manila. https://www.adb.org/sites/default/files/publication/180517/modernizing-sanitary-measures.pdf.

[243] Queensland Government Department of Agriculture and Fisheries. 2020. *Enhancing biosecurity capability and capacity in Queensland*. Brisbane. https://www.daf.qld.gov.au/business-priorities/biosecurity/enhancing-capability-capacity.

[244] M. Sagar. 2020. How Singapore government's communication keeps nation moving forward in crisis. *Open Gov*. 16 March. https://opengovasia.com/how-singapore-governments-communication-has-kept-the-nation-working-through-crisis/.

[245] C. Lan and W. Schultz-Henry. 2020. Cambodia's 115 Hotline: Successful COVID-19 Digital Response. *ICT Works*. 6 May. https://www.ictworks.org/cambodia-115-hotline-digital-response/#.X9MmN9gzY2w; WHO. 2020. Yangon uses media mix to boost solidarity against COVID-19. 27 October. https://www.who.int/news-room/feature-stories/detail/yangon-uses-media-mix-to-boost-solidarity-against-covid-19; and W. Agung. 2020. *Initiatives of Indonesian ICT Players in Combating Covid-19*. https://gcn.comsoc.org/initiatives-indonesian-ict-players-combating-covid-19.

[246] WEF. 2016. *Building Partnerships for Sustainable Agriculture and Food Security A Guide to Country-Led Action*. Cologny. http://www3.weforum.org/docs/IP/2016/NVA/NVAGuidetoCountryLevelAction.pdf.

[247] NAM. 2020. *COVID-19 Resources*. Washington, DC. https://www.nam.org/coronavirus/?_zs=Nw4kf1&_zl=faRa6.

c. **Strengthening coordination across Southeast Asia.** Given the significant intra-ASEAN trade of raw materials and processed products, it is important to enhance coordination among Southeast Asian countries. The ASEAN Ministers on Agriculture and Forestry pledged to minimize disruptions in regional food supply chains and provide timely information and have reaffirmed their commitment to ensuring food security in the region during the pandemic.[248]

5. **Pursue food-related circularity policies.** COVID-19 placed constraints on the current food system and there are opportunities to pursue a circular economy as countries rethink their economic models and figure out their recovery plans.[249] A sustainable model for the food system involves moving from the current linear model to a circular model to avoid food loss and waste (e.g., by shortening supply chains) and deploying food loss and waste for productive purposes like generating biogas.[250] Countries can tackle post-harvest and supply chain waste, including working with smallholder farmers to provide technical expertise and mechanisms to fund the purchase of capital-intensive equipment and storage. The Government of Indonesia is considering developing a large-scale cold storage warehouse, possibly costing Rp3 trillion ($207 million), which could help stabilize domestic prices and discourage farmers from throwing away their produce.[251] Governments can promote the productive use of food loss and waste, and necessary enablers, such as regular maintenance and supervision, should be set in place to ensure efficiency. A food processing industry that focuses on value-added products (e.g., tomato sauce) could help absorb the excess supply of agricultural products and reduce post-harvest waste.[252] Pilot efforts in Bali have demonstrated the use of cooking oil waste as fuel for school buses.[253] Beyond tackling food waste, the agro-processing industry could also rethink its plastic packaging usage. As food and beverage products typically utilize a significant share of plastic packaging, there are opportunities for the agro-processing industry to adopt circularity approaches.[254] Businesses could reduce the use of single-use plastics and incorporate higher degrees of recycled plastics in their packaging with the support of governments.[255]

Some of these recommendations can benefit from increased regional cooperation from the rest of Southeast Asia. For instance, promoting cross-border trade and harmonizing standards require collaboration and mutual agreement beyond the five focus countries. Table 7 summarizes the key policy recommendations and their relevance to each focus country (footnote 124).

[248] ASEAN Secretariat. 2020. Statement of ASEAN Ministers on Agriculture and Forestry in Response to The Outbreak of The Coronavirus Disease (Covid-19) to Ensure Food Security, Food Safety and Nutrition in ASEAN. Jakarta. https://asean.org/statement-asean-ministers-agriculture-forestry-response-outbreak-coronavirus-disease-covid-19-ensure-food-security-food-safety-nutrition-asean/.

[249] M. Wijayasundara. 2020. Opportunities for a circular economy post COVID-19. WEF. 22 June. https://www.weforum.org/agenda/2020/06/opportunities-circular-economy-post-covid-19/.

[250] Ellen MacArthur Foundation. 2021. *Food and the Circular Economy*. https://www.ellenmacarthurfoundation.org/explore/food-cities-the-circular-economy.

[251] R. Syukra. 2015. Govt Plans Rp3t Cold Storage Facility to Tackle Price Fluctuations. *Jakarta Globe*. 18 September. https://jakartaglobe.id/business/govt-plans-rp3t-cold-storage-facility-tackle-price-fluctuations/.

[252] Food Security and Food Justice. 2016. *Rotten tomatoes: the story of post-harvest food waste in Indonesia*. https://foodsecurityfoodjustice.com/2016/01/25/rotten-tomatoes-the-story-of-the-post-harvest-food-waste-in-indonesia/.

[253] I. Pusparani. 2018. Recycled Cooking Oil Powers Eco-friendly Buses in Bali. *Seasia*. 8 March. https://seasia.co/2018/03/08/recycled-cooking-oil-powers-eco-friendly-buses-in-bali.

[254] B. Geueke, K. Groh and J. Muncke. 2018. Food packaging in the circular economy: Overview of chemical safety aspects for commonly used materials. *Journal of Cleaner Production* Volume 193, 20 August 2018, pp. 491–505. https://www.sciencedirect.com/science/article/pii/S0959652618313325.

[255] P. Berg et al. 2020. The drive toward sustainability in packaging—beyond the quick wins. *McKinsey & Company*. 30 January. https://www.mckinsey.com/industries/paper-forest-products-and-packaging/our-insights/the-drive-toward-sustainability-in-packaging-beyond-the-quick-wins; and UNEP. 2020. *Perceptions on Plastic Waste: Insights, interventions and incentives to action from businesses and consumers in South-East Asia*. Bangkok. https://www.sea-circular.org/wp-content/uploads/2020/06/PERCEPTIONS-OF-PLASTIC-WASTE_FINAL.pdf.

Table 7: Summary of Recommendations for Agro-Processing

Key recommendations and their relevance to focus countries

Degree of relevance: ■ High ■ Medium ■ Low

		Cambodia	Indonesia	Myanmar	Philippines	Thailand
Making supply chains more efficient	Improve information flows and transparency of prices	Low	Medium	High	Low	Low
	Promote cross-border trade	High	High	High	Medium	High
	Upgrade infrastructure	High	High	High	High	Medium
Increasing the value-add of the industry	Expand food product range	Medium	Medium	Medium	Medium	Medium
	Expand sales channels	Medium	Medium	Medium	Medium	Medium
	Attract investment and companies into the industry	Medium	Medium	Medium	Medium	Medium
Pursuing steps to raise productivity rates	Focus on research and enabling policies to ensure a more consistent supply of raw materials	Medium	Medium	Medium	Medium	Medium
	Promote the adoption of processing equipment	High	Medium	Medium	Medium	Medium
	Equip workers with the right nondigital skillsets	Medium	Medium	Medium	Medium	Medium
	Facilitate digital transformation in the agro-processing industry	High	High	High	High	High
Building industry resilience	Streamline regulatory functions	High	High	High	High	High
	Strengthen local agro-processing ecosystem	High	High	Medium	High	Low
	Accelerate investments and improve communication policies to guard against risks	Medium	High	High	High	High
	Promote partnerships between agro-processing stakeholders	High	Low	Low	Low	Low
	Pursue food-related circularity policies	High	Medium	High	High	High

Note: This exercise is based on a broad assessment of the observed gaps and what countries have done (i.e., current responses in terms of presence and scope of policy measures).
Source: AlphaBeta analysis.

Box 5 provides an overview of some of the relevant country plans and ADB programs by country.

Box 5: Examples of ADB Country Programs on Agro-Processing

A review of the Asian Development Bank (ADB) Country Operations Business Plans (COBP) (2020-22) and the Country Partnership Strategies (CPS) for the five focus countries identified several lending and non-lending products and services related to the agro-processing industry and the policy recommendations:[a]

- *Trade and regulatory policy reforms.* In the Philippines, ADB supports trade and regulatory reforms aimed at raising agriculture productivity and competitiveness, expanding economic opportunities in farming, and reducing poverty in rural areas. It will help the government liberalize and facilitate the rice trade to increase market supply and make rice affordable.[b]
- *Improving supply chains and promoting private investments.* In the Philippines, ADB will support investments that support market linkages and market-oriented value chain development to increase business viability and more private sector participation. ADB will work to improve the production and aggregation of safe and quality agricultural products and facilitate linkages between high-value agriculture products and their corresponding global markets.-In Cambodia, through the Cambodia Country Partnership Strategy, 2019–2023, ADB will promote

continued on next page

Box 5 *continued*

sustainable and inclusive growth by developing agricultural value chains in the country. A $70 million loan was approved in 2020 to strengthen the agricultural value chain and enhance the food safety of key commodities (e.g., cashews, mangoes) in six provinces across Cambodia. In Thailand, ADB aims to train local communities and the private sector on agri-food quality and safety improvement and value addition to help the agricultural sector recover from the pandemic.

- *Productivity enhancements.* In the Philippines, ADB plans to work with micro, small, and medium-sized enterprises to help them develop market-oriented products by providing technical assistance on several issues, including how to enhance capacity for food processing, branding, and marketing. Furthermore, ADB works closely with the Department of Trade and Industry and Department of Agriculture on key policy measures and strategic project investments focusing on developing and promoting high value agriculture commodities that have a comparative edge in the market.
- *Reduced food loss.* In Thailand, ADB aims to enhance the competitiveness and resource efficiency of postharvest operations in highland agriculture, using modern technologies.[c] ADB aims to demonstrate the application of digital technologies to improve the traceability of agri-food products, which could reduce food loss along the value chain.

[a] The Country Operations Business Plans include:
- ADB. 2019. *Country Operations Business Plan: Cambodia (2020–2022).* Manila. https://www.adb.org/documents/cambodia-country-operations-business-plan-2020-2022.
- ADB. 2019. *Country Operations Business Plan: Indonesia (2020–2022).* Manila. https://www.adb.org/sites/default/files/institutional-document/526266/cobp-ino-2020-2022.pdf.
- ADB. 2019. *Country Operations Business Plan: Myanmar (2020–2022).* Manila. https://www.adb.org/sites/default/files/institutional-document/541976/cobp-mya-2020-2022.pdf.
- ADB. 2019. *Country Operations Business Plan: Philippines (2020–2022).* Manila.https://www.adb.org/sites/default/files/institutional-document/533741/cobp-phi-2020-2022.pdf.
- ADB. 2019. *Country Operations Business Plan: Thailand (2020–2022).* Manila. https://www.adb.org/sites/default/files/institutional-document/541811/cobp-tha-2020-2022.pdf.

The Country Partnership Strategies include:
- ADB. 2019. *Country Partnership Strategy: Cambodia, 2019–2023, Inclusive pathways to a competitive economy.* Manila. https://www.adb.org/sites/default/files/institutional-document/534691/cps-cam-2019-2023.pdf.
- ADB. 2020. *Country Partnership Strategy: Indonesia, 2020–2024, Emerging Stronger.* Manila. https://www.adb.org/sites/default/files/institutional-document/640096/cps-ino-2020-2024.pdf.
- ADB. 2017. *Country Partnership Strategy: Myanmar, 2017–2021, Building the foundations for inclusive growth.* Manila. https://www.adb.org/sites/default/files/institutional-document/640096/cps-ino-2020-2024.pdf.
- ADB. 2018. *Country Partnership Strategy: Philippines, 2018–2023, High and inclusive growth.* Manila. https://www.adb.org/sites/default/files/institutional-document/456476/cps-phi-2018-2023.pdf.
- ADB. 2013. *Country Partnership Strategy: Thailand, 2013–2016.* Manila. https://www.adb.org/sites/default/files/institutional-document/33990/files/cps-tha-2013-2016.pdf.

[b] ADB. 2020. *Proposed Programmatic Approach and Policy-Based Loan for Subprogram 1 Republic of the Philippines: Support for Competitive and Inclusive Agriculture Development Program.* Manila. https://www.adb.org/sites/default/files/project-documents/53353/53353-001-cp-en.pdf.

[c] ADB. 2020. *Kingdom of Thailand: Climate Change Adaptation in Agriculture for Enhanced Recovery and Sustainability of Highlands.* Manila. https://www.adb.org/sites/default/files/project-documents/53099/53099-001-tar-en.pdf.

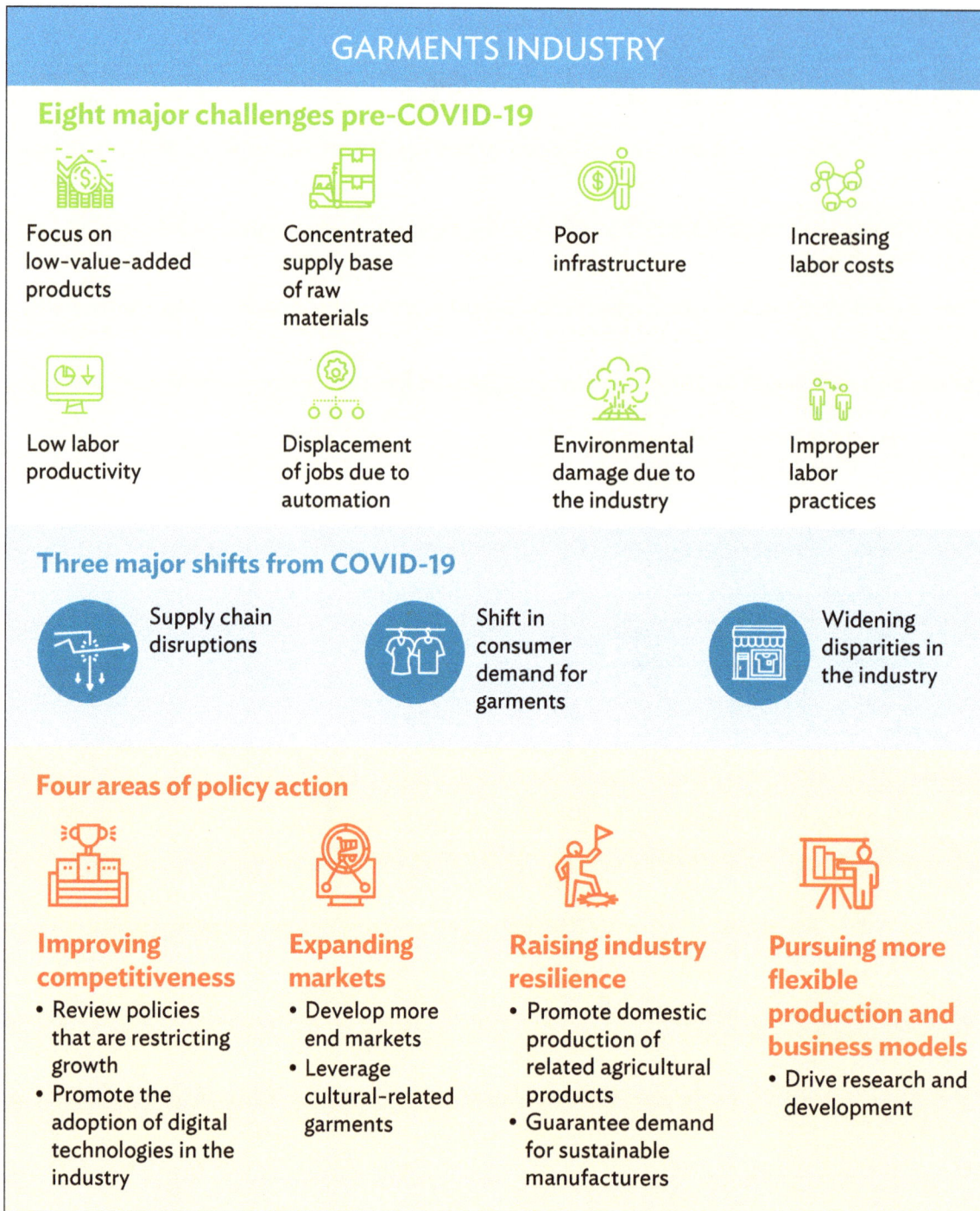

GARMENTS INDUSTRY

Eight major challenges pre-COVID-19

Focus on low-value-added products

Concentrated supply base of raw materials

Poor infrastructure

Increasing labor costs

Low labor productivity

Displacement of jobs due to automation

Environmental damage due to the industry

Improper labor practices

Three major shifts from COVID-19

Supply chain disruptions

Shift in consumer demand for garments

Widening disparities in the industry

Four areas of policy action

Improving competitiveness
- Review policies that are restricting growth
- Promote the adoption of digital technologies in the industry

Expanding markets
- Develop more end markets
- Leverage cultural-related garments

Raising industry resilience
- Promote domestic production of related agricultural products
- Guarantee demand for sustainable manufacturers

Pursuing more flexible production and business models
- Drive research and development

SECTION IV

Garments

▶ **Garments contribute to over 30% of exports in Myanmar and 65% in Cambodia.**

Covering textiles, apparel, and footwear, the garment industry plays an important role in the economies of many focus countries. According to the latest data from the National Institute for Statistics, this industry contributed 10% to Cambodia's nominal GDP in 2020.[256] The industry is labor-intensive and is the largest contributor to employment in Cambodia, employing 660,327 people.[257] This number becomes higher if employment in subcontracting factories is included. The industry is also an important source of employment for females, accounting for close to 20% of all female employment in Cambodia in 2019 (Figure 10).[258]

The garment industry is an important driver of exports (Figure 11). In 2019, garments and textile accounted for over 65% of Cambodia's total exports. All countries, except Thailand, have experienced annual growth in garment and textile exports from 2009 to 2019. Globally, among the focus countries, Indonesia, Thailand, and Cambodia were in the top 20 exporting countries of fashion goods including textiles and garments.[259]

Many Southeast Asian countries have competitive advantages in garment manufacturing due to relatively low labor costs, their strategic location, preferential market access, and supportive government policies. For instance, Cambodia benefited from the European Union (EU) "Everything but Arms" program granting least developed countries quota-free access for almost all products including garments.[260] This has driven significant demand from the EU. The Philippines introduced the "Textile-Garment Industry Roadmap 2020–2029" to boost manufacturing capabilities and drive exports.[261] Indonesia has set a target to increase the export value of textiles and garments to $75 billion by 2030.[262]

[256] National Institute for Statistics. 2020. National accounts. Phnom Penh. https://www.nis.gov.kh/nis/NA/NA2018_Tab_files/TAB1-2.htm.

[257] ILO Better Factories Cambodia. 2019. *Cambodia Garment and Footwear Sector Bulletin*, Issue 9. Phnom Penh. https://www.ilo.org/wcmsp5/groups/public/---asia/---ro-bangkok/documents/publication/wcms_714915.pdf.

[258] ILO. 2020. *The supply chain ripple effect: How COVID-19 is affecting garment workers and factories in Asia and the Pacific.* Geneva. https://www.ilo.org/wcmsp5/groups/public/---asia/---ro-bangkok/documents/briefingnote/wcms_758626.pdf.

[259] A. Teodoro and L. Rodriguez. 2020. Textile and garment supply chains in times of COVID-19: challenges for developing countries. *UNCTAD.* Geneva. https://unctad.org/news/textile-and-garment-supply-chains-times-covid-19-challenges-developing-countries.

[260] United Nations. 2020. *Preferential Market Access – European Union Everything But Arms Initiative.* New York. https://www.un.org/ldcportal/preferential-market-access-european-union-everything-but-arms-initiative/.

[261] J. Kastner. 2020. Philippines prepares for textile-garment industry roadmap. *Just-style.* 4 March. https://www.just-style.com/analysis/philippines-prepares-for-textile-garment-industry-roadmap_id138198.aspx.

[262] Global Business Guide Indonesia. 2020. "Indonesia's Upstream Textile Sector; On the Rise After a Slump." http://www.gbgindonesia.com/en/manufacturing/article/2017/indonesia_s_upstream_textile_sector_on_the_rise_after_a_slump_11803.php.

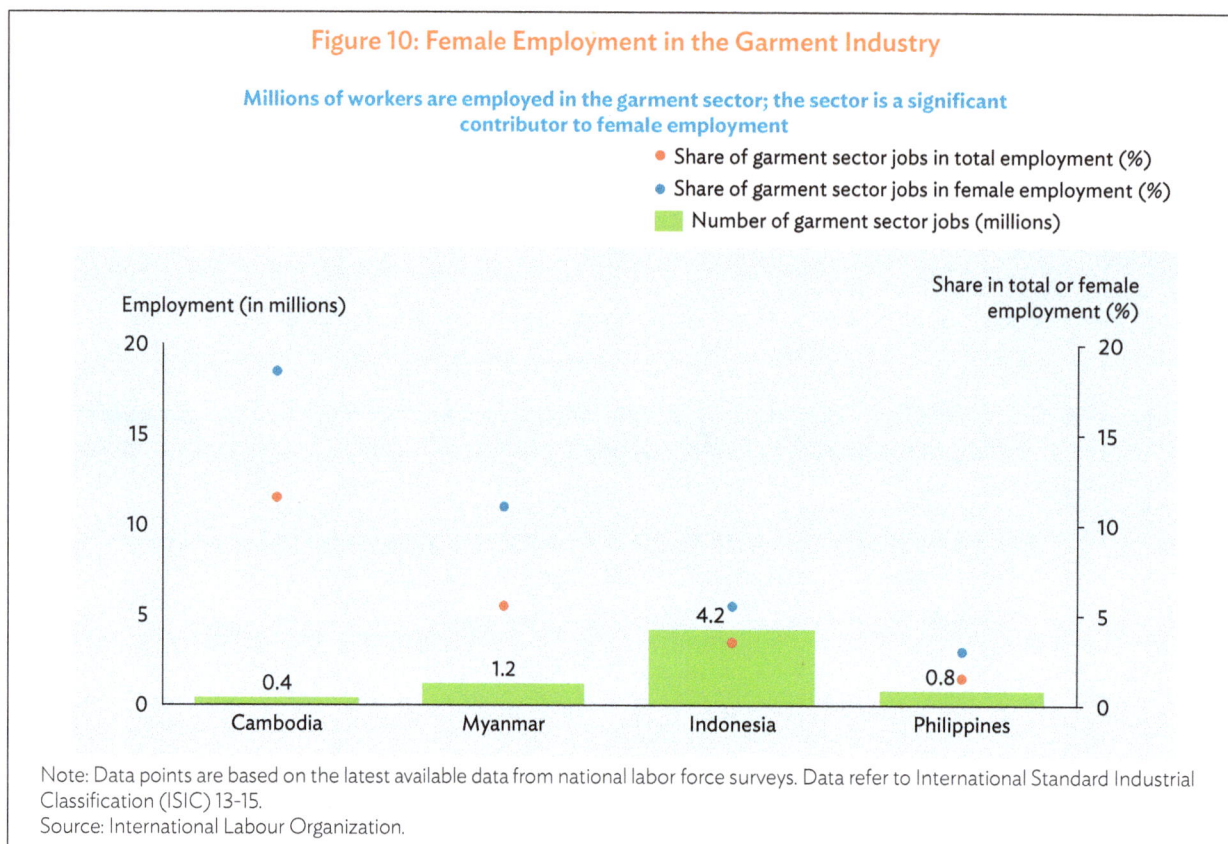

Figure 10: Female Employment in the Garment Industry

Millions of workers are employed in the garment sector; the sector is a significant contributor to female employment

- Share of garment sector jobs in total employment (%)
- Share of garment sector jobs in female employment (%)
- Number of garment sector jobs (millions)

Note: Data points are based on the latest available data from national labor force surveys. Data refer to International Standard Industrial Classification (ISIC) 13-15.
Source: International Labour Organization.

▶ **Several challenges contributed to the industry's low value addition.**

The garment industry faced eight structural challenges before the COVID-19 pandemic:

- **Focus on low-value and high-volume production.** Most of the focus countries are known to produce high volumes of low-value-added products. While countries in East Asia such as the PRC have moved toward higher value-added products (e.g., high-end shirts) and services (e.g., garment designing), countries like Cambodia and Myanmar still produce low value-added goods, relying on cheap labor as their primary competitive advantage.[263] The focus on Cut-Make-Pack/CMP (or Cut-Make-Trim) model as opposed to the Free-On-Board (FOB) model, is a primary driver for the low value add in the industry. Under the CMP system, factories focus on assembling imported raw materials such as cotton and buttons. They assume no responsibility for the more knowledge-intensive functions, such as product design, sourcing decisions of input materials, distribution arrangements, and marketing.[264] Conversely, under the FOB system, factories are responsible for the whole production process. In Myanmar, nearly all factories rely on the CMP model, driven by the tax exemptions on imports.[265] The CMP model offers limited profit margins for manufacturers

[263] P. Huynh. 2015. *Employment, wages and working conditions in Asia's garment sector: Finding new drivers of competitiveness.* ILO. Bangkok. https://www.ilo.org/asia/publications/WCMS_426563/lang--en/index.htm.
[264] OECD. 2013. *Aid for trade and value chains in textiles and apparel.* https://www.oecd.org/dac/aft/AidforTrade_SectorStudy_Textiles.pdf.
[265] SMART Myanmar. 2015. *SMART Myanmar Export Promotion Guide: For Myanmar Garment Manufacturers.* Yangon. https://smartmyanmar.org/files/wp-content/uploads/2015/10/SMART-Myanmar-Export-Promotion-Guide-Myanmar-Garment-Sector.pdf.

Figure 11: Garments and Textiles in Total Exports

Garment and textile exports account for a significant portion of the merchandise export earnings of Cambodia and Myanmar

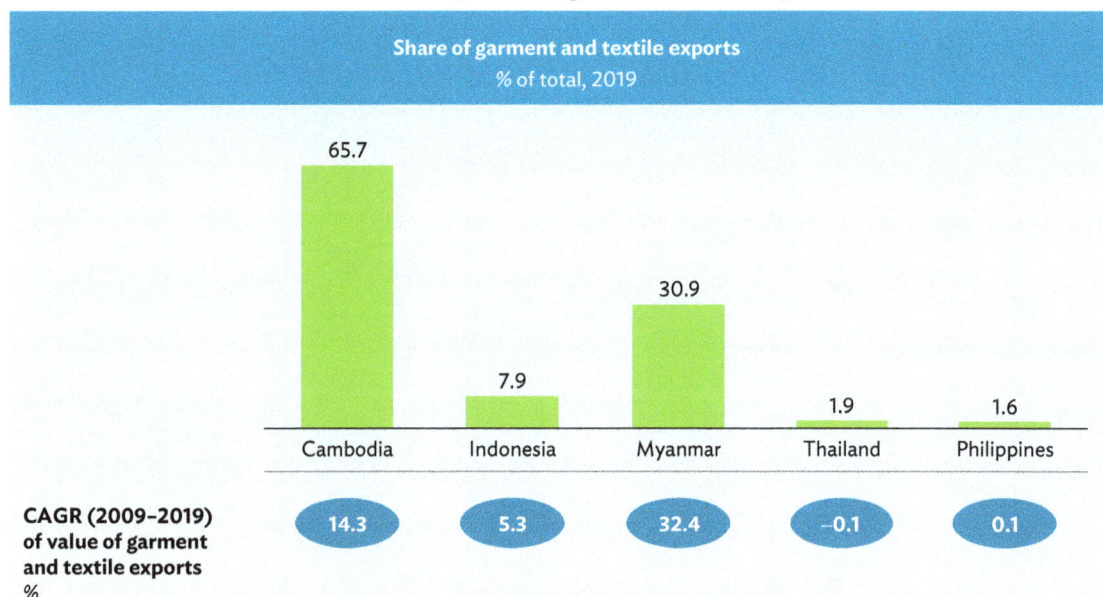

Share of garment and textile exports
% of total, 2019

Cambodia	Indonesia	Myanmar	Thailand	Philippines
65.7	7.9	30.9	1.9	1.6

CAGR (2009–2019) of value of garment and textile exports %

Cambodia	Indonesia	Myanmar	Thailand	Philippines
14.3	5.3	32.4	–0.1	0.1

CAGR = compound annual growth rate.
Note: Based on the export value of products with harmonized system (HS) codes 57 to 65.
Source: ASEAN Stats Data Portal.

since they occupy the low-value part of the value chain. The thin profit margins consequently limit their ability to invest in worker training, upgrading machinery, or factory expansion.

- **Concentrated supply base of raw materials.** Southeast Asian garment manufacturers are vulnerable to supply chain disruptions due to a heavy reliance on a few key raw materials suppliers such as the PRC. According to the ILO, the garment industry in Southeast Asia and the Pacific is the most vulnerable to input supply disruptions (footnote 258). The lack of local, high-quality input supply is also considered a key constraint to the industry's growth in Myanmar and Cambodia.[266] In addition to quality issues, manufacturers also find that the reliability, timing, and scale of local input production is insufficient, which deepens their dependence on foreign suppliers. For example, in Myanmar, garment manufacturers reported that inputs—buttons and trims along with chemicals—are almost entirely imported (footnote 266). Thread is either imported raw from the PRC or the Republic of Korea then dyed in Myanmar or sourced entirely from abroad.

- **Poor infrastructure.** Irregular electricity supply negatively impacts garment manufacturers in the focus countries. Garment factories in Yangon experience on average three to four electricity outages a day, leading to a significant loss of production time. Though most factories own a diesel generator, it usually takes at least 10 minutes to get the machinery working again, leading to a loss of 40 minutes and up to 2 hours for factories lacking a generator (footnote 266). Electricity can cost $0.04 to $0.09 per kilowatt hour (kWH) from the grid

[266] ILO. 2020. *The supply chain ripple effect: How COVID-19 is affecting garment workers and factories in Asia and the Pacific*. Geneva. https://www.ilo.org/wcmsp5/groups/public/---asia/---ro-bangkok/documents/briefingnote/wcms_758626.pdf; and *RIS News*. 2014. Opportunities and Challenges in Asia's Apparel and Textile Sector. 12 February. https://risnews.com/opportunities-and-challenges-asias-apparel-and-textile-sector.

in Myanmar.[267] This cost can go up nearly 10 times to $0.3 to $0.4 per kWh when a diesel generator is used as a power backup. Poor logistical infrastructure can also impose additional costs. The Terminal Handling Charge for a 20-feet container in Indonesia is more than double that in Viet Nam (Table 8).[268]

Table 8: Terminal Handling Charge in Selected Countries

The Terminal Handling Costs in Indonesia are significantly higher than those in other countries in the region

Terminal Handling Costs on ports
2018

Country	20 Feet Container $/container	40 Feet Container $/container
Ho Chi Minh, Viet Nam	46	135
Chittagong, Bangladesh	49	75
Bangkok, Thailand	60	95
North Port, Malaysia	64	97
Tanjung Priok, Indonesia	95	145

Source: Dialog Tekstil National (2018).

- **Increasing labor costs affect competitiveness.** Rising labor costs in the focus countries also add economic pressures. Figure 12 summarizes the monthly minimum wages of garment workers in 2018 showing most of the focus countries have relatively higher wages compared to global competitors.[269] Furthermore, minimum wages have risen over the past few years and are expected to continue increasing. In Indonesia, the minimum wage was increased by 8.5% in 2020.[270] In Cambodia, by 1 January 2021, the minimum wage increased from $190 to $192 per month.[271] Elsewhere, in Myanmar, the daily minimum wage was increased by 33% to $3.60 in 2018.[272]

- **Low labor productivity**. As shown in Figure 13, the labor productivity in Cambodia and Indonesia is nearly five and two times lower than that in Thailand, respectively.[273] There are several factors contributing to low

[267] D. Dapice. 2020. *Electricity Demand and Supply in Myanmar.* Ash Centre. Boston https://ash.harvard.edu/files/electricitydemand.pdf.

[268] D. Prasetyani et al. 2020. The Prospects and The Competitiveness of Textile Commodities and Indonesian Textile Product in the Global Market. *Etikonomi* Volume 19(1). http://journal.uinjkt.ac.id/index.php/etikonomi/article/viewFile/12886/pdf.

[269] N. McCarthy. 2019. Where Pay Is Lowest For Cheap Clothing Production. *Statista.* 7 May. https://www.statista.com/chart/17903/monthly-minimum-wage-in-the-global-garment-industry/.

[270] T. Sipahutar. 2020. Indonesia's Capital Raises Minimum Wages for Some Businesses. *Bloomberg.* 1 November. https://www.bloomberg.com/news/articles/2020-11-01/indonesia-s-capital-raises-minimum-wages-for-some-businesses?sref=kLmUAxRz.

[271] DFDL. Cambodia: Increase in Minimum Wage for 2021 – Textile, Garment & Footwear Sector (accessed 21 June 2021). https://www.dfdl.com/resources/legal-and-tax-updates/increase-in-minimum-wage-for-2021-textile-garment-footwear-sector/.

[272] N. Aung and P. Phyo. 2018. Government sets new daily minimum wage at K4800. *Myanmar Times.* 6 March. https://www.mmtimes.com/news/government-sets-new-daily-minimum-wage-k4800.html.

[273] ILO. 2015. *Strong export and job growth in Asia's garment and footwear sector.* Bangkok. https://www.ilo.org/wcmsp5/groups/public/---ed_protect/---protrav/---travail/documents/publication/wcms_419798.pdf.

Figure 12: Monthly Minimum Wages of Garment Workers in Selected Countries

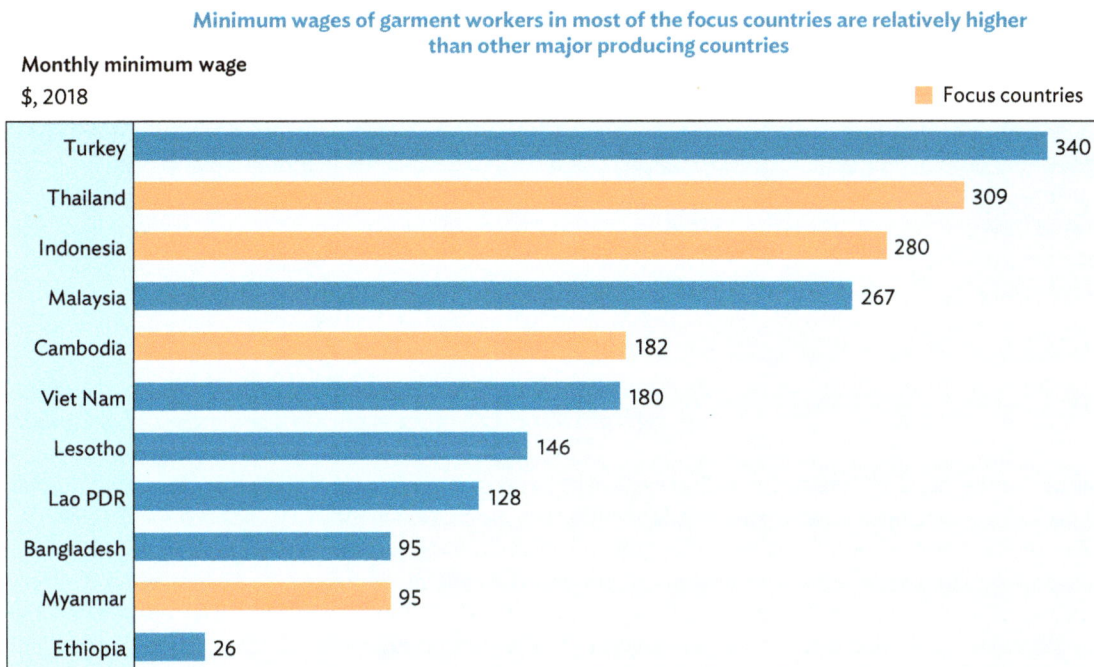

Minimum wages of garment workers in most of the focus countries are relatively higher than other major producing countries

Monthly minimum wage
$, 2018

■ Focus countries

Turkey	340
Thailand	309
Indonesia	280
Malaysia	267
Cambodia	182
Viet Nam	180
Lesotho	146
Lao PDR	128
Bangladesh	95
Myanmar	95
Ethiopia	26

Lao PDR = Lao People's Democratic Republic.
Source: Statista.

Figure 13: Labor Productivity of the Garment, Textile, and Fashion Sector

The labor productivity of the garment, textile, and fashion sector in Cambodia, Indonesia, and the Philippines is significantly lower than that in Thailand

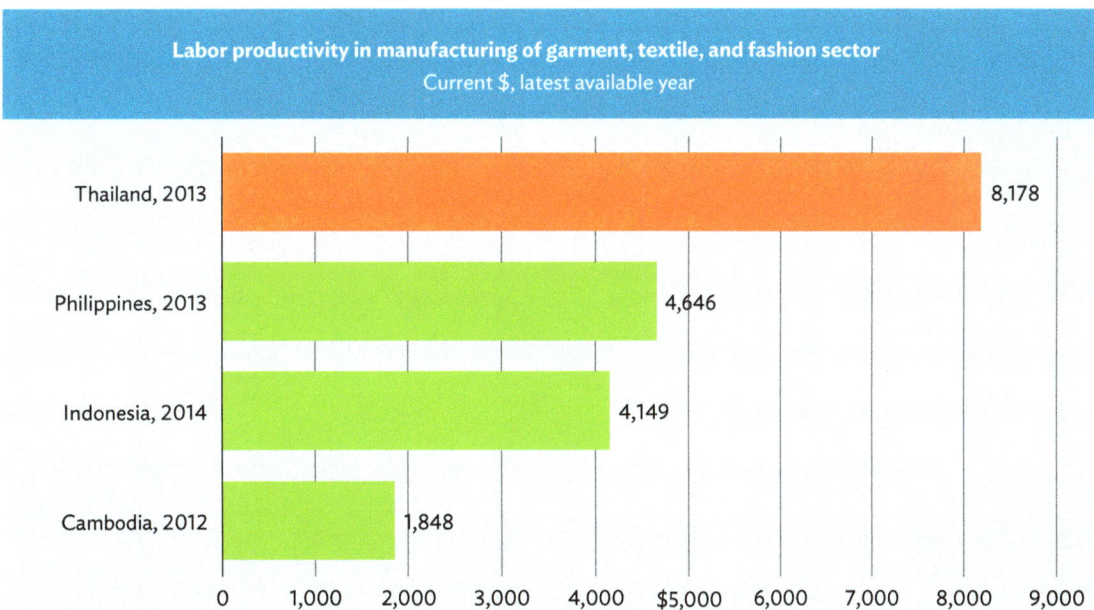

Labor productivity in manufacturing of garment, textile, and fashion sector
Current $, latest available year

Thailand, 2013	8,178
Philippines, 2013	4,646
Indonesia, 2014	4,149
Cambodia, 2012	1,848

0   1,000   2,000   3,000   4,000 $5,000   6,000   7,000   8,000   9,000

Source: International Labour Organization.

productivity. Lack of worker training is one.[274] Research has shown that the lack of adequate operator skills, lack of management skills, poor production planning, lack of data, and poor working conditions are some of the key factors for low productivity.[275] Additionally, the outdated technology used by factories also hurts productivity. For instance, in 2012, Indonesia's Ministry of Industry estimated that 70% of all machinery in use was 10–25 years old and outdated.[276]

- **Displacement of jobs due to automation.** A significant share of garment workers in Southeast Asia are at high risk of losing employment due to automation. Those at risk could be 64% in Indonesia and 88% in Cambodia (footnote 276). Based on an ADB study, 4IR technologies could displace 12% of Cambodia's garment manufacturing workforce (footnote 106). Automation could also facilitate growth in nearshoring, as garment manufacturing moves away from developing countries with cheap labor to developed end markets with access to advanced robotics and automation technologies (footnote 276). Automation could also be driven by a change in consumer preferences. Consumers are increasingly demanding more customized garments and faster turnaround times. Mass customization was previously cost and technically prohibitive, but Industry 4.0 technologies such as additive manufacturing can help make it less prohibitive. In 2017, Amazon filed a patent for an automated on-demand clothing factory that can process personalized orders on demand.[277]

- **Environmental damage due to the industry.** Garment production is one of the most resource-intensive and polluting industries in the world (footnote 140). The global textile industry uses around 93 billion cubic meters of water annually, representing 4% of global freshwater withdrawal. Close to 4,600 liters of water is required to produce one kilogram of cotton. The industry is also a major contributor to both water and air pollution. The garment industry is responsible for 10% of worldwide carbon emissions and 20% of all industrial water pollution globally as water leftover from the dyeing process is often released into local streams and rivers.[278] In 2018, close to 280 tons of toxic waste were dumped into Indonesia's Citarum river daily, including wastewater or effluent from textile-producing factories, contributing to decreasing land fertility.[279] A local waterway in West Jakarta was heavily polluted due to textile waste from a local factory.[280] In Cambodia, the Ministry of Environment fined a garment factory in Takeo province after villagers complained the factory was polluting nearby streams with untreated waste.[281] Moreover, increasing demand for viscose (a type of rayon fiber) contributed to deforestation in Indonesia.[282] Air pollution from textile factories reportedly led to negative health effects for villagers near factories producing synthetic fibers in Java, Indonesia.[283] The global demand for fast fashion goods is particularly responsible for the industry's waste and large environmental footprint. The average consumer in the world currently purchases

[274] ILO. 2016. *Wages and productivity in the garment sector in Asia and the Pacific and the Arab States.* Bangkok. https://www.ilo.org/wcmsp5/groups/public/---asia/---ro-bangkok/documents/publication/wcms_534289.pdf.

[275] S. Andersson, A. Machiels, and C. Bodwell. *Securing the competitiveness of Asia's garment sector: A framework for enhancing factory-level productivity.* ILO. Bangkok. https://www.ilo.org/wcmsp5/groups/public/---asia/---ro-bangkok/documents/publication/wcms_732907.pdf.

[276] J. Chang, G. Rynhart, and P. Huynh. 2016. *ASEAN in transformation: How technology is changing jobs and enterprises.* ILO. Bangkok. https://www.ilo.org/actemp/publications/WCMS_579553/lang--en/index.htm.

[277] CGS Blog. 2019. What Industry 4.0 Means for Apparel, Fashion, and Footwear Manufacturers. 12 February. https://www.cgsinc.com/blog/what-industry-4.0-means-apparel-fashion-and-footwear-manufacturers.

[278] M. McFall-Johnsen. 2020. These facts show how unsustainable the fashion industry is. *WEF.* 31 January. https://www.weforum.org/agenda/2020/01/fashion-industry-carbon-unsustainable-environment-pollution/#:~:text=Fashion%20production%20makes%20up%2010,of%20plastic%20into%20the%20ocean.

[279] Undark. 2017. *Worse for Wear: Indonesia's Textile Boom.* https://undark.org/2017/02/23/indonesia-textiles-citarum-river-pollution-2/

[280] *The Jakarta Post.* 2017. Textile waste pollutes West Jakarta waterways: Residents. https://www.thejakartapost.com/news/2017/09/11/textile-waste-pollutes-west-jakarta-waterways-residents.html.

[281] D. Chen. 2017. Garment factory fined after pollution claims. *The Phnom Penh Post.* 5 December. https://www.phnompenhpost.com/national/garment-factory-fined-after-pollution-claims.

[282] *BBC.* 5 fashion materials you didn't realise were bad for wildlife. https://www.bbcearth.com/blog/?article=fashion-materials-you-didnt-realise-were-bad-for-wildlife.

[283] La Croix International. 2018. *Indonesian villagers battle air, water pollution.* https://international.la-croix.com/news/indonesian-villagers-battle-air-water-pollution/7869.

60% more clothing items than 15 years ago, thus significantly increasing the quantity of pre-consumer and post-consumer textile waste.[284] A recent survey revealed that three in 10 Indonesians have thrown away clothing after wearing items only once.[285]

- **Improper labor practices.** Child labor, forced labor, noncompliance with minimum wage rates, lack of overtime regulations, unsafe working conditions, and the gender wage gap are examples of common labor issues. For instance, the ILO and World Bank found 10 cases of child labor in 2018 (down from 74 in 2014) in its survey of almost 500 licensed garment export factories in Cambodia.[286] The same survey found 12 forced labor-related practices out of 464 factories in Cambodia. Noncompliance with the minimum wage laws is widespread in the industry as shown in Figure 14 (footnote 274). In the Philippines, more than half the garment workers are not paid the minimum wage (footnote 274). The situation is worse for those with lower education. According to the ILO, in the focus countries, workers with primary education are more likely to receive a wage less than the minimum wage than those with secondary education.[287] Then, there is the gender wage gap, which is nearly 10% in the Philippines and Thailand, even after adjusting for demographic, educational, geographical, sub-industry, and occupational variances (footnote 274).

Figure 14: Noncompliance Rates in the Garment Sector

A large share of the garment workers in the focus countries do not receive minimum wages

Noncompliance rates with the minimum wage in the garment sector
%, latest available year

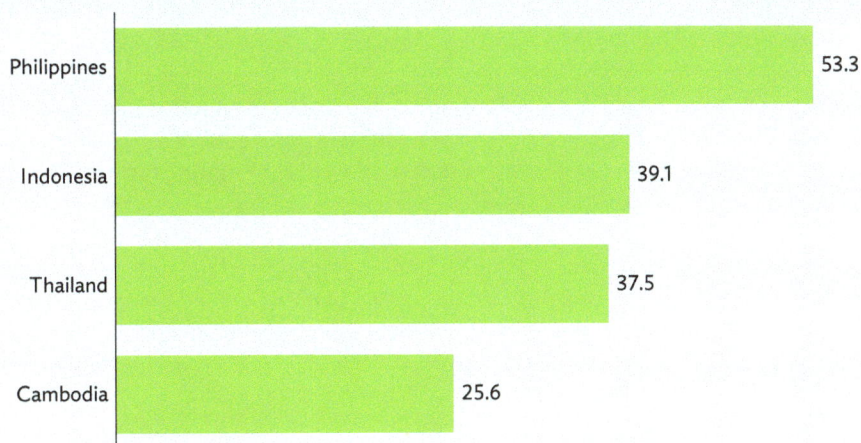

Philippines	53.3
Indonesia	39.1
Thailand	37.5
Cambodia	25.6

Source: Estimates from official national labor force surveys (various years).

284 McKinsey & Company. 2016. *Style that's sustainable: A new fast-fashion formula.* New York. https://www.mckinsey.com/business-functions/sustainability/our-insights/style-thats-sustainable-a-new-fast-fashion-formula.
285 *YouGov.* 2017. Fast fashion: 3 in 10 Indonesians have thrown away clothing after wearing it just once. 6 December. https://id.yougov.com/en-id/news/2017/12/06/fast-fashion/.
286 CARE International in Cambodia. 2020. Garment Worker Needs Assessment During COVID19. Phnom Penh. http://www.careevaluations.org/wp-content/uploads/CIC_garment-worker-need-assessment_EN_final_23072020.pdf.
287 ILO. 2016. Weak minimum wage compliance in Asia's garment industry. Bangkok. https://www.ilo.org/wcmsp5/groups/public/---ed_protect/---protrav/---travail/documents/publication/wcms_509532.pdf.

▶ **Supply chain disruptions due to COVID-19 increased the number of challenges.**

The garment industry has been severely affected by COVID-19. Order cancellations and production restrictions forced many companies across the focus countries to cease operations and lay-off employees. About 400 garment factories in Cambodia suspended operations, affecting the livelihoods of more than 150,000 workers.[288] The following pre-pandemic challenges were worsened by COVID-19 especially in:

- **Supply chain disruptions.** COVID-19 resulted in fluctuations and shortages of production factors like raw materials, impacting different parts of the value chain. According to the ILO, as of September 2020, an estimated 30% of foreign inputs into garment production were sourced from countries with closures of all but essential workplaces (footnote 258). These workplace closures prevented imported inputs from arriving on time, disrupting garment manufacturing, especially in Southeast Asia. The supply chain disruptions caused by the pandemic exposed the need to manufacture more inputs locally. The COVID-19 induced changes in transport logistics could also accelerate nearshoring or local production of inputs. For example, there has been a significant change in maritime transport networks. Due to the pandemic, ship operators witnessed massive service cancellations, leading to growing numbers of blank sailings.[289] Routes were also affected, particularly in Asia–Northern Europe, directly upsetting the trade of fashion goods (footnote 259). Moreover, shipping lines are reducing the number of ports of call they offer to adapt to declining demand.[290] Fashion brands and retailers could relocate to countries nearer demand-centers, including to the countries promoting re-shoring by providing corporate tax cuts and other incentives to further build up their resilience (footnote 289).

- **Shift in consumer demand for garments.** Studies suggest COVID-19 may lead to more demand for sustainable fashion products.[291] Consumer demand may shift from purchasing new garments to reusing them. Zalando, a European e-commerce company, reported that after the pandemic, consumers began purchasing more sustainable fashion products.[292] An uptake of garment reuse could lead to lower garment manufacturing, leading to a shift in jobs toward the downstream parts of the value chain. While reusing clothing is common in low to middle-income countries, such business models could extend the lifespan of fashion products among the growing consumer class in the focus countries and accelerate the growth of existing businesses that focus on reusing garments.[293] For instance, in Indonesia, online start-ups like Rentique and Style Theory provide garment rental services to consumers. A shift in consumer preferences could force the garment industry to rethink its current model of high-volume fast fashion, which could have significant implications for manufacturers based in the focus countries.

- **COVID-19 further widened disparities**. COVID-19 has also highlighted the lack of support services for vulnerable workers, exacerbating inequalities, with women appearing to be disproportionately affected. In the short term, the lack of access to necessities, unequal domestic responsibilities, gender-based hiring discrimination, and an increased risk of gender-based violence could make women workers in the industry

[288] *Xinhua.* 2020. 400 factories in Cambodia suspend operations, affecting over 150,000 workers due to COVID-19. 1 July. http://www.xinhuanet.com/english/2020-07/01/c_139180683.htm.
[289] UNESCAP. 2020. Transport and trade connectivity in the age of pandemics UN solutions for contactless, seamless and collaborative transport and trade. Bangkok. https://www.unescap.org/sites/default/files/ShippingPoliyBrief-30September2020-FINAL%20%281%29.pdf.
[290] G. Knowler. 2020. Container cargo imbalance from COVID-19 deepens. *JOC.* https://www.joc.com/maritime-news/container-lines/threat-container-cargo-imbalance-covid-19-builds_20200501.html.
[291] M. Ricchetti and R. Palma. 2020. *Will COVID-19 accelerate the transition to a sustainable fashion industry?* United Nations. 9 October. https://www.unido.org/stories/will-covid-19-accelerate-transition-sustainable-fashion-industry.
[292] Zalando. 2020. Zalando Expects Double-Digit Growth in 2020. 6 May. https://corporate.zalando.com/en/investor-relations/news-stories/zalando-expects-double-digit-growth-2020.
[293] N. Bairagi. 2018. *Recycling of Post-Consumer Apparel Waste in India: Channels for Textile Reuse.* https://www.hilarispublisher.com/open-access/recycling-of-postconsumer-apparel-waste-in-india-channels-for-textilereuse-2165-8064-1000331.pdf.

even more vulnerable.[294] At least 36% of respondents from a survey of 307 women garment workers in Cambodia reported that they bore a heavier workload than men during the pandemic and 13% identified an increase in unpaid care work among the top problems from the crisis (footnote 286). The same survey found that among women garment workers in Cambodia, 33% reported that COVID-19 increased tension and conflict in their homes. There are longer-term consequences, as limited access to social assistance, unregulated worker conditions, and reduced access to health services could diminish the economic and social empowerment of women (footnote 294). The pandemic may also severely impact child workers, as economic pressures and limited safety nets may push many children into child labor.[295] Economic pressures could lead to a lapse in worker welfare standards, disproportionately impacting informal workers.[296] However, some industry representatives also highlight that the pandemic may lead to a greater focus on worker health and working conditions. Additionally, COVID-19 may deepen the divide between workers employed by large, compliant, and profitable factories and those employed by smaller factories, which operate on thinner margins.

▶ **Four areas need policy response to strengthen the garment industry in the focus countries.**

In response to COVID-19, governments have implemented short-term measures such as wage support to mitigate adverse impacts. Trade unions have petitioned apparel buyers to honor their existing contracts and payments. In the longer term, policy responses could address the identified challenges and support the industry to achieve higher and more sustainable growth. The policy responses suggested below could help focus countries in four ways: (i) improving competitiveness, (ii) expanding markets, (iii) raising industry resilience, and (iv) pursuing more flexible production and business models.

(i) Improving Competitiveness

Enhancing competitiveness through productivity gains is important in maintaining the industry's growth, with the need to emphasize the following specific areas:

1. **Bridge infrastructure gaps.** There are areas where infrastructure gaps need bridging. Infrastructure gaps are a key barrier to relocate garment factories, especially in countries like Cambodia and Myanmar.[297] The lack of utilities and communication infrastructure led to higher power costs restricting the growth of the garment industry in the Philippines and Myanmar.[298] The lack of developed highways and ports inflated logistics costs and delivery schedules, and in Indonesia, garment exporters must navigate lengthy loading

---

[294] ILO. 2020. *Gendered impacts of COVID-19 on the garment sector.* Bangkok. https://www.ilo.org/wcmsp5/groups/public/---asia/---ro-bangkok/---sro-bangkok/documents/publication/wcms_760374.pdf.

[295] ILO and UNICEF. 2020. *COVID-19 and child labour: A time of crisis, a time to act.* https://www.unicef.org/press-releases/covid-19-may-push-millions-more-children-child-labour-ilo-and-unicef#:~:text=According%20to%20the%20brief%2C%20COVID,child%20labour%20in%20certain%20countries.

[296] ILO. 2020. *What next for Asian garment production after COVID-19?* Bangkok. https://www.ilo.org/wcmsp5/groups/public/---asia/---ro-bangkok/---sro-bangkok/documents/publication/wcms_755630.pdf.

[297] ERIA. 2010. *Fragmentation of Electronics and Textile Industries from Indonesia to CLMV Countries.* Jakarta. https://www.eria.org/uploads/media/Research-Project-Report/RPR_FY2009_7-3_Chapter_5.pdf; Konrad-Adenauer-Stiftung. 2020. *The Risks of Industry 4.0 on Cambodia's Garment Sector.* Phnom Penh. https://www.kas.de/en/web/kambodscha/single-title/-/content/the-risks-of-industry-4-0-on-cambodia-s-garment-sector; and Oxford Business Group. *Investment liberalisation positions Myanmar manufacturing subsectors for growth.* https://oxfordbusinessgroup.com/overview/turning-point-number-manufacturing-subsectors-are-positioned-growth-thanks-new-openness-investment.

[298] ILO. 2015. *Myanmar garment sub-sector value chain analysis.* Geneva. https://www.ilo.org/yangon/publications/WCMS_403359/lang--en/index.htm#:~:text=The%20Myanmar%20Garment%20Manufacturers%20Association,in%20the%20next%20three%20years; and J. Kastner. 2020. Philippines prepares for textile-garment industry roadmap. *Just-style.* 4 March. https://www.just-style.com/analysis/philippines-prepares-for-textile-garment-industry-roadmap_id138198.aspx.

and unloading processes at ports.[299] There are opportunities across the countries to improve overall infrastructure to ensure affordable electricity generation and reduce traveling time.[300] In the Philippines, under the Philippine Development Plan 2017–2022 and its "Build, Build, Build" program, there is an emphasis on enhancing roads, bridges, and port facilities.[301] Cambodia, Indonesia, Myanmar, and Thailand have also announced infrastructure development projects.[302] For instance, in Indonesia, there are programs to develop the Kuala Tanjung International Hub Port and Kijing Port. The next step will be to implement these plans. Except for Thailand, which made significant investments in manufacturing infrastructure to move up the value chain, the other focus countries still have much to do to upgrade their infrastructure. Countries could:

a. **Identify and prioritize the most urgent gaps.** Relevant authorities could identify and prioritize the most urgent infrastructure projects (e.g., ports, roads, airports). This would streamline operations and enable targeted policies.

b. **Raise capital to develop necessary infrastructure.** There are several channels that governments could tap to access funding, including:

   i. Expanding public–private partnerships (PPPs) to facilitate greater risk sharing among stakeholders. This would require critical enablers like clear regulations to attract investments both locally and globally. Countries can prioritize improving their rankings on global competitiveness indexes (e.g., World Bank Ease of Doing Business rankings, World Economic Forum).

   ii. Global Competitiveness Index to raise their value propositions and profiles on the international stage.

   iii. Tapping development partners like the World Bank, International Finance Corporation, and ADB. The ASEAN Secretariat, together with the World Bank and the ASEAN-Australia Development Cooperation Program Phase II, established the "Initial Pipeline of ASEAN Infrastructure Projects" across the transport, energy, and information sectors to consolidate prioritized infrastructure projects and sources of funding.[303] Countries in Southeast Asia can continue to identify relevant projects, with guidelines provided by the ASEAN Secretariat.

   iv. Using capital markets (e.g., bonds) to raise funds. However, for some countries with unsophisticated capital markets, efforts should also be spent on strengthening financial markets. The International Finance Corporation published important advice on how developing countries can adopt a systematic approach in building domestic capital markets.[304]

2. **Review policies that restrict growth.** Garment manufacturers face policy challenges contributing to high production costs. These include high raw material tariffs and cumbersome export permit procedures. In Indonesia, the industry depends heavily on imported inputs, accounting for up to 30% of production costs.[305] However, there have been higher tariffs for these inputs and garment manufacturers are not exempted. This is also the case of cotton fabrics in Cambodia (footnote 144). For example, the tariff imposed on imported cotton fabrics makes up 7% of the total price of materials. While the government allows special tax treatment to export-oriented producers, domestic-oriented MSMEs are required to pay import taxes for cotton fabrics.

[299]   A. Setyawati. 2015. Analysis: Indonesian textile industry faces formidable challenges. *The Jakarta Post.* 29 July. https://www.thejakartapost.com/news/2015/07/29/analysis-indonesian-textile-industry-faces-formidable-challenges.html.

[300]   ODI. 2019. *Economic transformation in Cambodia.* London. https://set.odi.org/wp-content/uploads/2019/04/Background-Note-ET-in-Cambodia.pdf.

[301]   NEDA. 2017. *Accelerating Infrastructure Development.* Manila. http://www.neda.gov.ph/wp-content/uploads/2018/10/PIP-2017-2022-19.pdf.

[302]   ASEAN Secretariat. 2019. *ASEAN identifies potential infrastructure projects.* Jakarta. https://asean.org/asean-identifies-potential-infrastructure-projects/; and Thailand Board of Investment. 2020. *Power Development Plan.* Bangkok. https://www.boi.go.th/index.php?page=electricity.

[303]   ASEAN Secretariat. 2019. *Enhancing ASEAN Connectivity: Initial Pipeline of ASEAN Infrastructure Projects.* Jakarta. https://asean.org/storage/2019/10/Booklet-1_Approach-and-Context.pdf.

[304]   IFC. 2020. *Creating Domestic Capital Markets in Developing Countries: Perspectives from Market Participants.* Washington, DC. https://openknowledge.worldbank.org/bitstream/handle/10986/33617/Creating-Domestic-Capital-Markets-in-Developing-Countries-Perspectives-from-Market-Participants.pdf?sequence=1&isAllowed=y.

[305]   D. Pane and D. Pasaribu. 2020. Indonesia's garment industry in crisis. *East Asia Forum.* 10 August. https://www.eastasiaforum.org/2020/08/10/indonesias-garment-industry-in-crisis/.

Furthermore, Cambodian exporters endure tedious paperwork for export permits (footnote 144). Countries could review their policies to simplify business processes for garment manufacturers. The Philippines recently provided clearer guidelines for the accreditation for garment firms and information on obtaining preferential tariffs.[306]

3. **Upgrade vocational curricula and increase access to training.** Gaps for technical and soft skills have been reported across the industry in some countries.[307] These range from procurement, production, maintenance, to managerial skills. Examples include the lack of adequate knowledge on sourcing and quality management, as well as technical know-how in machine maintenance.[308] Some Southeast Asian countries have detailed programs to address skills gaps for garment workers. For example, the Government of Indonesia sponsored the vocational training program "Sekolah Menengah Khusus" for high school students, including an internship at a garment factory with the potential to be hired on a permanent basis.[309] Thailand's Office of the Vocational Education Commission developed several certificates and diplomas in vocational education for the textile industry (e.g., in textile technology and garment technology).[310] In Cambodia, the Garment Manufacturers Association introduced the Cambodian Garment Training Institute with government support, to ensure that graduates meet industry needs.[311] The Ministry of Labor in Viet Nam partnered with the private sector and development partners to complete a detailed study of employer skills and education needs within the garment industry.[312] Furthermore, the government approved the establishment of the Hanoi Industrial Garment and Textile University to offer specialized programs.[313] Overall, there are opportunities to expand the scope of these upskilling initiatives across the five countries, particularly in rural areas.

4. **Promote the adoption of digital technologies.** There are relevant Industry 4.0 technologies, ranging from digital technologies enabling smart factories to additive manufacturing enabling mass product customization. McKinsey & Company estimated that productivity could be increased from 21% to 46% by adopting garment industry-relevant technologies like automatic sewing machines.[314] Another study found that applying new technologies to the industry could increase labor productivity by an average of 22% in the next five years (footnote 106). The focus countries must invest in hardware (e.g., relevant technologies), software (e.g., digital skills) and necessary enablers.
   a. **Invest in hardware.** Regarding hardware, there are several relevant Industry 4.0 technologies, ranging from those enabling smart factories to IoT to improve supply chain monitoring (Box 6). Cambodia's Ministry of Economy and Finance is finalizing the "Garment and Footwear Sector Development Strategy 2020–2025,

[306] *Fibre2Fashion.* 2017. Philippines govt issues guidelines for garment firms. 29 July. https://www.fibre2fashion.com/news/apparel-news/philippines-govt-issues-guidelines-for-garment-firms-207132-newsdetails.htm.

[307] P. Rodrigo. 2017. Cambodia clothing sector faces up to skills gap. *Just-style.* 17 May. https://www.just-style.com/analysis/cambodia-clothing-sector-faces-up-to-skills-gap_id130674.aspx, Fashion United. 2019. Apparel industry faces critical shortage of skills. 20 November. https://fashionunited.uk/news/business/apparel-industry-faces-critical-shortage-of-skills/2019112046286 and ILO. 2014. *Survey of ASEAN employers on skills and competitiveness.* Geneva. https://www.ilo.org/wcmsp5/groups/public/---asia/---ro-bangkok/---sro-bangkok/documents/publication/wcms_249982.pdf.

[308] NSDC. *Human Resource and Skill Requirements in the Textile Sector (2022).* New Delhi. https://nqr.gov.in/sites/default/files/Skill%20Gap%20Analysis%20Report.pdf.

[309] ILO. 2017. *A Market Systems Analysis of Working Conditions in Asia's Garment Export Industry.* Geneva. https://www.ilo.org/wcmsp5/groups/public/---ed_emp/---emp_ent/---ifp_seed/documents/publication/wcms_628430.pdf.

[310] Office of the Vocational Education Commission. Vocational courses. http://www.vec.go.th/en-us/aboutvec/vocationalcourses.aspx.

[311] CGTI. 2021. About Us. https://www.cgti-cambodia.org/about-us.

[312] Global Skills Ledger. 2017. *Textile and Garment Skills Roadmap.* 1 September. https://www.globalskillsledger.co.uk/2017/01/09/creating-a-skills-roadmap/.

[313] *Fibre2Fashion.* 2015. Garment and textile university to come up in Hanoi. https://www.fibre2fashion.com/news/textile-news/newsdetails.aspx?news_id=173002.

[314] McKinsey & Company. 2018. *Is apparel manufacturing coming home? Nearshoring, automation, and sustainability – establishing a demand-focused apparel value chain.* New York. https://www.mckinsey.com/~/media/McKinsey/Industries/Retail/Our%20Insights/Is%20apparel%20manufacturing%20coming%20home/Is-apparel-manufacturing-coming-home_vf.ashx.

Box 6: Key Technologies to Increase Garment Manufacturing Productivity

Industry 4.0 includes technologies that could increase productivity in garment manufacturing. Some examples:

- **Internet of Things.** IoT refers to a network of sensors and actuators embedded in machines and other physical objects connected with one another through the internet. Applications include data collection, monitoring, decision making, and process optimization.[a] It can be used in garment manufacturing for functions ranging from supporting location-based advertising to optimizing stock assortment and reducing out-of-stock rates.
- **Artificial intelligence and big data.** Big data refers to the ability to analyze extremely large volumes of data, extract insights, and act on them close to real-time. The benefits for garment manufacturing include being able to use predictive analytics to fine-tune production volumes and processes, while providing better supply chain management and greater insights into customer segments.
- **Industry robotics.** Industrial robots can significantly improve productivity in garment manufacturing. Sewing is currently the most labor-intensive step in creating each garment unit, accounting for more than half the total labor time. The potential for labor reduction varies by garment type, but as much as 90% of the sewing processes can potentially be automated.[b]
- **Additive manufacturing.** These are technologies that build three-dimensional (3D) objects by adding layer-upon-layer of material. Additive manufacturing allows for the creation of bespoke items with complex geometries and little wastage. Several companies are already experimenting with new apparel production systems linked to additive manufacturing. Boston-based apparel company Ministry of Supply uses thermal imaging, 3D printing, and 3D knitting technologies to create personalized blazers, shirts, dresses, and sweaters.[c] Similarly, a digital image of a pair of distressed jeans can be transformed into a basic pair of jeans with laser technology in just 90 seconds.[d]

[a] McKinsey Global Institute. 2014. *Southeast Asia at the crossroads: Three paths to prosperity.* https://www.mckinsey.com/~/media/McKinsey/Featured%20Insights/Asia%20Pacific/Three%20paths%20to%20sustained%20economic%20growth%20in%20Southeast%20Asia/MGI%20SE%20Asia_Executive%20summary_November%202014.ashx.
[b] ACT/EMP and ILO. 2017. *ASEAN in Transformation: How Technology is Changing Jobs and Enterprises – Cambodia Country Brief.* https://www.ilo.org/actemp/publications/WCMS_579672/lang--en/index.htm.
[c] McKinsey & Company. 2018. *Is apparel manufacturing coming home? Nearshoring, automation, and sustainability – establishing a demand-focused apparel value chain.* New York. https://www.mckinsey.com/~/media/mckinsey/industries/retail/our%20insights/is%20apparel%20manufacturing%20coming%20home/is-apparel-manufacturing-coming-home_vf.ashx.
[d] K. Masters. 2017. *The Impact of Industry 4.0 on the Automotive Industry.* https://blog.flexis.com/the-impact-of-industry-4.0-on-the-automotive-industry.

which will include a focus on shifting the sector to higher skill and value-added activities through the adoption of new technologies and upskilling."[315]

b. **Invest in digital skills.** Workers' digital skills must progress with technology adoption to enable effective implementation. This is important as technologies might displace garment workers if they do not have the appropriate skills to manage these technologies or transition to other complementary roles. In Indonesia, the government prioritized Industry 4.0 reforms for the garment industry and developed more vocational institutions partnering with local companies to train people to use the latest technology in production such as 3D printing.[316]

c. **Promote crucial enablers.** A crucial enabler is strengthening buyer-supplier relationships as garment manufacturers say these relationships tend to be transactional and depend heavily on middlemen, with minimal

[315] S. Sarath. 2020. Ministry releases five-year plan for garment and textile sector. *Khmer Times.* 31 July. https://www.khmertimeskh.com/50750542/ministry-releases-five-year-plan-for-garment-and-textile-sector/.
[316] *Fibre2Fashion.* 2020. Indonesian textiles industry likely to pull through global pandemic. May. https://www.fibre2fashion.com/industry-article/8679/indonesian-textiles-industry-likely-to-pull-through-global-pandemic; and A. Pathoni. 2019. Indonesia pushes Industry 4.0 reform onto receptive clothing industry. *Just-style.* 29 March. https://www.just-style.com/analysis/indonesia-pushes-industry-40-reform-onto-receptive-clothing-industry_id135847.aspx.

transparency and trust.[317] Buyers also tend to change suppliers often, reducing any incentives for suppliers to invest in technologies and innovate. Stronger buyer–supplier relationships may reduce risks associated with the increased cost of investing in digitalization and training, given higher trust for orders (footnote 296).

(ii)   Expanding Markets

Apart from cost reductions and productivity gains, the garment industry in Southeast Asia needs to distinguish itself from regional competitors. The measures to consider include:

1. **Develop more markets.** Currently, the focus countries export primarily to specific markets like the EU and the United States. This has been facilitated by trade preferences such as the "Everything but Arms" program. However, trade preferences can be removed, either due to violations or graduations of terms. Cambodia recently lost duty-free access for some exports including garments and footwear due to human rights concerns.[318] Such developments could hamper industry growth if the export markets are limited to a few countries. For example, Sri Lanka lost 10,000 workers or 4% of the garment labor force, and 1% of GDP, when it lost access to the EU developing country component of the Generalized System of Preferences due to human rights concerns (footnote 300). Indonesian manufacturers could consider new potential international markets like Australia with the ratification of the Indonesia–Australia Comprehensive Economic Partnership Agreement.[319]

2. **Expand product range.** The industry needs to pursue product differentiation and produce higher value garments to remain attractive. The need for product diversification is especially relevant for Cambodia and the Philippines. Currently, they produce low-cost basic commodity items, while Myanmar and Thailand manufacture higher value technical items.[320] While Cambodia specializes in trousers, sweatshirts, and t-shirts, Myanmar exports high-tech sportswear, formal shirts, and suits.[321] With consumers moving away from mass produced clothes, governments could incentivize companies to explore more sophisticated product offerings:[322]
    a. **Leveraging cultural-related garments.** Indonesia promotes Muslim fashionwear and Batik, where margins are potentially higher.[323] The government organized annual Islamic fashion shows like the International Indonesian Islamic Fashion Fair to showcase their products internationally.[324] There are also plans to coach and certify Muslim tailors and provide tools for entrepreneurs engaged in Muslim fashion.[325]

---

[317]   McKinsey & Company. 2011. *Bangladesh's ready-made garments landscape: The challenge of growth.* New York. https://www.mckinsey.com/~/ media/mckinsey/dotcom/client_service/consumer%20packaged%20goods/pdfs/bangladesh_ready_made_garment_landscape.ashx; and ADB. 2011. *Impediments to Growth of the Garment and Food Industries in Cambodia: Exploring Potential Benefits of the ASEAN-PRC FTA.* Manila. https://www.adb.org/sites/default/files/publication/29156/wp86-chheang-hamanaka-impediments-growth.pdf.

[318]   EC. 2020. *Cambodia loses duty-free access to the EU market over human rights concerns.* Brussels. https://ec.europa.eu/commission/presscorner/ detail/en/ip_20_1469.

[319]   Australian Government Department of Foreign Affairs and Trade. 2020. *Indonesia-Australia Comprehensive Economic Partnership Agreement.* Canberra. https://www.dfat.gov.au/trade/agreements/in-force/iacepa/Pages/indonesia-australia-comprehensive-economic-partnership-agreement.

[320]   ILO. 2017. *A Market Systems Analysis of Working Conditions in Asia's Garment Export Industry.* Geneva. https://www.ilo.org/wcmsp5/groups/ public/---ed_emp/---emp_ent/---ifp_seed/documents/publication/wcms_628430.pdf; and ODI. 2019. *Comparative country study of the development of textile and garment sectors.* London. https://www.odi.org/sites/odi.org.uk/files/resource-documents/12695.pdf.

[321]   ILO. 2016. *ASEAN In Transformation: Textiles, Clothing and Footwear: Refashioning the Future.* Geneva. https://www.ilo.org/wcmsp5/groups/ public/---ed_dialogue/---act_emp/documents/publication/wcms_579560.pdf.

[322]   McKinsey & Company. 2019. *The State of Fashion 2019.* New York. https://www.mckinsey.com/~/media/McKinsey/Industries/Retail/Our%20 Insights/The%20influence%20of%20woke%20consumers%20on%20fashion/The-State-of-Fashion-2019.ashx.

[323]   E. Maulia. 2019. Indonesia seeks lead in global modest-fashion industry. *Nikkei Asia.* 17 July. https://asia.nikkei.com/Spotlight/The-Big-Story/ Indonesia-seeks-lead-in-global-modest-fashion-industry; and J. Tandjung. 2020. Rescuing batik industry from COVID-19. *The Jakarta Post.* 8 June. https://www.thejakartapost.com/academia/2020/06/08/rescuing-batik-industry-from-covid-19.html.

[324]   *Global Business Guide Indonesia.* 2020. Indonesia Aiming to be the Islamic Fashion Capital by 2020. http://www.gbgindonesia.com/en/ manufacturing/article/2016/indonesia_aiming_to_be_the_islamic_fashion_capital_by_2020_11646.php.

[325]   Salama. 2018. Industry Ministry focuses on making Indonesia world's Muslim fashion center. *Halal Focus.* 16 December. https://halalfocus.net/ industry-ministry-focuses-on-making-indonesia-worlds-muslim-fashion-center/.

b. **Promoting made-to-measure items.** Demand for garment customization has been increasing, and apparel brands are piloting mass customization models.[326] As COVID-19 exposed significant risks for mass production manufacturers, governments could review business operations and assess the potential to switch from mass to made-to-measure production by providing technology, marketing, and financing support.[327]

(iii)   Raising Industry Resilience

COVID-19 demonstrated that the garment industry is vulnerable to supply chain shocks. Improving productivity and adopting better production technologies can strengthen the sector's resilience against these shocks, and some policies that can enhance resiliency include:

1. **Developing capabilities to participate across the garment supply chain.** The focus countries, particularly Cambodia and Myanmar, are reliant on the CMP mode of manufacturing as opposed to the FOB mode.[328] They focus mainly on labor-intensive garment cutting and sewing processes and do not get the full value added. There are two weaknesses in the supply chain. First, participation in the upstream section is often limited in the focus countries. Indonesia depends heavily on imported raw materials like cotton (almost 100%) (footnote 262). Second, the midstream section (fabric production and dyeing) is also not developed. The focus countries are reliant on imported inputs such as fabrics and yarns. Garment factories in most of developing Asia import over 80% of fabrics and yarns from more advanced Asian countries.[329] In Cambodia, there is significant production of downstream (e.g., cotton) and upstream products (e.g., cotton shirts) (footnote 144). However, there are no midstream manufacturers in the whole value chain, resulting in no domestic supply of textiles and fabrics. Cotton plants in Cambodia cannot produce cotton fabrics and must export cotton overseas for processing. The pandemic highlighted the importance of maintaining the continuous operation of supply lines. Countries relying heavily on upstream and midstream imports found it challenging given the border restrictions. There will be more emphasis on shorter supply chains, local alternative supplies, and local markets. To overcome the two weaknesses, countries could:

    a. **Incentivize shifts to FOB.** Countries are already progressing to FOB for higher returns. The garment industry in Myanmar had plans to partner with their government to do this.[330] Challenges include the lack of capital investment, limited technologies, and gaps in production skills. To increase industry resilience, governments could support transitions from CMP, including providing funding for machinery, upskilling workers, attracting foreign investors to facilitate more value-added production techniques, and providing incentives for FOB. In India, the government introduced the Scheme for Remission of Duties and Taxes on Exported Products where companies can claim rebates as a percentage of the FOB value of exports.[331]

    b. **Promote domestic production of related agricultural products.** Indonesia's Ministry of Industry encourages the domestic textile industry to use locally grown natural fibers like banana and pineapple to reduce the country's dependence on polyester and rayon imports.[332] Countries could also identify

---

[326] H. Hayes. 2019. Apparel Brands Are Testing the Waters of Mass Customization. *Sourcing Journal.* 5 June. https://sourcingjournal.com/topics/technology/personalization-report-investments-adaptations-152409/.

[327] Centre for the Promotion of Imports. 2020. *How to respond to COVID-19 in the apparel sector.* The Hague. https://www.cbi.eu/market-information/apparel/how-respond-covid-19-apparel-sector#change-from-mass-production-to-made-to-measure.

[328] ILO. 2015. *Myanmar garment sub-sector value chain analysis.* Geneva. https://www.ilo.org/yangon/publications/WCMS_403359/lang--en/index.htm#:~:text=The%20Myanmar%20Garment%20Manufacturers%20Association,in%20the%20next%20three%20years.

[329] S. Lu. 2020. Asia's garment industry should drive post-COVID economic recovery. *Nikkei Asia.* 25 July. https://asia.nikkei.com/Opinion/Asia-s-garment-industry-should-drive-post-COVID-economic-recovery.

[330] MGMA. 2018. *Myanmar Garment Industry: 10-Year Strategy 2015–2024.* Yangon. https://www.myanmargarments.org/wp-content/uploads/2018/12/Myanmar-garment-industry-10-year-strategy-Aug-2015.pdf?__cf_chl_jschl_tk__=ac1212388824544c0 6849c53965664ff685f51d4-1607566274-0-AYugitHk9BRLIZQ0GUS5a66BhKntNwQWu_-V66WcVFw9wqH4BqAK73- cfz1Wu7GuctuzYLWmVoBwmDPyb5NgNbM3lg_p3yyAwJDOhZvYw3q6mhaXsaWCADNcCl1RomnRjcqdQd152ue0lqUIN8TnAI7G RP-iHP9yRprYPS_p5tkF0ONz9hkGMtf3iA9STVucXWU21UngDlnKvpQ-YzAAKk5XyHg8Sn4If-isQ3DHyM9y1G92SRh_-Uw4OhVpLD_ kO_z6x5vjwxQ9JG7uuiqZl-jToRZACaeHNm53pRT3j4tusCtIfGDpm6DE0U7OxeRZQjClApfHzMzgdTQsqPcneS5ESnGON2EfGsKB0u WcHQcYv4FzniuKPMXV47mtH3h_a9hwEpoX7eomvycdqLu0Xbhnn394BJYEjyp6ji4rnAVc.

[331] M. Nayyar, A. Chawla, and A. Pagaria. 2020. Textile & Apparel Industry: The Change Agent of India. *Invest India.* 9 July. https://www.investindia.gov.in/siru/textile-apparel-industry-change-agent-india.

[332] *Fibre2Fashion.* 2014. Indonesia encourages use of natural fibres in textiles. 15 February. https://www.fibre2fashion.com/news/textile-news/newsdetails.aspx?news_id=159823.

potential alternative raw materials feasibly grown locally. Modal fabric, a bio-based fabric from beech tree cellulose, is considered an eco-friendlier alternative to cotton as beech trees require less water.[333]

c. **Transition to higher value-added services.** Garment manufacturers could go into quality control testing and original design manufacturing, which includes overseeing design and product development, or original brand manufacturing, including marketing the final products (footnote 309). Cambodia is increasing textile testing capabilities in Phnom Penh to reduce costs of testing abroad and build local capabilities.[334]

2. **Transitioning toward a circular economy.** Circular economy adoption is a sustainable way to pursue recovery across industries, including garment manufacturing.[335] While governments generally have policies on textile waste management, there is a lack of emphasis on circular economy approaches. In Indonesia, the "Standar Industri Hijau" (Green Industrial Standard) contains provisions on raw materials, auxiliary materials, energy, production processes, products, business management, and waste management for 17 industries, including garments.[336] Figure 15 illustrates the potential of the Indonesian garment industry to adopt circular principles through a simple "5Rs" framework applicable across Southeast Asia.

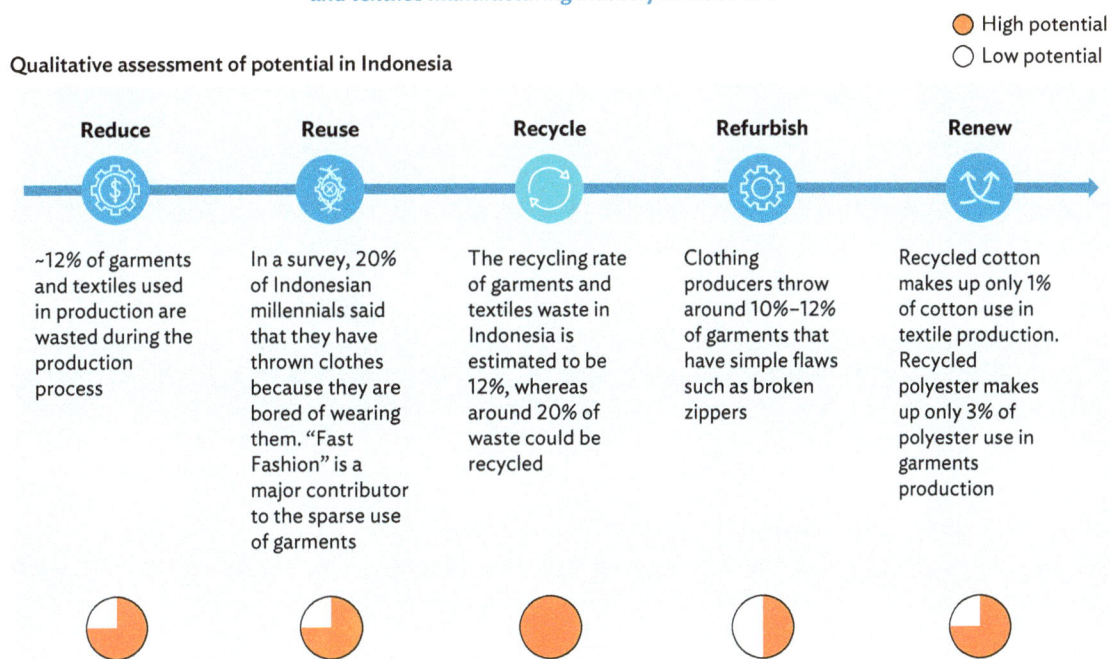

Figure 15: Recycling's Potential for Circularity in the Indonesian Garment Industry

The "Recycle" approach offers the highest potential for circularity in garments and textiles manufacturing industry in Indonesia

⬤ High potential
◯ Low potential

Qualitative assessment of potential in Indonesia

Reduce	Reuse	Recycle	Refurbish	Renew
~12% of garments and textiles used in production are wasted during the production process	In a survey, 20% of Indonesian millennials said that they have thrown clothes because they are bored of wearing them. "Fast Fashion" is a major contributor to the sparse use of garments	The recycling rate of garments and textiles waste in Indonesia is estimated to be 12%, whereas around 20% of waste could be recycled	Clothing producers throw around 10%–12% of garments that have simple flaws such as broken zippers	Recycled cotton makes up only 1% of cotton use in textile production. Recycled polyester makes up only 3% of polyester use in garments production

Sources: Ellen MacArthur Foundation; Guardian; YouGov; AlphaBeta.

---

[333] *MasterClass.* 2020. Fabric Guide: What Is Modal Fabric? Understanding How Modal Is Made and Whether Modal Is an Environmentally Conscious Choice. 8 November. https://www.masterclass.com/articles/fabric-guide-what-is-modal-fabric#what-is-modal-fabric.

[334] SGS. 2019. *SGS Invests in New Textile Testing Capabilities in Phnom Penh, Cambodia.* 8 January. https://www.sgs.com/en/news/2019/01/sgs-invests-in-new-textile-testing-capabilities-in-phnom-penh-cambodia.

[335] M. Wijayasundara. 2020. Opportunities for a circular economy post COVID-19. *WEF.* 22 June. https://www.weforum.org/agenda/2020/06/opportunities-circular-economy-post-covid-19/; and Centre for the Promotion of Imports. 2020. *How to respond to COVID-19 in the apparel sector.* The Hague. https://www.cbi.eu/market-information/apparel/how-respond-covid-19-apparel-sector#change-from-mass-production-to-made-to-measure.

[336] Kementerian Perindustrian. 2016. *Standar Industri hijau (SIH) untuk 17 Jenis Industri.* Jakarta. http://bppi.kemenperin.go.id/blog/standar-industri-hijau-sih-untuk-17-jenis-industri/.

The "5Rs" framework says to (i) Reduce (e.g., removing waste in production and the supply chain); (ii) Reuse (e.g., sharing assets); (iii) Recycle (e.g., recycling materials); (iv) Refurnish (e.g., prolonging product lifespan through maintenance); and (v) Renew (e.g., prioritizing renewable energy and materials). A report shows that the adoption of a circular economy in the garment industry could lead to an additional Rp19.5 trillion ($1.4 billion) of GDP by 2030.[337]

While Indonesia committed to creating a National Circular Economy Strategy for five sectors, including textiles,[338] none of the other focus countries has a coherent and comprehensive strategy for improving circularity in the garment industry. Some potential measures to promote circularity adoption include:

a. **Providing financial and partnership support.** Using more sustainable materials, such as organic cotton, hemp, linen, recycled material, and Tencel though these require the retooling of garment production processes. This may be especially difficult for MSMEs, who may not have sufficient access to capital to modify their production systems. Governments could provide financial support to encourage textile factories, especially MSMEs, to upgrade their machinery. Support could also help garment manufacturers market sustainably produced clothes through funding (e.g., media advertising, roadshows) or partnerships. The authorities could help companies adopting circularity approaches to identify and pitch to local and international buyers.

b. **Guaranteeing demand for sustainable manufacturers.** Providing guaranteed public procurement is a possible way to support domestic demand and help reduce the risks for manufacturers who invest in circular production methods. Governments could pledge orders of school uniforms, military uniforms, and government staff uniforms. The Netherlands has demonstrated this in their own textile industry. [339]

3. **Reforming the labor welfare system.** There are several pressing issues with the labor welfare system—poor working conditions, the lack of labor rights, low adherence to minimum wage recommendations, and significant gender discrimination. Several high-profile incidents in recent years have put the spotlight on the negative social aspects of the industry. They include the Rana Plaza collapse which affected five garment factories, killed more than 1,100 people, and revealed the poor working conditions of ready-made garment factory workers in Bangladesh, who work long hours in unventilated facilities that do not meet even local safety standards and are without proper fire exits (footnote 140). Furthermore, there is a large group of informal workers with no contracts or protection of their rights. The focus countries need to continuously address the welfare of garment workers given increasing pressure from consumers and major export countries. Perceived issues on political and labor rights resulted in Cambodia losing its duty-free access to the European market for some exports including garments and footwear.[340] Fortunately, there are some efforts to improve the working conditions of garment workers. Myanmar drafted the Labour Organization Law to increase the minimum wage and allow workers to unionize.[341] The process has been slow, and the country's minimum wage is still one of the lowest in Asia. There is now an increased partnership between the industry and government on labor welfare. The "Call to Action" initiative was negotiated between the International Organization of Employers, the International Trade Union Confederation, and IndustriALL Global Union, with the 125-plus signatories committing to promote sustainable systems of social protection for workers (footnote 258). Apart from facilitating unionization and enforcing minimum wages, other potential policies to consider include:

---

[337] BAPPENAS and UNDP. 2021. *The Economic, Social, and Environmental Benefits of a Circular Economy in Indonesia.* Jakarta. https://alphabeta.com/wp-content/uploads/2021/03/210127-designed-english-full-report-web.pdf.

[338] UNDP. 2020. *UNDP, Bappenas and Denmark collaborate to support the development of Circular Economy in Indonesia.* 3 March. https://www.id.undp.org/content/indonesia/en/home/presscenter/pressreleases/2020/Circular-Economy.html.

[339] Ministry of Infrastructure and Environment, Netherlands. *Public Procurement of textiles in the Netherlands.* https://ec.europa.eu/environment/gpp/pdf/Textiles_webinar_28_june_pratical_experiences.pdf.

[340] EC. 2020. *Cambodia loses duty-free access to the EU market over human rights concerns.* Brussels. https://ec.europa.eu/commission/presscorner/detail/en/ip_20_1469; and EC. 2020. Commission Delegated Regulation (EU) 2020/550. *Official Journal of the European Union.* https://eur-lex.europa.eu/legal-content/EN/TXT/PDF/?uri=CELEX:32020R0550&from=EN.

[341] L. Hogan. 2018. The True Cost of Myanmar's Growing Garment Industry. *The New Humanitarian.* 25 May. https://deeply.thenewhumanitarian.org/womensadvancement/articles/2018/05/25/the-true-cost-of-myanmars-growing-garment-industry.

a. **Mandating certifications.** Some nongovernment organizations introduced labels for apparel production like "Sweat-free Communities," "Garments without Guilt," "Better Factories," and "Better Work" to certify products meeting minimum standards on ethical production and improved labor conditions. [342] Governments can mandate these certifications to put pressure on companies to improve working conditions.

b. **Emphasizing gender-specific policies.** Studies show that women, the majority of the garment industry's workers, are more likely to face gender-specific challenges like discrimination, gender pay gaps, and sexual harassment.[343] Governments should ensure female workers receive appropriate protection from these challenges, by analyzing data segregated by gender, establishing dedicated working groups, and strengthening the monitoring capacity of working conditions.[344] Most focus countries do not have gender-specific policies, and reports indicate the need to develop policies along these lines.[345] In Cambodia, women are still underrepresented in leadership roles and face challenges such as restricted opportunities for skill development, though there has been some progress since 2011.[346]

(iv) Pursuing More Flexible Production and Business Models

The pandemic's impact on the garment industry has shown how a thriving industry can be severely affected by simultaneous demand and supply shocks, revealing a need for greater flexibility in production and business models to respond to future shocks. In Indonesia and Cambodia, garment factories attempted to produce personal protective equipment, but they faced raw material shortages and difficulties getting the necessary certifications.[347] The ability of garment factories to switch across production types to meet changing consumer demand needs flexible factory designs. Governments could:

a. **Drive research and development.** Factories require extensive technologies and financing capital for innovation, and governments could spearhead such efforts. In Singapore, the Agency for Science, Technology and Research leads the Advanced Remanufacturing and Technology Centre, to develop new technologies and applications.[348] One project does research on creating robots that can manufacture different products in a limited space based on varying demands.

b. **Equip workers with transferable skills.** Factories also require workers with multiple relevant skillsets and transferable skills. As discussed previously, there are skill gaps in both nondigital and digital skills, making reskilling and upskilling programs more important.

Many of these policy recommendations apply to the five focus countries. However, some recommendations can benefit from increased regional cooperation, as the adoption of circular production methods requires collaboration and mutual agreement among countries in the region, especially as some share common water bodies like the Mekong River.

[342] ADB. 2016. *Working Conditions, Work Outcomes, and Policy in Asian Developing Countries.* Manila. https://www.adb.org/sites/default/files/publication/198551/ewp-497.pdf.

[343] ILO. 2016. *Progress and Potential: How Better Work is improving garment workers' lives and boosting factory competitiveness.* Geneva. https://betterwork.org/wp-content/uploads/2016/09/BW-Progress-and-Potential_Web-final.pdf.

[344] ILO. 2012. *Action-oriented research on gender equality and the working and living conditions of garment factory workers in Cambodia.* Geneva. https://www.ilo.org/wcmsp5/groups/public/---asia/---ro-bangkok/---sro-bangkok/documents/publication/wcms_204166.pdf.

[345] A. Imron et al. 2017. Why is Gender Inequality Still Appearing in Garment Factories, in Indonesia? *Advances in Economics, Business and Management Research,* volume 36.

[346] ILO. 2012. *Action-oriented research on gender equality and the working and living conditions of garment factory workers in Cambodia.* Geneva. https://www.ilo.org/wcmsp5/groups/public/---asia/---ro-bangkok/---sro-bangkok/documents/publication/wcms_204166.pdf; and Better Work. 2020. *New report 'shines a light' on gender dynamics in Cambodia's garment factories.* https://betterwork.org/2018/03/07/new-report-shines-a-light-on-gender-dynamics-in-cambodias-garment-factories/.

[347] *The Jakarta Post.* 2020. COVID-19: Textile factories face hurdles as they switch to producing medical gear. 30 March. https://www.thejakartapost.com/news/2020/03/30/covid-19-textile-factories-face-hurdles-as-they-switch-to-producing-medical-gear.html; and *Khmer Times.* 2020. Cambodian government gives approval for garment factories to produce masks and PPE's. 17 May. https://www.khmertimeskh.com/723913/cambodian-government-gives-approval-for-garment-factories-to-produce-masks-and-ppes/.

[348] EDB. 2017. *Singapore's advanced manufacturing avatar "Industry 4.0."* 10 July. https://www.edb.gov.sg/en/news-and-events/insights/manufacturing/singapores-advanced-manufacturing-avatar--industry-4-0.html.

Table 9 summarizes the key policy recommendations and their relevance to each focus country (footnote 124).

Table 9: Summary of Recommendations for Garment Manufacturing

Key recommendations and their relevance to focus countries

Degree of relevance: ▮ High ▮ Medium ▮ Low

		Cambodia	Indonesia	Myanmar	Philippines	Thailand
Improving competitiveness	Bridge infrastructure gaps	High	High	High	High	Medium
	Review policies that are restricting growth	High	Medium	Medium	Low	Low
	Upgrade vocational curriculum and increase access to training	High	Medium	High	Medium	Medium
	Promote digital technologies in the garments manufacturing industry	High	High	High	High	High
Expanding markets	Develop more end markets	High	High	High	High	Medium
	Expand product range	High	Medium	Medium	High	High
Raising industry resilience	Develop capabilities to participate across the garments supply chain	High	High	High	High	High
	Transit toward a circular economy	High	Medium	High	High	High
	Reform the labor welfare system	High	High	High	High	High
Pursuing more flexible production and business models	Pursuing more flexible production and business models	High	High	High	High	High

Note: This exercise is based on a broad assessment of the observed gaps and what countries have done (i.e., current responses in terms of presence and scope of policy measures).
Source: AlphaBeta analysis.

Box 7 provides an overview of some of the relevant country plans and ADB programs by country.

Box 7: Examples of ADB Country Programs on Garment Manufacturing

A review of the Asian Development Bank (ADB) Country Operations Business Plan (COBP) (2020–2022) and the Country Partnership Strategies (CPS) for the five focus countries identified some sources of assistance provided by ADB related to the garment industry and the policy recommendations:[a]

- **Economic competitiveness.** ADB currently supports the Government of Cambodia in improving the competitiveness of prioritized industries, which includes garments. ADB aims to understand the prioritized sectors' barriers to growth, employment generation, and investment to improve supply chain competitiveness and enable the growth of micro, small, and medium-sized enterprises (MSMEs).
- **Human capital investment.** As part of its Country Partnership Strategy for Cambodia, ADB aims to ensure lifelong learning for wage employment workers, by enabling them to upskill and reskill continuously. To achieve this, ADB focuses on education and skills, investing in science, technology, engineering, and mathematics education in upper secondary schools, as well as teacher qualification, revising curricula, and enhancing student assessment.
- **Inclusive growth.** ADB prioritized two opportunities in Myanmar's textile and clothing sector in 2018 as part of its "Bangladesh and Myanmar: Inclusive Textiles and Clothing: Mapping Inclusive Business Opportunities in the Textile and Clothing Sector in Asia" project to ensure the sector improves the livelihood of the low-income population of the country.[b] First, ADB proposed creating a handloom hub, to improve the competitiveness of the local supply chain. Second, it proposed the creation of self-help groups to help build the capacity of factory workers, particularly women, in education, financial management, health care, and other issues.

[a] The Country Operations Business Plans include:
- ADB. 2019. *Country Operations Business Plan: Cambodia (2020–2022)*. Manila. https://www.adb.org/documents/cambodia-country-operations-business-plan-2020-2022.
- ADB. 2019. *Country Operations Business Plan: Indonesia (2020–2022)*. Manila. https://www.adb.org/sites/default/files/institutional-document/526266/cobp-ino-2020-2022.pdf.
- ADB. 2019. *Country Operations Business Plan: Myanmar (2020–2022)*. Manila. https://www.adb.org/sites/default/files/institutional-document/541976/cobp-mya-2020-2022.pdf.
- ADB. 2019. *Country Operations Business Plan: Philippines (2020–2022)*. Manila.https://www.adb.org/sites/default/files/institutional-document/533741/cobp-phi-2020-2022.pdf.
- ADB. 2019. *Country Operations Business Plan: Thailand (2020–2022)*. Manila. https://www.adb.org/sites/default/files/institutional-document/541811/cobp-tha-2020-2022.pdf.

The Country Partnership Strategies include:
- ADB. 2019. *Country Partnership Strategy: Cambodia 2019–2023, Inclusive pathways to a competitive economy*. Manila. https://www.adb.org/sites/default/files/institutional-document/534691/cps-cam-2019-2023.pdf.
- ADB. 2020. *Country Partnership Strategy: Indonesia 2020–2024*. Manila. https://www.adb.org/sites/default/files/institutional-document/640096/cps-ino-2020-2024.pdf.
- ADB. 2017. *Country Partnership Strategy: Myanmar, 2017–2021*, Building the foundations for inclusive growth. Manila. https://www.adb.org/sites/default/files/institutional-document/237161/cps-mya-2017-2021.pdf.
- ADB. 2018. *Country Partnership Strategy: Philippines, 2018–2023, High and inclusive growth*. Manila. https://www.adb.org/sites/default/files/institutional-document/456476/cps-phi-2018-2023.pdf.
- ADB. 2013. *Country Partnership Strategy: Thailand 2013–2016*. Manila. https://www.adb.org/sites/default/files/institutional-document/33990/files/cps-tha-2013-2016.pdf.

[b] ADB. 2018. *Bangladesh and Myanmar: Inclusive Textiles and Clothing: Mapping Inclusive Business Opportunities in the Textile and Clothing Sector in Asia (Co-financed by the Government of Sweden)*. Manila. https://www.adb.org/sites/default/files/project-documents/46240/46240-001-tacr-en_1.pdf.

ELECTRONICS INDUSTRY

Four major challenges pre-COVID-19

Lack of diversification across the electronics supply chain

Relatively low economic value-add of stage in value chain and type of electronics produced

Disruptive technologies

Rapid changes in electronics technology and consumption trends

Two major shifts from COVID-19

Production delays

Acceleration in changing landscape of consumer demand

Two areas of policy action

Upgrading special economic zones
- Adopt zone specialization to maximize industry linkages
- Develop supportive policies specific to the electronics industry

Develop human capital
- Create dedicated strategies and government agencies
- Incentivize local companies to engage in research and development

SECTION V

Electronics

▶ **Electronics manufacturing employed more than 3.7 million people across Southeast Asia in 2019.**

Electronics manufacturing has been a significant driver of economic activity in the five focus countries, particularly in Indonesia, the Philippines, and Thailand.[349] The industry contributed close to 2% of GDP in these countries and accounted for 9% to 15% of gross value added in the manufacturing sector.[350] The industry also increased the countries' roles in the global value chains, generating export sales and attracting foreign direct investment (FDI).[351] The total accrued investment capital for the industry in Cambodia in December 2017 was over $226 million.[352] The net FDI inflow in electronics manufacturing in Thailand was nearly $2 billion in 2019.[353] In 2019, the total electronics exports was around $40 billion in both Thailand and the Philippines, and approximately $9 billion in Indonesia. Figure 16 shows that Indonesia is the only country where electronics' share of exports declined over the past decade. Elsewhere, the 10-year annualized growth rates of electronics exports were considerably high, with electronics' export share going over 50% in the Philippines in 2019.

The industry provides several economic benefits. For example, in the Philippines, every ₱1.00 increase in electronics export sales could generate at least ₱0.12 in additional indirect taxes for the economy, and ₱0.11 to ₱0.25 of additional household income. Every ₱1 billion increase in investment in the sector could create between 600 to 1,400 additional jobs.[354] In Southeast Asia, the industry directly employs more than 3.7 million workers in 2019 (Figure 17). Among the focus countries, Thailand has the highest number of employed workers in electronics, accounting for 12% of manufacturing's total workforce, about 750,000 people. The Philippines is second, employing over half a million people and over 14% of manufacturing's total workforce. The industry is also a significant employer of women. In Indonesia and Thailand, more than half of the workers are women (footnote 351). Though women account for nearly 43% of occupations requiring higher skills (e.g., managers, professionals, technicians, and associate professionals), they are nearly 59% of the workers in occupations requiring lower skills (e.g., assembly workers, craft, and related trades workers).

---

[349] The industry is defined as a combination of two subsectors found in national statistics: "Manufacture of computer, electronic and optical products" and "Manufacture of electrical equipment."

[350] The data was sourced from national statistics from the three countries.

[351] ILO. 2019. *The electronics industry in Indonesia and its integration into global supply chains*. Geneva. https://www.ilo.org/wcmsp5/groups/public/---ed_dialogue/---sector/documents/publication/wcms_732119.pdf.

[352] V. Seyhah and H. Vutha. 2019. *Cambodia in the Electronic and Electrical Global Value Chains*. CDRI. Phnom Penh. https://cdri.org.kh/storage/pdf/wp119e_1617247939.pdf.

[353] Bank of Thailand. EC_XT_059 Foreign Direct Investment Classified by Business Sector of Thai Enterprises (US$) 1. https://www.bot.or.th/App/BTWS_STAT/statistics/ReportPage.aspx?reportID=656&language=eng.

[354] A. Awan. 2017. *Philippines Electronic Components Manufacturing*. ISC HBS. Boston. https://www.isc.hbs.edu/Documents/resources/courses/moc-course-at-harvard/pdf/student-projects/Philippines_Electronics_2017.pdf.

Figure 16: Electronics Export Contributions in Focus Countries

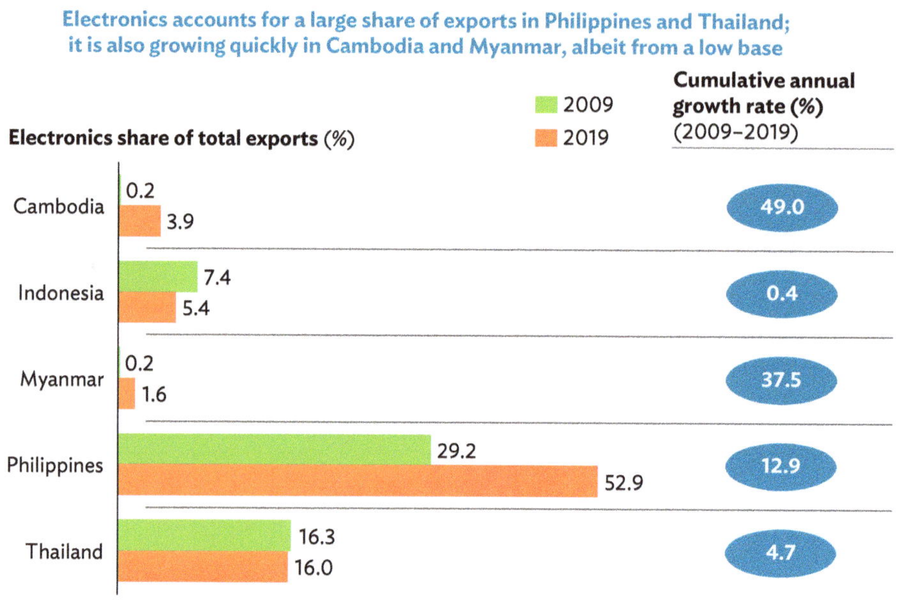
Electronics accounts for a large share of exports in Philippines and Thailand;
it is also growing quickly in Cambodia and Myanmar, albeit from a low base
Electronics share of total exports (%)
2009
2019
Cumulative annual growth rate (%) (2009–2019)
Cambodia
0.2
3.9
49.0
Indonesia
7.4
5.4
0.4
Myanmar
0.2
1.6
37.5
Philippines
29.2
52.9
12.9
Thailand
16.3
16.0
4.7

Note: Includes harmonized system (HS) codes [85] Electrical machinery and equipment and parts thereof; sound recorders and reproducers; television image and sound recorders and reproducers, parts and accessories of such articles, and [90] Optical, photographic, cinematographic, measuring, checking, medical or surgical instruments and apparatus; parts and accessories.
Sources: ASEAN Stats Data Portal; AlphaBeta analysis.

Figure 17: Electronics Employment in Southeast Asia

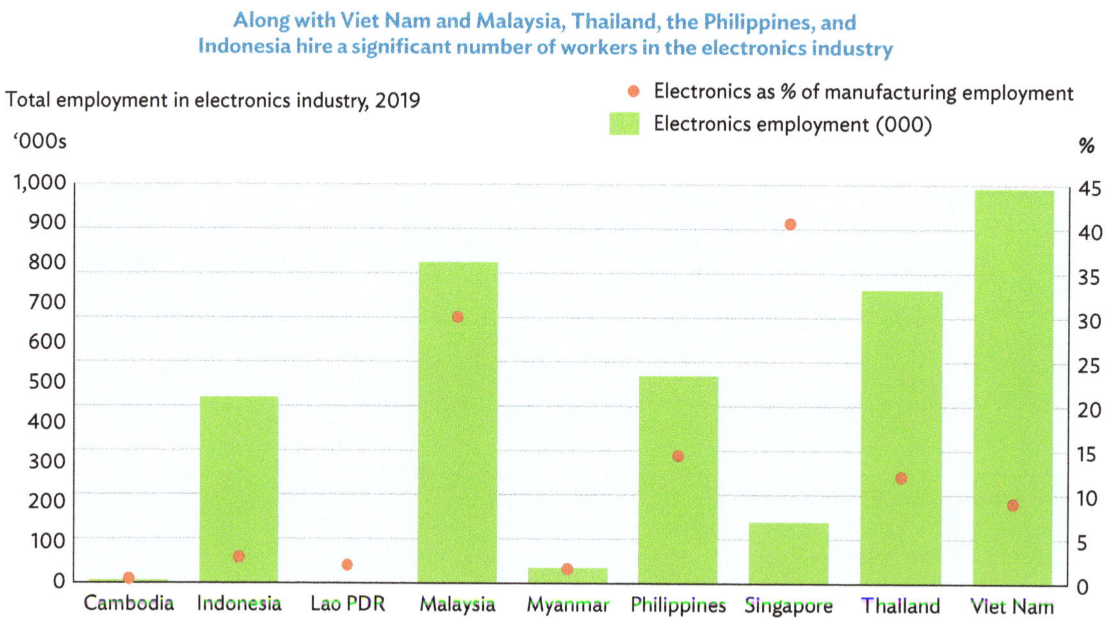
Along with Viet Nam and Malaysia, Thailand, the Philippines, and
Indonesia hire a significant number of workers in the electronics industry
Total employment in electronics industry, 2019
'000s
Electronics as % of manufacturing employment
Electronics employment (000)
%
1,000
900
800
700
600
500
400
300
200
100
0
45
40
35
30
25
20
15
10
5
0
Cambodia
Indonesia
Lao PDR
Malaysia
Myanmar
Philippines
Singapore
Thailand
Viet Nam

Lao PDR = Lao People's Democratic Republic.
Note: Include products under the International Standard Industrial Classification of All Economic Activities (ISIC, Rev. 4) Divisions 26 ('Computer, electronics, and optical products'), 27 ('Electrical equipment'), and 28 ('Machinery and equipment). Total manufacturing refers to ISIC, Rev. 4, Section C, Divisions 10-33. Insufficient data for Brunei Darussalam and Timor-Leste.
Sources: International Labour Organization, SingStat, and AlphaBeta analysis.

While electronics plays an important role in the economy of several focus countries, its production scope varies by country (Table 10). For instance, Thailand's production is typically capital-intensive, and focuses on electronic hardware components, particularly hard disk drives (HDDs) and semiconductors and integrated circuits (ICs). Thailand is one of the world's largest manufacturers of HDDs, accounting for about 30% of the global market.[355] In Cambodia, the industry is focused on more labor-intensive electrical components production like wires, cables, and transformers, accounting for 45% of the country's total electronics export value (footnote 352). The Philippines is involved primarily in the component stage (particularly ICs) of the value chain, accounting for over two-thirds of its exports and firms (footnote 354). In Indonesia, the industry largely caters to the domestic market due to the rise in local purchasing power. The main manufacturing activities in the Indonesian electronics industry are assembly and quality control, especially regarding consumer electronics (footnote 351).

Table 10: Differences of Electronics Production across Southeast Asia

Southeast Asian countries produce a range of electronics, from low-end cables and wires to high-end semiconductors and silicon wafers

Country	Key Production	Major Players
Cambodia	Wires, cables, transformers	General Cable, Southwire, Furukawa
Indonesia	Integrated circuits (ICs), semi-conductor, printed circuit boards (PCBs)	Toshiba, LG, Sony, Panasonic, Samsung
Malaysia	Semiconductors, microchips, conductors, valves, household appliances, radio equipment, solar cells, PCBs	Bosch, Fairchild, Hewlett Packard, Hitachi, Silterra, Intel
Philippines	ICs, semiconductor, electronic data processing (PCBs, printers, hard disk)	Texas Instruments, Fairchild, Amkor, Toshiba, Epson, Fujitsu
Singapore	Semiconductors, silicon wafers, hard-disk components	Avago, Fairchild, Micron, Seagate, Hitachi, Flextronics, Sanmina, Lite-On, Wistron
Thailand	Hard-disk drives, ICs, microchips, air conditioning units, refrigerators	Fujitsu, LG Electronics, Samsung, Seagate, Sony, Western Digital Bosch, Daikin, Electrolux, LG, Panasonic, Samsung, Siemens, Toshiba
Viet Nam	ICs, semiconductor, PCBs	Intel, Microsoft, LG, Panasonic, Samsung, Hitachi, Active-Semi, Hanel, Fuji, Xerox

Sources: Adapted from *ASEAN in Transformation. Electrical and Electronics: On and Off the Grid* by the International Labour Organization, AlphaBeta analysisSources: ASEAN Stats Data Portal; AlphaBeta analysis.

▶ **Challenges faced by the electronics industry include changing consumption trends and the impact of disruptive technologies on employment.**

• **Lack of diversification across the supply chain.** Like other industries, electronics manufacturing in the focus countries has inadequate industrial systems and lacks the complete upstream and downstream portions of the value chains.[356] The countries' underlying lack of competitiveness in this sector can be seen in Figure 18, which shows the industry's trade balance with the PRC over the last decade; all five

---

[355] Thailand Board of Investment. 2017. *Thailand's smart electronics.* https://www.boi.go.th/upload/content/BOI_Smart%20Electronics_W1_5b6bb13a126e9.pdf.

[356] Think China. 2020. *Wake-up call for ASEAN countries: Curb over-reliance on China and seize opportunities of global supply chain restructuring.* https://www.thinkchina.sg/wake-call-asean-countries-curb-over-reliance-china-and-seize-opportunities-global-supply-chain.

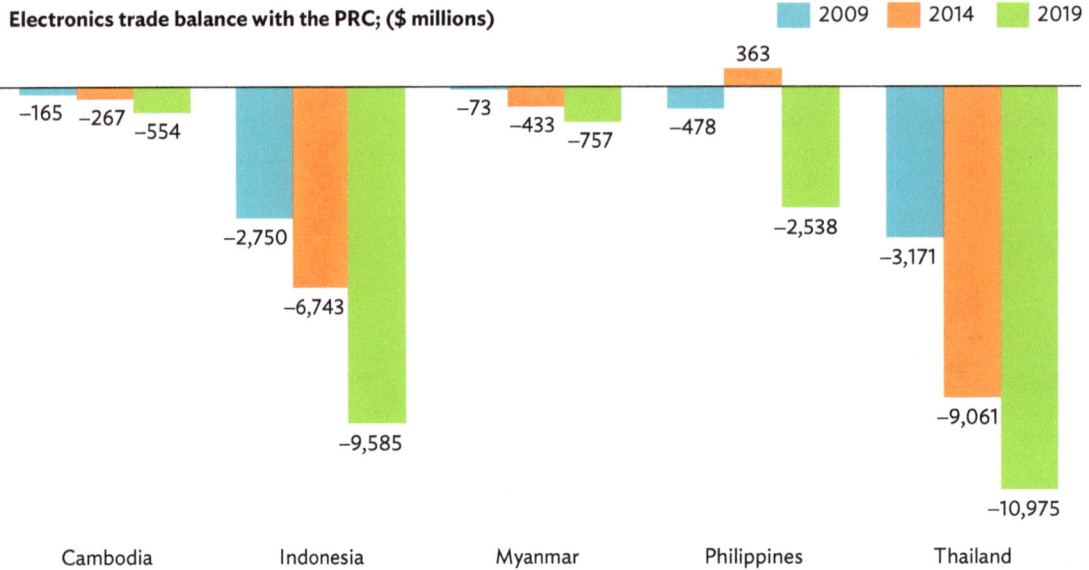

Figure 18: Trade Deficits with the People's Republic of China

In the electronics industry, the focus countries are running increasingly large trade deficits with the PRC

Electronics trade balance with the PRC; ($ millions)

2009   2014   2019

Cambodia: −165, −267, −554
Indonesia: −2,750, −6,743, −9,585
Myanmar: −73, −433, −757
Philippines: −478, 363, −2,538
Thailand: −3,171, −9,061, −10,975

PRC = People's Republic of China.
Note: Includes harmonized system (HS) codes [85] Electrical machinery and equipment and parts thereof; sound recorders and reproducers; television image and sound recorders and reproducers, parts and accessories of such articles, and [90] Optical, photographic, cinematographic, measuring, checking, medical or surgical instruments and apparatus; parts and accessories.
Sources: ASEAN Stats Data Portal; AlphaBeta analysis.

countries are running increasingly large deficits with the PRC. Upstream, electronics manufacturers continue to rely heavily on a PRC-centric global industrial chain, particularly for raw materials and intermediate products. Semiconductors and Electronics Industries in the Philippines Incorporated, the largest industry association of electronics companies in the country, reported that semiconductor factories source 40% of their raw materials from the PRC; Hong Kong, China; and Taipei,China. Further downstream, a strong customer concentration also poses risks to the industry. For instance, in 2019, the top five export destinations made up the following percentages of the total electronics exports for these countries: 78% for Cambodia, 54% for Indonesia, 74% for Myanmar, 68% for the Philippines, and 55% for Thailand.

• **Relatively low economic value-add in value chain and type of electronics produced.** This challenge stems from two characteristics of electronics manufacturing in the five focus countries. First, they have a relatively stronger focus on the assembly and testing stage of the industry value chain, versus upstream stages generating higher economic value-add such as research and development (R&D) and product design. For example, of the top ten technology and electronics companies globally by revenue, only two have their R&D centers in the five focus countries. Second, production in these countries tends to mainly focus on less complex electronics like storage devices, as compared to high-tech electronics such as semiconductors (except for the Philippines) generating greater economic benefits. For example, over the last decade in Indonesia, although the value-add from high-tech industries increased fourfold and currently accounts for over 40% of total manufacturing value-add, the share of manufacturing firms engaged in high-tech manufacturing has remained constant at around 30%. The government recognized this challenge and now aims to increase employment in the overall manufacturing sector to 20% of the total workforce by 2024 by exporting more high-tech electronics products under the "Making Indonesia 4.0" policy.[357] Two key factors drive the low economic value-add currently observed in this sector:

– A predominantly low-skilled labor force led to the lack of capacity to transition beyond assembly operations. For example, in Thailand, 80% of the total workforce in the industry are low-skilled, holding positions such as assembly workers or plant and machinery operators.[358] A study on Myanmar showed that the country faced a severe demand–supply gap for semiskilled labor; this gap was estimated at 13 million workers in the manufacturing, retail, logistics, and administrative services sectors.[359]

– Strong competitive pressures from countries in the region led to further outsourcing of low-cost and labor-intensive activities. For example, with strong government and private sector investments to enhance Malaysia's electronics sector R&D capabilities over the past decade, a resultant increased focus on capital-intensive operations in the country triggered a shift of labor-intensive activities to Indonesia and Thailand.[360]

• **Disruptive technologies and the potential impact on labor.** The adoption of digital technologies in electronics could have widespread implications for the labor market. Electronics manufacturing companies in the focus countries are increasingly required to adopt new technologies, driven by a range of industry trends like the growing interconnectedness of global supply chains, the need for more complex designs and shorter delivery times, and increasing focus on the reliability of production systems. These technologies include the Internet of Things, Artificial Intelligence, and machine learning technologies; industry robotics (allowing the automation of repetitive tasks like components assembly); and additive manufacturing (more commonly known as 3D printing, these allow for the mass customization of goods).[361] Research by ADB and AlphaBeta found that in the Philippines's electronics manufacturing sector, approximately 24% of jobs are at risk of displacement with the adoption of these technologies (footnote 106). An ILO study estimates even higher displacement rate if such technologies were to be fully adopted, predicting that more than 60% of workers could be displaced by technologies in this sector in Indonesia, the Philippines, and Thailand.[362] Though this could be potentially offset by jobs created due to the productivity effects of such technologies,[363] workers who stay in the sector are likely to experience major shifts in daily tasks and the associated skills required. The research for the Philippines predicted that the share of working time spent on routine physical tasks could almost be halved due to the large share of assembly line work, with a high potential to be automated (footnote 106). Employer demand for computer literacy skills is also expected to rise significantly, as workers will need to have basic digital know-how to operate new factory technologies

[357] A. Medina. 2020. "Indonesia's Manufacturing Sector: Practical Information for Investors." *ASEAN Briefing.* 31 March. https://www.aseanbriefing.com/news/indonesias-manufacturing-sector-practical-information-investors/.

[358] ILO. 2017. *Electrical and electronics manufacturing in Thailand: Exploring challenges and good practices in the workplace.* Geneva. https://www.ilo.org/wcmsp5/groups/public/---asia/---ro-bangkok/---sro-bangkok/documents/publication/wcms_575610.pdf.

[359] McKinsey & Company. 2018. *Sustaining Economic Momentum in Myanmar.* https://www.mckinsey.com/~/media/McKinsey/Featured%20Insights/Asia%20Pacific/Sustaining%20economic%20momentum%20in%20Myanmar/Sustaining-economic-momentum-in-Myanmar.pdf.

[360] *Invest in ASEAN.* 2020. "Electronics: Every Chip in Place." 10 December. http://investasean.asean.org/index.php/page/view/electronics.

[361] McKinsey & Company. 2018. *Industry 4.0: Reinvigorating ASEAN Manufacturing for the Future.* fhttps://www.mckinsey.com/~/media/mckinsey/business%20functions/operations/our%20insights/industry%204%200%20reinvigorating%20asean%20manufacturing%20for%20the%20future/industry-4-0-reinvigorating-asean-manufacturing-for-the-future.ashx; McKinsey Global Institute. 2014. *Southeast Asia at the crossroads: Three paths to prosperity.* https://www.mckinsey.com/~/media/McKinsey/Featured%20Insights/Asia%20Pacific/Three%20paths%20to%20sustained%20economic%20growth%20in%20Southeast%20Asia/MGI%20SE%20Asia_Executive%20summary_November%202014.ashx; *International Federation of Robotics.* 2018. Automation boom in electrical/electronics industry drives 30% increase in sales of industrial robots. 7 November. https://ifr.org/post/automation-boom-in-electrical-electronics-industry-drives-30-increase-in-sa.

[362] ILO. 2016. *ASEAN in Transformation. Electrical and Electronics: On and Off the Grid.* https://www.ilo.org/wcmsp5/groups/public/---ed_dialogue/---act_emp/documents/publication/wcms_579559.pdf.

[363] Sometimes called a "scale effect," "productivity effect" refers to when automation improves productivity and lowers production costs. Under normal conditions, this lowers the price of goods and services, which raises demand for them. To the extent that increased demand requires hiring more workers, it could offset the displacement effect from automation.

(footnote 106). Moreover, job displacement could disproportionately affect females; the same research on the Philippines found that 55% of jobs at risk of displacement in this sector were currently held by women, who tend to occupy manual assembler roles (footnote 106).

- **Rapid changes in electronics technology and consumption trends.** With the speed at which technologies used in electronics devices and equipment develop, matched by the similarly fast pace of change in consumer demand for them, the types of components and manufacturing processes required to produce them regularly evolve. These trends push manufacturers to constantly upgrade and adapt their manufacturing inputs and processes, which can be cost-prohibitive in the long term. For example, in the early 2010s, the shift within the data storage segment from HDDs toward solid state drives (SSD) in lightweight consumer electronics had adverse implications for Thailand.[364] Owing largely to this shift in the data storage market, Thailand saw its electronics export value dip during this period; in 2016, this value was identical to levels posted a decade before when B1.1 trillion ($30.7 billion) worth of electronics were shipped annually (footnote 364).

▶ COVID-19 led to two additional challenges.

COVID-19 accelerated digital transformations globally. The widespread adoption of technologies such as fifth generation (5G), IoT, machine learning, and AI will drive the demand for electronics components and semiconductors. The diversification of manufacturing out of traditional locations like the PRC due to economic and geopolitical considerations presents the focus countries with compelling opportunities to increase their electronics manufacturing footprint. To successfully develop a "PRC plus One" plan, requiring attracting corporations who are targeting such strategies, the focus countries need to resolve some structural challenges faced by the industry aside from the two additional challenges to the electronics industry:

- **Production delays.** Many electronics manufacturers, including those in the focus countries, face delays in production due to supply chain interruptions, resulting in the failure to meet the rising demand for some consumer electronics during the pandemic. In a survey by IPC, a nonprofit industry association formerly known as the Institute of Printed Circuits and then the Institute for Interconnecting and Packaging Electronic Circuits, the interruptions in manufacturing and shipping led to a domino effect on transportation, sales, prototyping, and the launches of new products across the industry.[365] For example, Apple delayed the launch of its iPhone 12 series in 2020 by at least a month. A separate study on electronics sourcing conducted by Dimensional Research also indicates that global supply chain disruptions attributed to COVID-19 significantly drove up component costs.[366]

- **Quickly changing landscape of consumer demand.** The pandemic forced consumers to adopt new ways of working and living, fundamentally changing the demand for electronics components. Therefore, the challenge is consistently understanding these shifts in demand. For example, there has been a considerable rise in demand for personal computers and other home office electronics due to the increasing need to do remote work, though it is unclear how long this will last. Beyond the consumer, policy considerations in key public sectors like education and health may also affect the mix of future electronics demand. The pandemic revealed weaknesses in public service delivery. For instance, schooling in some countries was completely stopped for months, which had significant implications on curricula. As governments begin to focus on digitalizing public services, this will invariably lead to changing demands for electronic products and components.

[364] Oxford Business Group. 2017. *Thailand's Manufacturing Sector to Move Further Up the Value Chain.* (from *The Report: Thailand 2017.* https://oxfordbusinessgroup.com/overview/upwards-march-raft-well-performing-industries-manufacturing-sector-set-move-further-value-chain.
[365] T. Katsabaris. 2020. 9 timely strategies for electronics marketers: Tackling the challenges of COVID-19. *Insider.* https://useinsider.com/9-strategies-for-electronics-marketers-facing-covid-19/.
[366] *EE Times.* 2020. Pandemic Delays Electronic Product Launches. https://www.eetimes.com/pandemic-delays-electronic-product-launches/.

▶ **Two areas need policy reform to strengthen competitiveness in the electronics industry.**

The market disruptions due to COVID-19 show the increasing urgency for electronic industries in the focus countries to move up the production value chain. For instance, countries could consider shifting to high-tech electronics manufacturing like semiconductor fabrication or higher value-added activities such as research and development. To address the identified challenges and improve the competitiveness of the electronics industry, policies should:

1. **Upgrade special economic zones.** SEZs are areas where governments facilitate industrial activity through fiscal and regulatory incentives and infrastructure support.[367] SEZs aim to cluster firms so that scale economies can be reaped, while potentially facilitating spillovers in technology, labor skills, and market opportunities. In countries like Cambodia, the private sector leads SEZ development. SEZs became prominent after the establishment of the ASEAN Economic Community (2015) to attract investment and facilitate border trade.[368] Thailand commenced the development of 10 SEZs to target priority industries including electronics, medical equipment, automobiles and parts, and textiles.[369] Indonesia operates 13 SEZs and has another seven under development (footnote 368). The Philippines classifies 12 SEZs into manufacturing, tourism, digital parks, and medical tourism parks. Cambodia has 31 SEZs across the country mostly focusing on garments and textiles, although major electronic companies such as Apple and IBM have established a presence at the Phnom Penh SEZ. Finally, the Thilawa SEZ in Myanmar, a joint project between the governments of Myanmar and Japan, had around 90 foreign firms in operation (footnote 368).

    Despite financial incentives and concessions, performance remains below expectations. This includes an unsustained boost in economic growth, the lack of spillover benefits outside these enclaves, and negative social and environmental impacts (footnote 367). This finding extends to both publicly and privately led SEZs. The reasons for poor performance are many and differ across focus countries, but two stand out in general. First, inadequate and/or the lack of legal enforcement in these SEZs contributed to overall poor management. This was a key reason for human rights and environmental disruption in Myanmar's SEZs.[370] Second, the lack of hard infrastructure and poor connectivity hampered the effectiveness of SEZs in focus countries. For example, many Cambodian SEZs do not have linkages to the domestic economy. Elsewhere, Thailand's Tak SEZ mainly serves the domestic market, with few global linkages.[371] In Myanmar and Cambodia, many privately operated SEZs have major infrastructural gaps (e.g., unstable electricity supply) impeding foreign investment (footnote 371). The general lack of connectivity in focus country ports can be seen from the Liner Shipping Connectivity Index produced by the UNCTAD which measures countries' level of integration into the existing global liner shipping network. Figure 19 shows that apart from Thailand (ranked 27th), the other focus countries rank relatively low in the latest scores update, with Cambodia (ranked 109th) and Myanmar (ranked 121st) in the bottom half globally. More open economies such as Singapore, Malaysia, and Viet Nam are in the top quartile of the rankings.

---

[367] World Investment Report. 2019. *Special Economic Zones*. https://unctad.org/system/files/official-document/WIR2019_CH4.pdf.

[368] ASEAN Briefing. 2020. *Special Economic Zones in ASEAN: Opportunities for US Investors*. https://www.aseanbriefing.com/news/special-economic-zones-in-asean-opportunities-for-us-investors/.

[369] Open Development Thailand. 2018. *Special Economic Zones*. https://thailand.opendevelopmentmekong.net/topics/special-economic-zones/.

[370] *Myanmar Times*. 2017. Lack of Accountability and Clarity in SEZ Law highlighted in Dawei. https://www.mmtimes.com/business/26788-lack-of-accountability-and-clarity-in-sez-law-highlighted-in-dawei.html.

[371] Open Development Mekong. 2019. *SEZs, Infrastructure Development, and Official Development Aid*. https://opendevelopmentmekong.net/topics/sezs-infrastructure-development-and-official-development-aid/.

Figure 19: Shipping Connectivity across Focus Countries

Apart from Thailand, the other focus countries rank poorly on the Liner Shipping Connectivity Index

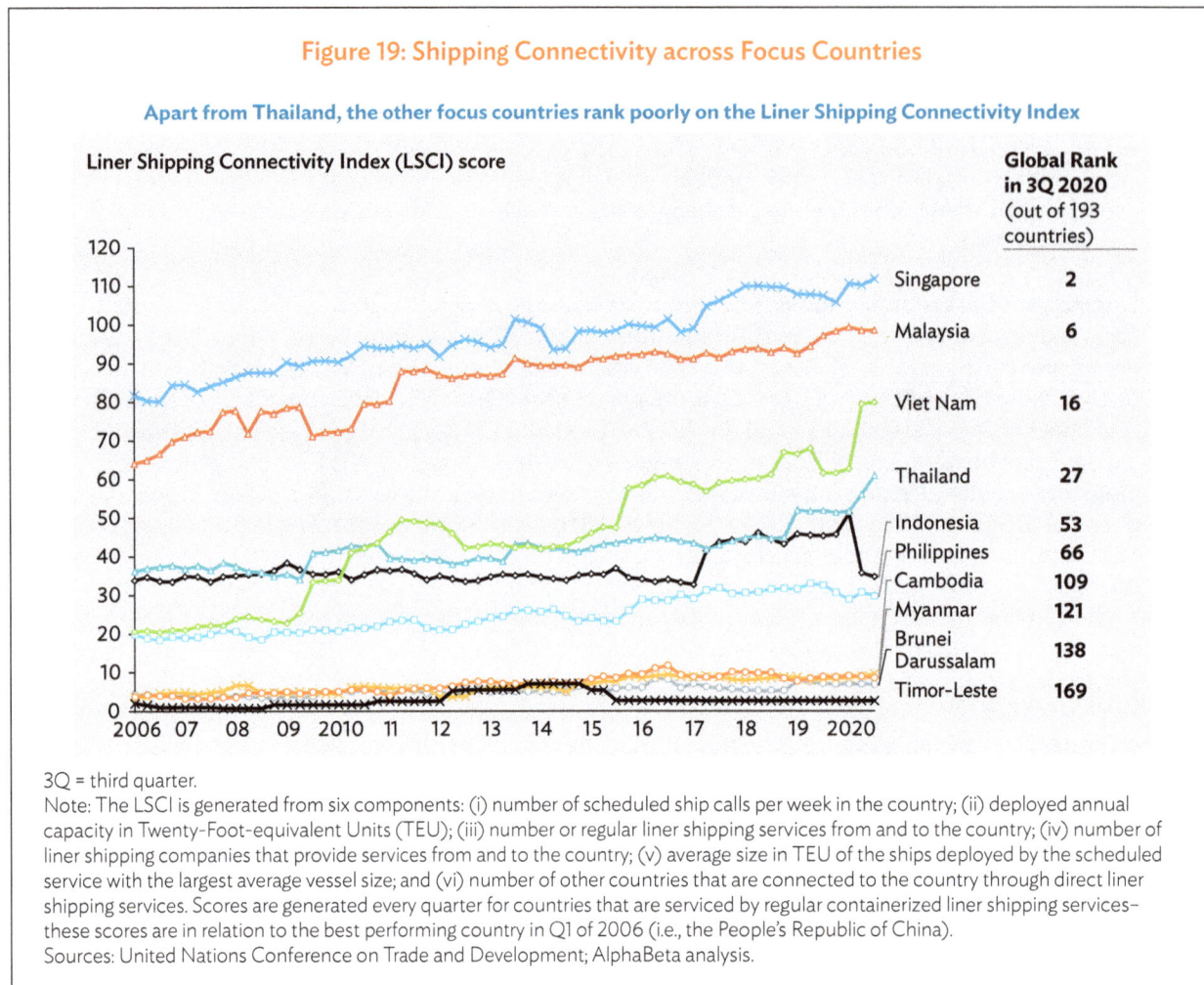

Liner Shipping Connectivity Index (LSCI) score

	Global Rank in 3Q 2020 (out of 193 countries)
Singapore	2
Malaysia	6
Viet Nam	16
Thailand	27
Indonesia	53
Philippines	66
Cambodia	109
Myanmar	121
Brunei Darussalam	138
Timor-Leste	169

3Q = third quarter.
Note: The LSCI is generated from six components: (i) number of scheduled ship calls per week in the country; (ii) deployed annual capacity in Twenty-Foot-equivalent Units (TEU); (iii) number or regular liner shipping services from and to the country; (iv) number of liner shipping companies that provide services from and to the country; (v) average size in TEU of the ships deployed by the scheduled service with the largest average vessel size; and (vi) number of other countries that are connected to the country through direct liner shipping services. Scores are generated every quarter for countries that are serviced by regular containerized liner shipping services—these scores are in relation to the best performing country in Q1 of 2006 (i.e., the People's Republic of China).
Sources: United Nations Conference on Trade and Development; AlphaBeta analysis.

Some recommendations to improve SEZs to move the electronics industry up the value chain include:
  a. **Getting basics right.** Several SEZs are hampered by sub-optimal planning and designs. According to UNCTAD, many SEZ failures can be traced to factors like poor site locations (e.g., being far away from labor sources or transport hubs), shortage in utilities (e.g., power supplies), inadequate facilities or maintenance, or red tape. Governments in the focus countries could review the challenges and incorporate more stringent design principles in future SEZs.
  b. **Adopting zone specialization to maximize industry linkages.** One idea is developing an exclusive SEZ for the electronics industry, where the clustering of firms can lead to more collaboration and pooling of resources while promoting competition. India, which has ambitions for net zero imports in electronics, emphasizes the development of coastal-based electronics SEZs. The Tamil Nadu government is developing four Electronics Manufacturing Clusters in Chennai, Tiruvallur, Hosur and Kancheepuram by 2023 in addition to eight existing electronic hardware manufacturing SEZs in the state.[372] In most of the focus countries, there are SEZs dedicated to electronics. The focus countries could provide supporting measures like design guidelines and special permits to enhance

---

[372] The New Indian Express. 2019. *Tamil Nadu to set up four Electronics Manufacturing Clusters.* https://www.newindianexpress.com/business/2019/dec/30/tn-to-set-up-4-electronics-manufacturing-clusters-2082646.html.

adoption and promote zone specialization in future SEZs. SEZs or their sub-areas could also be designed based on specific products which could have different requirements. For instance, semiconductor manufacturing might require different policies and enablers as compared to cable manufacturing.

c. **Developing supportive policies specific to electronics.** Governments should review existing policies on the electronics industry to plug existing gaps and develop supportive policies, aside from providing financial incentives like tax breaks and preferential land leasing regulations. For example, export promotion could be aided by FTAs to promote duty-free markets for electronics. Other components to help boost value addition may include investor incentives to set up R&D facilities and establish vocational training facilities close to the SEZs to ensure a supply of skilled labor.

d. **Increasing collaboration between government and the industry.** COVID-19 will accelerate change in the global demand for electronic products due to changes in the behaviors of consumers, businesses, and governments. The transition toward high-value activities within the electronics supply chain requires policy makers to work closely with local players and foreign investors. As the private sector is likely more aware of industry trends (e.g., new manufacturing techniques, consumer behavior, policy changes in other countries, and others), policy makers need to communicate frequently with industry associations so that policies can respond promptly to industry needs.

2. **Develop human capital.** The lack of skilled workers has been an issue for the electronics industry, exacerbated by the rapid evolution of technologies requiring new technical knowledge. Soft skills like critical thinking and problem solving are also lacking in most electronics manufacturing labor forces. This might impede foreign direct investments (FDIs) for the electronics industry. Countries need to actively develop human capital to remain competitive and transit to manufacturing higher value-added electronics. Several policies to consider include:

a. **Providing appropriate and continuous training.** Governments could spearhead training programs by dedicating resources to industry-specific programs and partnering with other stakeholders. These can also help the workforce adopt digital technologies and improve productivity. Applying new technologies could result in labor productivity increasing by an average of 40% in the next 5 years (footnote 106).

   - **Creating dedicated strategies and government agencies.** Governments need to prioritize upskilling and reskilling workers. One way is having clear roadmaps with targets and specific actions. The Philippines launched strategies like the Philippine Development Plan 2017–2022, which aims to accelerate human capital development, and the National Technical Education and Skills Development Plan 2018–2022, which serves to prepare the workforce for new technologies.[373] Another option is creating dedicated government agencies to oversee industry development. In India, under the National Policy on Electronics, the Electronics Sector Skills Council was established to directly oversee capacity building and enhance the availability of skilled manpower.[374] There is still a large scope for the other focus countries to implement such measures.

   - **Partnering with industry and learning institutions.** Partnering with stakeholders like the private sector and learning institutions allows tailored apprenticeships and curricula for potential electronics manufacturing employees to have relevant skills. Thailand's National Science Technology and Innovation Policy Office introduced the "Work-Integrated Learning Program," which aims to provide 50,000 skilled workers to the industrial sector over the next few years (footnote 358). The program, with inputs from the industry, requires participants to undergo

---

[373] National Economic and Development Authority of the Philippines. 2017. *Philippine Development Plan 2017–2022*. Manila. https://pdp.neda.gov.ph/wp-content/uploads/2017/01/PDP-2017-2022-07-20-2017.pdf and TESDA. 2018. *National Technical Education and Skills Development Plan*. Manila. http://www.tesda.gov.ph/About/TESDA/47.

[374] Government of India Ministry of Electronics & Information Technology. 2020. Human Resource Development. https://www.meity.gov.in/human-resource-development.

vocational training in line with industry needs. The Government of the Philippines partnered with the Semiconductors and Electronics Industries in the Philippines, Incorporated promoting apprenticeships and immersion programs among firms and training schools.[375] The other focus countries could consider such partnerships.

b. **Incentivizing local companies to engage in research and development.** While FDIs have led to the transfer of technical knowledge and enhancing the skills of local workers, the significant skill gaps suggest that more needs to be done.[376] A long-standing issue is the lack of knowledge and technology transfer to the host community, as advanced and high-valued functions such as research and development are kept in investors' home countries. Countries could create more equal partnerships between local and international companies, with mutually agreeable clauses for knowledge transfer. Governments could also provide incentives for local companies to engage in research and development, to concurrently build up local skills. Other emerging manufacturing areas such as biotechnology might provide case studies for the electronics industry. In Singapore, the government launched the Research, Innovation and Enterprise 2020 plan, focusing on four key industries including health and biomedical science and allocating S$4 billion (equivalent to $2.9 billion based on 2016 exchange rate), including funding for local firms to venture into research and development.[377]

Many of these policy recommendations apply to the five focus countries. However, some recommendations can benefit from increased regional collaboration within Southeast Asia. Regional cooperation and integration can increase industry resilience by diversifying economic and trade structures, upgrading competitiveness, and speeding up regulatory reforms.[378] For instance, given the significant investment and skill requirements, there could be regional programs to drive research and development for electronics manufacturing in Southeast Asia. Table 11 summarizes the key policy recommendations and their relevance for each focus country (footnote 124).

---

[375] Department of Trade and Industry. 2020. Electronics. http://industry.gov.ph/industry/electronics/.

[376] C. Newman. 2015. Technology transfers, foreign investment and productivity spillovers. *European Economic Review* Volume 76, May 2015, pp. 168-187. https://www.sciencedirect.com/science/article/pii/S0014292115000367.

[377] KPMG. 2016. *Growing Singapore's biomedical R&D.* 3 March. https://home.kpmg/sg/en/home/media/press-contributions/2016/03/growing-singapore-biomedical-r-and-d.html.

[378] ADB. 2018. *Building Complementarity and Resilience in ASEAN amid Global Trade Uncertainty.* Manila. https://www.adb.org/sites/default/files/publication/456931/adb-brief-100-asean-resilience-global-trade-uncertainty.pdf.

Table 11: Summary of Recommendations for Electronics

Key recommendations and their relevance to focus countries

Degree of relevance: ■ High ■ Medium ■ Low

		Cambodia	Indonesia	Myanmar	Philippines	Thailand
Upgrading special economic zones	Get the basics right	High	High	High	High	High
	Adopt zone specialization to maximize industry linkages	Low	Medium	Medium	Low	Low
	Develop supportive policies specific to the electronics industry	High	Medium	Medium	Medium	Medium
	Increase collaboration between government and industry	Medium	Medium	Medium	Medium	Medium
Develop human capital	Provide appropriate and continuous training	High	High	High	Low	Low
	Incentivize local companies to engage in research and development	High	High	High	Medium	Medium

Note: This exercise is based on a broad assessment of the observed gaps and what countries have done (i.e., current responses in terms of presence and scope of policy measures).
Source: AlphaBeta analysis.

Box 8 provides an overview of some of the relevant country plans and ADB programs by country.

Box 8: Examples of ADB Country Programs on Electronics

A review of the Asian Development Bank (ADB) Country Operations Business Plan (COBP) (2020–2022) and the Country Partnership Strategies (CPS) for the five focus countries identified ADB assistance and the policy recommendations related to the electronics industry:[a]

- **Economic competitiveness.** ADB partnered with Bappenas in Indonesia to develop the "Policies to Support the Development of Indonesia's Manufacturing Sector During 2020–2024" report.[b] This report aims to boost the competitiveness of the manufacturing sector, including electronics manufacturing, and identify key enablers to support the growth.
- **Human capital investment.** ADB aims to enhance the skills of Cambodia's industrial labor force and develop skilled labor for four priority sectors including electronics manufacturing. The project aims to strengthen technical training institutes and support partnerships with the industry.

[a] The Country Operations Business Plans include:
  - ADB. 2019. *Country Operations Business Plan: Cambodia (2020–2022)*. Manila. https://www.adb.org/documents/cambodia-country-operations-business-plan-2020-2022.
  - ADB. 2019. *Country Operations Business Plan: Indonesia (2020–2022)*. Manila. https://www.adb.org/sites/default/files/institutional-document/526266/cobp-ino-2020-2022.pdf.
  - ADB. 2019. *Country Operations Business Plan: Myanmar (2020–2022)*. Manila. https://www.adb.org/sites/default/files/institutional-document/541976/cobp-mya-2020-2022.pdf.
  - ADB. 2019. *Country Operations Business Plan: Philippines (2020–2022)*. Manila. https://www.adb.org/sites/default/files/institutional-document/533741/cobp-phi-2020-2022.pdf.
  - ADB. 2019. *Country Operations Business Plan: Thailand (2020–2022)*. Manila. https://www.adb.org/sites/default/files/institutional-document/541811/cobp-tha-2020-2022.pdf.

  The Country Partnership Strategies include:
  - ADB. 2019. *Country Partnership Strategy: Cambodia 2019–2023, Inclusive pathways to a competitive economy*. Manila. https://www.adb.org/sites/default/files/institutional-document/534691/cps-cam-2019-2023.pdf.
  - ADB. 2020. *Country Partnership Strategy: Indonesia 2020–2024*. Manila. https://www.adb.org/sites/default/files/institutional-document/640096/cps-ino-2020-2024.pdf.
  - ADB. 2017. *Country Partnership Strategy: Myanmar, 2017–2021, Building the foundations for inclusive growth*. Manila. https://www.adb.org/sites/default/files/institutional-document/237161/cps-mya-2017-2021.pdf.
  - ADB. 2018. *Country Partnership Strategy: Philippines, 2018–2023, High and inclusive growth*. Manila. https://www.adb.org/sites/default/files/institutional-document/456476/cps-phi-2018-2023.pdf.
  - ADB. 2013. *Country Partnership Strategy: Thailand 2013–2016*. Manila. https://www.adb.org/sites/default/files/institutional-document/33990/files/cps-tha-2013-2016.pdf.

[b] ADB. 2019. *Policies to Support the Development of Indonesia's Manufacturing Sector During 2020–2024*. Manila. https://www.adb.org/sites/default/files/publication/481506/policies-manufacturing-sector-indonesia-2020-2014.pdf.

DIGITAL TRADE

Five major challenges pre-COVID-19

Risk of automation
89% of Filipino BPO workers are at high risk of automation

Limited connectivity
Fixed broadband speeds are 20.2 megabits per second (Mbps) in Indonesia and 49.5 Mbps in the Philippines, which are up to **ten times slower** than the speed in Singapore

Low level of small and medium-sized enterprises (smes) digitalization
In Thailand, just **1.7%** of businesses received Internet orders, with the lowest rates among SMEs

Tax base erosion
Taxation of digital payments could slow down growth

Risk of restrictive digital regulation
Macroeconomic costs of forced data localization range between **0.7%** and **1.1%** of GDP

Five areas of policy action

Develop an IT-BPO road map
• Introduce industry transformation maps (ITMs)

Enhance connectivity
• Leverage non-broadband infrastructure projects such as road construction

Support skills development
• Provide financial incentives

Enable SMEs to go digital
• Design toolkits for SMEs to assess their digital readiness

Rethink digital regulation
• Raise de minimis thresholds
• Enact data localization reforms

SECTION VI

Digital Trade

The amount of cross-border bandwidth used has grown 45 times since 2005. It is projected to increase by an additional nine times over the next 5 years as flows of information, searches, communication, video, transactions, and intra-company traffic continue to surge.[379] Yet, the importance of digital trade and exports has received limited attention to date in many Southeast Asian countries, including the five focus countries. Traditional economic metrics failed to keep pace with the digital economy's rapid growth, and there is a lack of robust data measuring the importance of digital trade for exports. Recent estimates suggest that digital exports are already very important to the focus countries (e.g., it already ranks the 6th largest export sector in the Philippines and the 11th in Indonesia) and could grow as much as nine times in these countries by 2030.[380] These are also economic activities and jobs more amenable to remote working and more resilient to COVID-19. These benefits may prove elusive unless supporting policy measures and programs addressing a range of barriers, including skills development, data localization, and connectivity are in place.

> ▶ **Digital trade is increasingly vital for the five focus countries.**

Digital exports include digitally enabled products (apps and e-commerce), digitally enabled services (online advertising and business process outsourcing), and indirect digital services, as shown in Box 9. Already, these are large sectors for many economies in Southeast Asia (Figure 20). In Indonesia, it represents the 11th largest sector, accounting for 1.2% of exports.[381] In the Philippines, it represents an even larger share of exports, being the 6th largest export sector accounting for 5.4% of exports.[382]

The source of digital trade value varies significantly by country. For example, much of the digital exports for the Philippines are driven by its information technology business processing outsourcing (IT-BPO) sector.[383] In Viet Nam, much of the growth has been driven by e-commerce and app development.[384]

---

[379] McKinsey Global Institute. 2016, *Digital globalization: The new era of global flows.* https://www.mckinsey.com/business-functions/digital-mckinsey/our-insights/digital-globalization-the-new-era-of-global-flows.

[380] Hinrich Foundation and AlphaBeta. 2017. *The Digital Komodo: How Indonesia can capture the digital trade opportunity at home and abroad.* https://alphabeta.com/wp-content/uploads/2019/02/digitrade_indo_eng_1-pg-view.pdf; and Hinrich Foundation and AlphaBeta. 2019. *The Data Revolution: How the Philippines can capture the digital trade opportunity at home and abroad.* https://alphabeta.com/wp-content/uploads/2019/06/digitrade_philippines_1-pg-view.pdf.

[381] Note: this is a conservative estimate of digital exports. For example, the value of digitally enabled products only focuses on Fast Moving Consumer Goods (FMCG) and not other categories of goods where e-commerce could be important. Similarly, the value of digitally enabled services only focuses on a subset of services where robust data is available. As a result, the potential value of digital exports could be more than 10 times as large if some of these broader impacts were included according to estimates by the Hinrich Foundation. See Hinrich Foundation and AlphaBeta. 2017. *The Digital Komodo: How Indonesia can capture the digital trade opportunity at home and abroad.* https://alphabeta.com/wp-content/uploads/2019/02/digitrade_indo_eng_1-pg-view.pdf.

[382] Hinrich Foundation and AlphaBeta. 2019. *The Data Revolution: How the Philippines can capture the digital trade opportunity at home and abroad.* https://alphabeta.com/wp-content/uploads/2019/06/digitrade_philippines_1-pg-view.pdf. Unfortunately, digital export data is currently not available for Cambodia, Myanmar, and Thailand.

[383] Hinrich Foundation and AlphaBeta. 2017. *The Data Revolution: How the Philippines can capture the digital trade opportunity at home and abroad.* https://alphabeta.com/wp-content/uploads/2019/06/digitrade_philippines_1-pg-view.pdf.

[384] Hinrich Foundation and AlphaBeta. 2017. *The Data Revolution: How Vietnam can capture the digital trade opportunity at home and abroad.* https://alphabeta.com/wp-content/uploads/2019/03/digitaltrade_vietnam-en_1-pg-view-hi-res.pdf.

Box 9: What We Mean by Digital Trade and Exports

There is no universal definition of digital trade or exports, due to its rapid development. In the World Trade Organization, the term "electronic commerce" has generally been used rather than "digital trade" and understood to mean "the production, distribution, marketing, sale or delivery of goods and services by electronic means."[a] The United States International Trade Commission definition includes the provision of e-commerce platforms and related services but excludes the value of sale of physical goods ordered online, as well as physical goods with a digital counterpart (such as books, movies, music, and software sold as downloads or on CDs or DVDs).[b] The United Nations Economic and Social Commission for Asia and the Pacific (UN ESCAP) takes a broad approach to measure the value of digital exports, seeking to capture digital infrastructure related to exports, as well as digital goods and services. (footnote a) A definition used by the Hinrich Foundation includes the following components for digital exports:[c]

1. **Digitally enabled products.** These are "content" products like software, books, music, films, and games that can be traded in a physical form but are now traded electronically via the Internet, as well as apps and e-commerce.
2. **Digitally enabled services.** These are services provided using digital technologies. Most services currently adopted digital technologies and are selling e-services to varying degrees. This includes business process outsourcing, online advertising (viewed from abroad), and the export of data processing and online software consultancy services. It also includes other direct e-service exports such as online booking and electronic banking; however, these categories are not measured robustly.
3. **Indirect digital services (embedded in other exports).** These refer to imported digital services used in exporting other products and services. Examples include telecommunication services such as email, video conferencing, digital file-sharing, and Voice Over Internet Protocol (VOIP) services used by mining firms exporting overseas.

a UNESCAP. 2016. *Internal trade in a digital age.* http://www.unescap.org/sites/default/files/aptir-2016-ch7.pdf.
b United States International Trade Commission. 2017. *Global Digital Trade 1: Market Opportunities and Key Foreign Trade. Restrictions.* https://www.usitc.gov/publications/332/pub4716.pdf.
c Further information available at: https://www.hinrichfoundation.com/research/project/digital-trade-research-project/.

In the five focus countries there are considerable opportunities to drive greater digital trade:

- **Cambodia.** Cambodia's digital trade is still relatively young, but there is strong potential. While English language skills are a challenge for BPO opportunities, other opportunities exist in data analysis and document processing.[385] E-commerce is also limited to date. For example, only about 20% of small firms (under 20 employees) have a website.[386]

- **Indonesia.** Indonesia can grow across all aspects of digital trade. Less than 7% of Indonesian businesses were engaged in exporting in 2015 (versus 11% in Malaysia)[387] and only 2% of Indonesia's total domestic retail sales are done via the internet.[388] Many MSMEs lack the resources to research international sales opportunities, build global business networks, and promote their products overseas. Indonesia's low financial inclusion and smartphone penetration rates also limit the development of domestic e-commerce. App development is still emerging, particularly compared to economies such as Viet Nam. Digital services, including IT-BPO and online video creating, is still low compared to those in other economies. There is a large potential for growth in IT-BPO as Indonesia ranks 3rd in AT Kearney's Global Services Location Index.[389]

385 *Phnom Penh Post.* 2016. "An inside track on outsourcing." https://www.phnompenhpost.com/business/inside-track-outsourcing.
386 World Bank Group. 2019. Enterprise Surveys (database). www.enterprisesurveys.org.
387 The Balance – Small Business (2018) *Export Potential in Indonesia.* https://www.thebalancesmb.com/export-potential-in-indonesia-1953479; and World Bank Enterprise Surveys. http://www.enterprisesurveys.org/Custom-Query.
388 AusTrade-Australia Unlimited (2018), *E-commerce in Indonesia.*
389 AT Kearney. 2019. *2019 Kearney Global Services Location Index.* https://www.kearney.com/digital-transformation/gsli/2019-full-report.

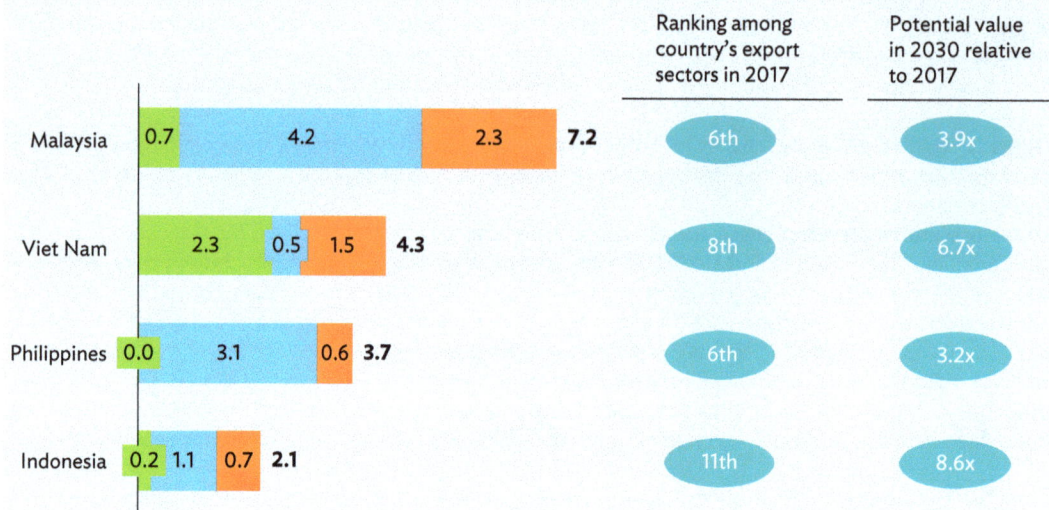

Figure 20: Value of Digital Exports in Select Southeast Asian Economies

If digital were a sector, it would be among the largest export sectors for many Southeast Asian economies, with large potential for growth

Current and projected annual values of digital exports
$ billion, 2017

- Digitally-enabled products
- Digitally-enabled services
- Indirect digital services

	Value	Ranking among country's export sectors in 2017	Potential value in 2030 relative to 2017
Malaysia	0.7 / 4.2 / 2.3 → 7.2	6th	3.9x
Viet Nam	2.3 / 0.5 / 1.5 → 4.3	8th	6.7x
Philippines	0.0 / 3.1 / 0.6 → 3.7	6th	3.2x
Indonesia	0.2 / 1.1 / 0.7 → 2.1	11th	8.6x

Note: Values converted to $ from local currency using average exchange rates in 2017.
Sources: Hinrich Foundation and AlphaBeta. 2017 (various reports).

- **Myanmar.** As of January 2021, the IT-BPO sector was limited, with investments needed in communication infrastructure to support its growth. E-commerce is also limited to date with only about 10% of small firms (under 20 employees) with a website (footnote 386). While internet penetration is rising, social media use (which can increasingly support e-commerce as a sales channel) was low with less than a quarter of the population using social media.[390]

- **The Philippines.** Digital exports in the Philippines are dominated by its IT-BPO sector. The industry's annual average growth rates have been estimated at 17% to 18%.[391] Between 2000 and 2015, IT-BPO's contribution to total gross domestic product increased from less than 1% to 6% (footnote 391). The industry's rapid development was driven by a large pool of service-minded and English-speaking workforce, supportive government policies, and supportive business association policies (footnote 391). According to the IT and Business Process Association of the Philippines (IBPAP), the industry contributed 2.7% to total employment in the Philippines in 2016 and accounted for 10% to 15% of the global IT-BPO market share. IBPAP expects the sector to recover faster than others, projecting up to $32 billion in revenues by 2022.[392] Compared to IT-BPO's success, e-commerce exports are limited. Although the Philippines's economy is 1.4 times the size of Viet Nam's in terms of GDP, the latter's e-commerce export revenues are estimated to be 110 times that of the Philippines in 2017 (footnote 383).

[390] We Are Social. 2017. Digital in Southeast Asia in 2017. https://wearesocial.com/sg/blog/2017/02/digital-southeast-asia-2017/.

[391] ACT/EMP and ILO. 2017. ASEAN in Transformation—How Technology is Changing Jobs and Enterprises—The Philippines Country Brief. https://www.ilo.org/actemp/publications/WCMS_579667/lang--en/index.htm.

[392] Newsbytes. 2020. Local BPO sector issues 'recalibrated' growth figures for next 3 years. 10 February. https://newsbytes.ph/2020/02/10/local-bpo-sector-issues-recalibrated-growth-figures-for-next-3-years/; and O. V. Campos. 2020. BPO sector expects recovery with revenue of $29B by 2022. Manila Standard. 20 November. https://manilastandard.net/business/it-telecom/340042/bpo-sector-expects-recovery-with-revenue-of-29b-by-2022.html.

- **Thailand.** Thailand is becoming a growing IT-BPO hub, already ranking 7th in the AT Kearney Global Services Location Index (footnote 389). E-commerce is a mixed picture. For example, while over 40% of small firms have a website (rising to over 70% for large firms) and social media use is high (with over 60% of individuals using social media) (footnote 390), less than 10% of small firms (and less than 20% of large firms) received orders over the Internet in 2018.[393]

▶ **Key challenges in digital trade must be addressed.**

There are several challenges potentially impeding the growth of digital trade in these countries:

- **Automation.** Industry 4.0 technologies represent both an opportunity and a threat to the IT-BPO industry. Digital technologies spurred the growth of IT-BPO and could further increase the productivity of workers by providing real-time insights. However, the increasing sophistication of AI could potentially remove, to a large degree, the need for human involvement in many IT-BPO functions. For example, the use of chatbots (i.e., a bot that interacts with business customers just like a living person) can be used as an artificial agent to talk with the customers and can give adequate advice when a live agent is unavailable. This is a risk facing 89% of Filipino BPO workers (footnote 391). The skills required by workers in this industry will need to change markedly, with digital and technical skills, and skills related to critical thinking and adaptive learning, expected to increase significantly in demand. Much of this needs to come from on-the-job training (footnote 106). Concerningly, there appears to be severe misalignment between training institutions' assessment of graduate preparedness for work, and employers' expectations about the skills graduates require to perform well in entry-level roles, along with their general and job-specific skills. For example, only 52% of employers in the IT-BPO industry in the Philippines believe that graduates are adequately prepared for entry-level positions, versus the 90% believed by training institutions (footnote 106). Closer partnerships between training institutions and employers are crucial in ensuring appropriate skills development.

- **Connectivity.** Mobile and broadband connectivity is critical, but there are gaps in both access and speed in the focus countries. The five countries can be clustered into two groups based on internet connectivity. The "partial Internet usage" cluster comprises Thailand and the Philippines, with roughly 50% to 60% of their population using the Internet. The "low usage" cluster comprises Cambodia, Indonesia, and Myanmar with roughly 25% to 35% of their population online.[394] Fixed broadband usage is much lower—in the case of Myanmar, less than 1% of the population has access to fixed broadband. There is also a significant rural-urban divide in terms of internet connectivity, and download speeds continue to be an issue. According to the Speedtest Global Index by Ookla, an Internet metrics company, in 2022, fixed broadband speeds are 20.2 Mbps in Indonesia and 49.5 Mbps in the Philippines, which are up to 10 times slower than the speed in Singapore at 192.7 Mbps.[395]

- **MSMEs development.** Less than a tenth of MSMEs in Asia and the Pacific currently export.[396] Many MSMEs lack the resources to research international sales opportunities, build a global business network, and promote their products overseas. Digital technologies can help MSMEs reduce costs involved in exporting by 82% and the time involved in exporting by up to 29%.[397] However, many MSMEs lack the

---

[393] World Bank Group. 2019. Enterprise Surveys (database). www.enterprisesurveys.org; *The Nation Thailand*. 2019. Thailand fares badly in business digitalisation: UNCTAD. https://www.nationthailand.com/business/30375882; and OECD. 2019. *Southeast Asia Going Digital: Connecting SMEs*. Paris. https://www.oecd.org/digital/broadband/southeast-asia-connecting-SMEs-note.pdf.

[394] OECD. 2019. *Southeast Asia Going Digital: Connecting SMEs*. Paris. https://www.oecd.org/digital/broadband/southeast-asia-connecting-SMEs-note.pdf.

[395] Ookla. 2022. Speedtest Global Index. https://www.speedtest.net/global-index.

[396] Oxford Economics. 2017. Local Business Global Ambition: How the internet is fueling SME exports in Asia-Pacific. http://www.oxfordeconomics.com/google/local_global.

[397] Asia Pacific MSME Trade Coalition. 2018. *Micro-revolution: The new stakeholders of trade in APAC*. https://alphabeta.com/wp-content/uploads/2020/06/singles-msme-report-apac.pdf.

understanding of the available digital technologies and trade opportunities, and costs can also be a concern. The digital divide is significant. The usage gap, meaning the difference between small and large firms in their use of the Internet, is 62% in Indonesia and 63.5% in Myanmar.[398] In Thailand, just 1.7% of businesses received Internet orders.[399]

- **Tax base erosion.** Many policy makers fear that digital trade makes it easier for companies to shift profits to low tax jurisdictions to avoid paying taxes. As government officials have increasingly acknowledged, an international approach to tackling base erosion and profit shifting is needed. Some countries have discussed digital taxes. Since mid-2020, Indonesia has been collecting a 10% value-added tax on digital products and services from internet-based firms. However, caution is needed to avoid retaliatory taxes from other countries and to not undermine the growth of digital products and services. For example, taxation of digital payments could slow down growth, reducing the number of people brought into the formal economy, undermining future tax collection efforts.[400]

- **Digital regulation.** A range of digital regulations is being introduced to address concerns ranging from data privacy to economic competitiveness. However, some risk remains. For example, the macroeconomic costs of forced data localization range between 0.7% and 1.1% of GDP, and data localization has been associated with investment decreases of up to 4%.[401] Digital trade constraints often fall hardest on MSMEs. Past research has found that local companies would be required to pay 30%–60% more for their computing needs from strictly enforced data localization policies.[402]

▶ An enabling environment is necessary to accelerate digital trade growth.

Some key recommendations to support an enabling environment for digital trade are to:

- **Develop an IT-BPO road map.** IT-BPO requires a road map of emerging technology opportunities, skills requirements, and detailed policies. Singapore's industry transformation maps provide information on technology impacts, career pathways, the skills required for different occupations, and reskilling options for different industries.[403] In the Philippines, industry groups have collaborated to understand skills requirements and provide suggested reforms.[404]

- **Enhance connectivity.** The underdevelopment of fixed broadband networks in the focus countries is due in part to a lack of access to other infrastructure such as the electrical grid. For instance, it was reported that only 68% of Myanmar's population had access to electricity in 2019. Cambodia made significant strides in this area. The most recent Electricity Authority of Cambodia report on the salient features of Cambodia's power sector reported that 97.4% of the over 14,000 villages in Cambodia had a connection to the grid, but only around 80% of households had electricity. Greater investments are needed in expanding energy grids and finding innovative ways of reducing the cost of broadband installation (e.g., adopting policies for

398 World Bank. 2019. Enterprise Surveys (database). www.enterprisesurveys.org/.
399 UNCTAD. 2017. UNCTADStat (database). http://unctadstat.unctad.org.
400 A. Maherali. 2017. Financial Inclusion, Digital Payments and Their Impact on Income and Tax Revenue Around the World. Master's thesis, Harvard Extension School. https://dash.harvard.edu/handle/1/33826588.
401 M. Bauer et al. 2014. The costs of data localisation: Friendly fire on economic recovery, European Centre for International Political Economy (ECIPE) Occasional Paper No. 3/2014. https://ecipe.org/wp-content/uploads/2014/12/OCC32014__1.pdf.
402 Leviathan Security Group. 2014. Quantifying the costs of forced localisation. Seattle. https://static1.squarespace.com/static/556340ece4b0869396f21099/t/559dad76e4b0899d97726a8b/1436396918881/Quantifying+the+Cost+of+Forced+Localization.pdf.
403 SkillsFuture. 2019. Skills framework. https://www.skillsfuture.gov.sg/skills-framework.
404 An example of this study is: IBPAP. 2014. Talent Deep Dive: An Analysis of Talent Availability for the Information Technology and Business Process Management Industry in 10 Provinces in the Philippines.

encouraging the efficient deployment of broadband by leveraging non-broadband infrastructure projects such as road construction).

- **Support skills development.** A range of initiatives is needed, starting with greater responsiveness in curricula, along with greater industry involvement, to ensure that key skills such as English language, critical thinking, and complex problem solving are included in courses. Support for employers by raising their awareness of available courses and providing financial incentives to support their usage is needed to ensure more and higher-quality training in the workplace (footnote 106). As already highlighted, industry partnerships with training institutions are crucial to ensure their alignment on priority skills to develop.

- **Enable MSMEs to go digital.** Focused programs to support MSMEs going digital could be useful. Some good examples include New Zealand's Business Growth Agenda and Singapore's "Go Digital" plan to boost the global competitiveness of MSMEs. Singapore's plan includes toolkits for MSMEs to assess digital readiness, technical support, potential to participate in pilot projects, and a set of pre-approved and/or curated digital solutions.[405] Adopting digital technologies could improve the worker productivity. In Southeast Asia, applying new technologies could result in labor productivity increasing by 51% on average in the next 5 years (footnote 106).

- **Raise de minimis thresholds.** Raising de minimis thresholds on custom duties for digital products is important, particularly for MSMEs.[406] A de minimis threshold of $200 could generate over $30 billion in economic benefits for all 21 Asia-Pacific Economic Cooperation (APEC) members.[407] Indonesia leads this area, having increased its de minimis threshold from $50 to $1,001 in 2017.[408] While the Philippines has a threshold above $200, other focus countries can improve, especially considering Cambodia's and Thailand's thresholds were around $50, and Myanmar's was zero.[409]

- **Enact data localization reforms.** Governments could rethink data localization laws given the potential economic costs and the limited benefits. In Indonesia, Government Regulation 82 of 2012 (GR 82) requires electronic system providers offering public services to place data centers and disaster recovery centers within Indonesia, for law enforcement and customer protection purposes.[410] Academic research showed that recently proposed or enacted legislation on data localization could potentially reduce GDP by around 0.5%, possibly reaching 0.7% of GDP if economy-wide restrictions are introduced (footnote 401). Myanmar and Cambodia have no data localization provisions, but Thailand and the Philippines have some areas of ambiguity in their laws which could see possible application in data localization.[411] Countries with data localization laws should review their policies, understand the potential impacts, and enact reforms where applicable to facilitate greater digital trade. For countries considering such laws, efforts should be made to fully understand the trade-offs and learn from best practices. Countries could consider adopting bilateral (or multilateral) approaches to data flows. A useful starting point would be to adopt the APEC Privacy Framework, join the APEC Cross Border Data Privacy Rules System, and adopt International Organization for Standardization (ISO) Standards like ISO 27018

---

[405] Government of Singapore. 2020. SMEs Go Digital (web page), https://www.imda.gov.sg/smesgodigital.

[406] The International Chamber of Commerce, also referred to as the World Business Organization, defines "de minimis" as a valuation ceiling for goods, including documents and trade samples, below which no duty or tax is charged and clearance procedures, including data requirements, are minimal. United Nations. 2012. De minimis. https://tfig.unece.org/contents/de-minimis.htm.

[407] S. Holloway and J. Rae. March 2012. "De minimis thresholds in APEC," World Customs Journal, Vol.6 # 1.

[408] UPS. 2017. Indonesia increases the De Minimis threshold on inbound shipments. Georgia. https://www.ups.com/vn/en/about/news/apac-de-minimis.page.

[409] Information sourced from: https://docs.zonos.com/guides/de-minimis-values; and *Rappler*. 2016. Aquino signs law increasing tax-exempt value of balikbayan boxes. 31 May. https://www.rappler.com/nation/aquino-signs-customs-modernization-act-balikbayan-boxes.

[410] B. McKenzie. 2018. *Indonesia - changes to data localization provisions for electronic system operators*. Illinois. https://www.lexology.com/library/detail.aspx?g=a3b371a0-1b95-4ebc-86a1-2cbcda491eda.

[411] *ASEAN Post*. 2019. Southeast Asia's data localization. https://theaseanpost.com/article/southeast-asias-data-localisation.

that specifies controls to protect personal data.[412] This could be supported by encouraging interoperability between digital frameworks, particularly on payment gateways, to avoid the costs of companies having to customize their approaches for every single market. Finally, within ASEAN, it will be important for countries to progress on the data management initiative under the Master Plan on ASEAN Connectivity 2025, which aims to improve transparency and accountability on data regulation requirements in ASEAN and identify areas to enhance performance and coordination.[413]

Many of these policy recommendations apply to the five focus countries, but some recommendations will benefit from increased regional collaboration within Southeast Asia. Regional sharing of best practices and learning on data localization reforms and de minimis thresholds could help promote trade in Southeast Asia. Table 12 summarizes the key policy recommendations and their relevance to each focus country (footnote 124).

Table 12: Summary of Recommendations for Digital Trade

Key recommendations and their relevance to focus countries

Degree of relevance: High (blue), Medium (green), Low (orange)

	Cambodia	Indonesia	Myanmar	Philippines	Thailand
Develop an IT-BPO road map	High	High	Medium	Medium	High
Enhance connectivity	High	High	High	Medium	Medium
Support skills development	High	High	High	High	High
Enable SMEs to go digital	High	Medium	High	High	Medium
Raise de minimis thresholds	High	Low	High	Low	High
Enact data localization reforms	Low	High	Low	Medium	Medium

IT-BPO = information technology and businss process outsourcing, SMEs = small and medium-sized enterprises.
Note: This exercise is based on a broad assessment of the observed gaps and what countries have done (i.e., current responses in terms of presence and scope of policy measures).
Source: AlphaBeta analysis.

[412] Hinrich Foundation. 2019. *The Digital Komodo Dragon: How Indonesia can capture the digital trade opportunity at home and abroad.* https://alphabeta.com/wp-content/uploads/2019/02/digitrade_indo_eng_1-pg-view.pdf.

[413] ASEAN Secretariat. 2016. *Master Plan on ASEAN Connectivity 2025.* https://asean.org/wp-content/uploads/2016/09/Master-Plan-on-ASEAN-Connectivity-20251.pdf.

Box 10 provides an overview of some of the relevant country plans and ADB programs by country.

Box 10: Examples of Country Strategies and ADB Country Programs on Digital Trade

A review of the Asian Development Bank (ADB) Country Operations Business Plan (COBP) (2020-22) and the Country Partnership Strategies (CPS) for the five focus countries and the country strategies identified several lending and non-lending products and services, and national plans related to the digital trade sector and the policy recommendations:[a]

- **IT-BPO Roadmap.** The Government of Indonesia launched the "Making Indonesia 4.0" road map in 2018 focusing on five key technological advances: Internet of Things, artificial intelligence, human-machine interface, robot and sensor technology, and three-dimensional printing. In the Philippines, industry representatives developed the IT-BPO Roadmap 2022, projecting that the sector could increase revenues from $22.9 billion in 2016 to $38.9 billion in 2022 by prioritizing five high-value subsectors: contact centers and BPO, IT services, health information management, animation and game development, and global in-house centers.[b]
- **Skill development.** In Cambodia, the Asian Development Bank (ADB) developed the blueprint for secondary education and human resource development for 2020–2030 and is working with the Cambodian Federation of Employers and Business Associations and training institutes in Singapore to boost the quality of skills training and integrate digital skills into technical and vocational education and training schemes. In Myanmar, ADB supported the implementation of secondary education subsector curriculum reforms and the expansion of new competency based technical and vocational education and training programs targeted at disadvantaged youth and unskilled workers. In Indonesia, ADB provided a loan worth $80 million to invest in two higher education institutes in East Java to help the country build skills for the Fourth Industrial Revolution (4IR).[c]
- **Electricity infrastructure.** In Cambodia, ADB invested in solar energy through competitive tenders promoting public–private partnerships and mobilizing energy efficiency investments through grid extensions, including cross-border power imports. In Myanmar, one of the key focus areas for ADB was building a power transmission and distribution network. In Indonesia, access to sustainable and reliable energy has been a key focus for ADB, with the Sustainable Energy Access in Eastern Indonesia: Electricity Grid Development Program and the Sustainable Energy Access in Eastern Indonesia: Power Transmission Sector Project accounting for 31% of ADB's total lending in 2020.
- **Digital transition for micro, small, and medium-sized enterprises (MSMEs).** The Government of Indonesia aimed to have 10 million MSMEs go digital by the end of 2020 to minimize the financial distress faced by the firms due to the pandemic.[d] To promote regional cooperation, the ASEAN Coordinating Committee on Micro, Small and Medium Enterprises launched "Go Digital ASEAN: Digital skills to address the economic impact of COVID-19" to equip MSMEs with critical ICT skills to leverage the digital economy in the region.[e]
- **Data localization.** The Government of Indonesia eased data localization requirements in November 2019 by limiting its application to "public electronic systems operators" after dissatisfaction from the private sector on the previous localization requirements.[f] Elsewhere, Thailand issued the Personal Data Protection Act in 2019, which also mandates companies to comply with data localization regulations.[g]

ASEAN = Association of Southeast Asian Nations, BPO = business process outsourcing, COVID-19 = coronavirus disease 2019, ICT = information and communications technology, IT = information technology.
[a] The Country Operations Business Plans include:
- ADB. 2019. *Country Operations Business Plan: Cambodia (2020–2022)*. Manila. https://www.adb.org/documents/yancambodia-country-operations-business-plan-2020-2022.
- ADB. 2019. *Country Operations Business Plan: Indonesia (2020–2022)*. Manila. https://www.adb.org/sites/default/files/institutional-document/526266/cobp-ino-2020-2022.pdf.
- ADB. 2019. *Country Operations Business Plan: Myanmar (2020–2022)*. Manila. https://www.adb.org/sites/default/files/institutional-document/541976/cobp-mya-2020-2022.pdf.
- ADB. 2019. *Country Operations Business Plan: Philippines (2020–2022)*. Manila.https://www.adb.org/sites/default/files/institutional-document/533741/cobp-phi-2020-2022.pdf.
- ADB. 2019. *Country Operations Business Plan: Thailand (2020–2022)*. Manila. https://www.adb.org/sites/default/files/institutional-document/541811/cobp-tha-2020-2022.pdf.

continued on next page

Box 10 *continued*

The Country Partnership Strategies include:

- ADB. 2019. *Country Partnership Strategy: Cambodia, 2019–2023, Inclusive pathways to a competitive economy.* Manila. https://www.adb.org/sites/default/files/institutional-document/534691/cps-cam-2019-2023.pdf.
- ADB. 2020. *Country Partnership Strategy: Indonesia, 2020–2024, Emerging Stronger.* Manila. https://www.adb.org/sites/default/files/institutional-document/640096/cps-ino-2020-2024.pdf.
- ADB. 2017. *Country Partnership Strategy: Myanmar, 2017–2021, Building the foundations for inclusive growth.* Manila. https://www.adb.org/sites/default/files/institutional-document/237161/cps-mya-2017-2021.pdf.
- ADB. 2018. *Country Partnership Strategy: Philippines, 2018–2023, High and inclusive growth.* Manila. https://www.adb.org/sites/default/files/institutional-document/456476/cps-phi-2018-2023.pdf.
- ADB. 2013. *Country Partnership Strategy: Thailand, 2013–2016.* Manila. https://www.adb.org/sites/default/files/institutional-document/33990/files/cps-tha-2013-2016.pdf.

[b] IBPAP et al. 2018. *Accelerate PH Future-read Roadmap 2022: The Philippines IT-BPM sector - Executive Summary.* https://boi.gov.ph/wp-content/uploads/2018/03/Executive-Summary-Accelerate-PH-Future-Ready-Roadmap-2022_with-corrections.pdf.

[c] ADB. 2020. *Indonesia: Higher Education for Technology and Innovation Project.* Manila. https://www.adb.org/projects/52332-001/main#project-pds.

[d] E. Eloksari. 2020. Govt aims for 10 million MSMEs to go digital by year end. *The Jakarta Post.* 2 July. https://www.thejakartapost.com/news/2020/07/01/govt-aims-for-10-million-msmes-to-go-digital-by-year-end.html.

[e] ASEAN. 2020. Factsheet - "Go Digital ASEAN: Digital skills to address the economic impact of COVID-19" Project. Jakarta. https://asean.org/storage/2020/06/Factsheet-Go-Digital-ASEAN-as-of-19-June-2020_final.pdf.

[f] A. Assegaf, Z. Husein, and M. Sirie. 2019. Indonesia: Government Relaxes Data Localisation Requirement. *Mondaq.* https://www.mondaq.com/data-protection/861082/government-relaxes-data-localisation-requirement.

[g] Watson Farley & Williams. 2020. Thailand's personal data protection act: a business checklist. https://www.wfw.com/articles/thailands-personal-data-protection-act-a-business-checklist/.

SECTION VII

Conclusion

The policy recommendations in this report contribute to achieving the operational priorities in ADB's Strategy 2030.[414] For example, one of ADB's operational priorities is "promoting rural development and food security" by "improving market connectivity and agricultural value chain linkages" and "increasing agricultural productivity and food security." The recommendations for the agro-processing sector in the report can help address this. For instance, improving information flows and transparency and promoting cross-border trade can increase market connectivity in the focus countries. By expanding the food product range and attracting investment into the industry, the countries could increase their agricultural productivity. Elsewhere, this report could also meet ADB's operational priority of "fostering regional cooperation and integration." For example, the policy recommendations for tourism and agro-processing suggest the need to strengthen coordination among Southeast Asian countries to boost post-pandemic economic recovery.

To execute the sector-specific policy recommendations in this report, focus countries could consider a four-step approach. First, to further understand and implement the recommendations, countries should establish sector-specific multistakeholder task forces with representatives from the government, the private sector, academia, and civil society. For instance, Singapore established the Tourism Recovery Action Task Force, comprising government agencies (e.g., Singapore Tourism Board) and tourism industry associations (e.g., Singapore Hotel Association) to streamline plans for recovery and future growth.[415] Existing working groups and industry associations like the Boracay Inter-Agency Task Force, Cambodia Hotel Association, and the Indonesian Retail Merchants Association (APRINDO) could help shorten the timeline.

Second, established task forces could conduct deeper diagnostic exercises to understand the proposed recommendations, including learning potential costs and benefits if a certain policy measure is rolled out.

Third, there is a need to prioritize recommendations based on the local context, available funding, and urgent needs. For instance, for the garment sector, a task force could focus first on reviewing policies restricting growth, like tariffs in the short term, rather than emphasizing flexible production models requiring further research and key enablers like advanced equipment. In the digital trade sector, a task force might want to focus first on enhancing connectivity in the short term while planning studies on de minimis thresholds and data localization reforms.

Finally, a task force should oversee the implementation of the selected recommendations and undertake monitoring and evaluations of its policies and refine them accordingly.

---

[414] ADB. 2018. *Strategy 2030*. Manila. https://www.adb.org/sites/default/files/institutional-document/435391/strategy-2030-main-document.pdf.

[415] STB. 2020. STB rallies tourism sector to face biggest challenge since SARS. 11 February. https://www.stb.gov.sg/content/stb/en/media-centre/media-releases/stb-rallies-tourismsectortofacebiggestchallengesincesars.html.

Appendix

Three-Step Approach on Prioritizing Sectors in Focus Countries

A three-step approach was taken to prioritize sectors.

1. **Develop criteria to evaluate the sectors of the five focus countries.**
   Five criteria were used:
   (i)   **Contribution to Gross Domestic Product (GDP) pre-pandemic:** Measures the sector's share of GDP before the pandemic, using data from the Asian Development Bank (ADB) or National Statistics Offices.[1]
   (ii) **Contribution to employment pre-pandemic:** Measures the sector's total employment figures using official labor statistics from ADB and International Labour Organization (ILO) databases.
   (iii) **Impact of COVID-19:** Measures the economic impact on the sectors using national accounts data from the National Statistics Offices. Where data is available, the total of second quarter 2020 (2Q 2020) and third quarter 2020 (3Q 2020)'s sector contribution to GDP was compared to 2019's to assess the magnitude of change. For countries with a high reporting lag (Cambodia and Myanmar), the impact was informed by existing assessments by ADB and ILO.
   (iv) **Competitive advantage:** Measures the sector's competitiveness in each country. For tradeable sectors, the World Bank's Revealed Comparative Advantage index was used. For non-tradeable sectors, a wider range of competitiveness factors (e.g., demographics and capacity of the labor force, unit labor costs, size of domestic market and others) were assessed.
   (v)   **Alignment with future growth drivers:** Measures a sector's relevance to future trends such as urbanization and growing consuming class, and alignment with national development plans.

2. **Evaluate sector importance based on systematic scoring criteria.**
   The sectors are based on the International Standard Industrial Classification (ISIC). Due to the size and diversity of the manufacturing sector, it was split into three subsectors: (i) labor-intensive manufacturing and processing, (ii) resource and energy-intensive processing, and (iii) innovative and high-end manufacturing.

---

[1]   ADB. 2020. *Key Indicators Database*. Manila. https://kidb.adb.org/kidb/.

Table A1 summarizes how sectors were scored, and Tables A2 to A7 illustrate the scoring outcomes across the five focus countries.

Table A1: Scoring Criteria and Matrix for Sector Assessment

Sectors are scored based on this scoring matrix

#	Criteria	Scores ("low" to "high")		
Points awarded to form total score:		**Low** ⚪	**Medium** 🟢	**High** ⚪
		0	1	2
1	Contribution to GDP pre-pandemic	Below 5% of GDP in 2019	Between 5% to 10% of GDP in 2019	Above 10% of GDP in 2019
2	Contribution to employment pre-pandemic	Less than 5% of national employment	5% to 10% of national employment	More than 10% of national employment
3	Impact of COVID-19	Limited impact (positive y/y increase in economic output)	Moderate impact (single digit y/y decline in economic output)	Strong impact (double digit y/y decline in economic output)
4	Competitive advantage	RCA score of below 1; limited scope to compete (e.g., poor endowment of natural resources for mineral processing)	RCA score of above 1; moderate scope to compete (e.g., moderately skilled labor force for manufacturing, but faced with rapidly rising wages)	RCA score of above 1; strong scope to compete (e.g., cheap and young labor force for manufacturing)
5	Alignment with future growth drivers	Limited alignment	Moderate alignment	Strong alignment

COVID-19 = coronavirus disease 2019, GDP = gross domestic product, RCA = revealed comparative advantage.
Source: Authors.

Table A2: Scoring Outcome for Cambodia

Assessment of Cambodia

Prioritization of sectors[a]	GDP Share	Employment	COVID-19 Impact	Competitive Advantage	Future Trends	Total Score[b]
Agriculture, forestry, and fishing	High	High	Low	Medium	Medium	6
Mining and quarrying	Low	Low	Medium	Medium	Low	2
Labor-intensive manufacturing and processing	High	High	High	Medium	High	9
Resource-and energy-intensive processing	Low	Low	Low	Medium	Low	1
Innovative and high-end manufacturing	Low	Low	Low	Medium	Medium	2
Electricity, gas, steam, and air-conditioning supply	Low	Low	Low	Low	Medium	1
Water supply; sewerage, waste management, and remediation activities	Low	Low	Low	Low	Medium	1
Construction	High	Medium	High	Medium	High	8
Wholesale and retail trade; repair of motor vehicles and motorcycles	Medium	High	Low	High	High	7
Accommodation and food service activities	Low	Low	Medium	High	High	5
Transportation and storage	Medium	Low	Medium	Medium	Medium	4
Information and communication	Low	Low	Medium	Low	High	3
Financial and insurance activities	Low	Low	High	Low	Medium	3
Real estate activities	Medium	Low	High	Low	Medium	4
Professional, scientific, and technical activities	Low	Low	Low	Low	Low	0
Administrative and support service activities	Low	Low	Low	Low	Low	0
Public administration and defense; compulsory social security	Low	Low	Medium	Low	Low	1
Education	Low	Low	Low	Low	Medium	1
Human health and social work activities	Low	Low	Low	Medium	Medium	2
Arts, entertainment, and recreation	Low	Low	Low	Medium	Medium	2

Degree of importance: ■ High ■ Medium ■ Low

COVID-19 = coronavirus disease 2019, GDP = gross domestic product.
a   Manufacturing has been split into three categories depending on the labor and technology intensities.
b   A score of 2 is given if the degree of importance is "High," a score of 1 is given if the degree of importance is "Medium," and a score of 0 is given if the degree of importance is "Low."
Sources: Literature review; AlphaBeta analysis.

Table A3: Scoring Outcome for Indonesia

Assessment of Indonesia

Prioritization of sectors[a]

Degree of importance: ■ High ■ Medium ▢ Low

	GDP Share	Employment	COVID-19 Impact	Competitive Advantage	Future Trends	Total Score[b]
Agriculture, forestry, and fishing	High	High	Low	Medium	Medium	7
Mining and quarrying	Medium	Low	High	Low	Medium	4
Labor-intensive manufacturing and processing	High	Medium	Medium	High	High	8
Resource-and energy-intensive processing	Low	Low	Medium	Medium	Low	2
Innovative and high-end manufacturing	Medium	Low	Low	Medium	Medium	3
Electricity, gas, steam, and air-conditioning supply	Low	Low	Medium	Low	High	4
Water supply; sewerage, waste management, and remediation activities	Low	Low	Low	Medium	Low	1
Construction	High	Low	High	Medium	Medium	8
Wholesale and retail trade; repair of motor vehicles and motorcycles	High	High	High	High	High	10
Accommodation and food service activities	Low	Medium	High	Medium	Medium	7
Transportation and storage	Medium	Low	High	Low	Medium	4
Information and communication	Low	Low	Low	Medium	High	3
Financial and insurance activities	Low	Low	Low	Medium	High	3
Real estate activities	Low	Low	Low	Low	Medium	1
Professional, scientific, and technical activities	Low	Low	Medium	Low	Medium	2
Administrative and support service activities	Low	Low	Medium	Low	Low	1
Public administration and defense; compulsory social security	Low	Low	Medium	Low	Low	1
Education	Low	Low	Low	Medium	Medium	2
Human health and social work activities	Low	Low	Low	Low	High	2
Arts, entertainment, and recreation	Low	Low	Medium	Medium	Medium	3

COVID-19 = coronavirus disease 2019, GDP = gross domestic product.

a Manufacturing has been split into three categories depending on the labor and technology intensities.

b A score of 2 is given if the degree of importance is "High," a score of 1 is given if the degree of importance is "Medium," and a score of 0 is given if the degree of importance is "Low."

Sources: Literature review; AlphaBeta analysis.

Table A4: Scoring Outcome for Myanmar

Assessment of Myanmar

Prioritization of sectors[a] Degree of importance ■ High ■ Medium ■ Low

Sector	GDP Share	Employment	COVID-19 Impact	Competitive Advantage	Future Trends	Total Score[b]
Agriculture, forestry, and fishing	High	High	Medium	High	Medium	8
Mining and quarrying	Medium	Medium	Low	High	Medium	5
Labor-intensive manufacturing and processing	High	High	High	High	High	10
Resource-and energy-intensive processing	Low	Low	Medium	High	High	5
Innovative and high-end manufacturing	Low	Low	Medium	Low	Low	1
Electricity, gas, steam, and air-conditioning supply	Low	Low	Low	Low	Medium	1
Water supply; sewerage, waste management, and remediation activities	Low	Low	Low	Low	Medium	1
Construction	Medium	Medium	Low	Low	Medium	4
Wholesale and retail trade; repair of motor vehicles and motorcycles	High	High	Medium	High	High	9
Accommodation and food service activities	Low	Low	High	High	High	6
Transportation and storage	High	Medium	High	Low	Medium	6
Information and communication	Low	Low	Low	Low	High	2
Financial and insurance activities	Low	Low	Low	Low	Medium	1
Real estate activities	Low	Low	Low	Medium	Medium	2
Professional, scientific, and technical activities	Low	Low	Low	Low	Low	0
Administrative and support service activities	Low	Low	Low	Medium	Low	1
Public administration and defense; compulsory social security	Low	Low	Low	Medium	Medium	2
Education	Low	Low	Low	Low	Medium	1
Human health and social work activities	Low	Low	Low	Low	Medium	1
Arts, entertainment, and recreation	Low	Low	Medium	Medium	Medium	3

COVID-19 = coronavirus disease 2019, GDP = gross domestic product.

[a] Manufacturing has been split into three categories depending on the labor and technology intensities.

[b] A score of 2 is given if the degree of importance is "High," a score of 1 is given if the degree of importance is "Medium," and a score of 0 is given if the degree of importance is "Low."

Sources: Literature review; AlphaBeta analysis.

Table A5: Scoring Outcome for the Philippines

Assessment of the Philippines

Prioritization of sectors[a]   Degree of importance ▮ High ▮ Medium ▮ Low

	GDP Share	Employment	COVID-19 Impact	Competitive Advantage	Future Trends	Total Score[b]
Agriculture, forestry, and fishing	Medium	High	Low	Low	Low	4
Mining and quarrying	Low	Low	Medium	Low	Low	1
Labor-intensive manufacturing and processing	High	Medium	High	Low	High	8
Resource-and energy-intensive processing	Low	Low	Medium	Low	Medium	2
Innovative and high-end manufacturing	Medium	Medium	Medium	Low	High	6
Electricity, gas, steam, and air-conditioning supply	Low	Low	Medium	Medium	Low	2
Water supply; sewerage, waste management, and remediation activities	Low	Low	Medium	Low	Medium	2
Construction	Medium	Medium	Low	Low	Low	4
Wholesale and retail trade; repair of motor vehicles and motorcycles	High	High	High	Low	Medium	9
Accommodation and food service activities	Low	Low	High	Low	High	6
Transportation and storage	Low	Medium	Medium	Low	Medium	4
Information and communication	Low	Low	Medium	High	High	5
Financial and insurance activities	Medium	Low	Low	Medium	Low	3
Real estate activities	Medium	Low	High	Low	Low	4
Professional, scientific, and technical activities	Medium	Low	Low	Medium	Medium	4
Administrative and support service activities	Low	Low	Low	High	Medium	3
Public administration and defense; compulsory social security	Low	Medium	Low	Low	Medium	2
Education	Low	Low	Medium	High	Medium	4
Human health and social work activities	Low	Low	Medium	Medium	Medium	3
Arts, entertainment, and recreation	Low	Low	Medium	Medium	Medium	3

COVID-19 = coronavirus disease 2019, GDP = gross domestic product.

[a] Manufacturing has been split into three categories depending on the labor and technology intensities.

[b] A score of 2 is given if the degree of importance is "High," a score of 1 is given if the degree of importance is "Medium," and a score of 0 is given if the degree of importance is "Low."

Sources: Literature review; AlphaBeta analysis.

Table A6: Scoring Outcome for Thailand

Assessment of Thailand

Prioritization of sectors[a] — Degree of importance: ■ High ■ Medium ■ Low

Prioritization of sectors[a]	GDP Share	Employment	COVID-19 Impact	Competitive Advantage	Future Trends	Total Score[b]
Agriculture, forestry, and fishing						6
Mining and quarrying						0
Labor-intensive manufacturing and processing						4
Resource-and energy-intensive processing						2
Innovative and high-end manufacturing						8
Electricity, gas, steam, and air-conditioning supply						1
Water supply; sewerage, waste management, and remediation activities						1
Construction						4
Wholesale and retail trade; repair of motor vehicles and motorcycles						10
Accommodation and food service activities						8
Transportation and storage						4
Information and communication						5
Financial and insurance activities						4
Real estate activities						2
Professional, scientific, and technical activities						4
Administrative and support service activities						2
Public administration and defense; compulsory social security						2
Education						3
Human health and social work activities						4
Arts, entertainment, and recreation						4

COVID-19 = coronavirus disease 2019, GDP = gross domestic product.
[a] Manufacturing has been split into three categories depending on the labor and technology intensities.
[b] A score of 2 is given if the degree of importance is "High," a score of 1 is given if the degree of importance is "Medium," and a score of 0 is given if the degree of importance is "Low."
Sources: Literature review; AlphaBeta analysis.

Table A7: Summary of Top 5 Scoring Sectors across Focus Countries

	Cambodia	Indonesia	Myanmar	Philippines	Thailand
Agriculture, forestry, and fishing	✓	✓	✓		✓
Labor-intensive manufacturing and processing	✓	✓	✓	✓	
Innovative and high-end manufacturing				✓	✓
Construction	✓	✓			
Wholesale and retail trade; repair of motor vehicles and motorcycles	✓	✓	✓	✓	✓
Accommodation and food service activities	✓	✓	✓	✓	✓
Information and communication				✓	✓
Transport and storage			✓		

Sources: Literature review; AlphaBeta analysis.

3. **Refinement for more targeted analysis**

   Using ISIC allows for quantitative analysis for scoring purposes, and there were instances where it was more useful to narrow down the sector to subsectors (or industries). For instance, labor-intensive manufacturing and processing remained quite large and diverse, consisting of several subsectors such as food products, beverages, textiles, and paper products. Other critical industries like tourism might not be effectively captured by ISIC as tourism-related activities cut across a range of sectors. Based on extensive engagement with country experts in ADB, the final list of priority subsectors or industries is summarized in Table A8.

Table A8: Final Prioritized Industries

#	Prioritized Industries	Sector Coverage
1	Tourism	Wholesale and retail trade; Accommodation and food service activities
2	Agro-processing	Agriculture, forestry, and fishing; Labor-intensive manufacturing
3	Garments manufacturing	Labor-intensive manufacturing
4	Electronics manufacturing	Innovative and high-end manufacturing
5	Digital trade	Information and communication, which includes Business Process Outsourcing (BPO), e-commerce, and digital apps and services

Sources: Literature review; AlphaBeta analysis.